THE ANXIETY WORKBOOK FOR SUPPORTING TEENS WHO LEARN DIFFERENTLY

T0385125

of related interest

The Incredible Teenage Brain
Everything You Need to Know to Unlock Your Teen's Potential
Bettina Hohnen, Jane Gilmour and Tara Murphy
Illustrated by Douglas Broadley
Foreword by Sarah Jayne Blakemore
ISBN 978 1 78592 557 3
eISBN 978 1 78450 952 1

The Mentally Healthy Schools Workbook
Practical Tips, Ideas, Action Plans and Worksheets
for Making Meaningful Change
Pooky Knightsmith
Foreword by Norman Lamb
ISBN 978 1 78775 148 4
eISBN 978 1 78775 149 1

**The Big Book of Therapeutic Activity
Ideas for Children and Teens**
Inspiring Arts-Based Activities and
Character Education Curricula
Lindsey Joiner
ISBN 978 1 84905 865 0
eISBN 978 0 85700 447 5

The Big Book of Dyslexia Activities for Kids and Teens
100+ Creative, Fun, Multi-sensory and
Inclusive Ideas for Successful Learning
Gavin Reid, Nick Guise and Jennie Guise
ISBN 978 1 78592 377 7
eISBN 978 1 78450 725 1

My Anxiety Handbook
Getting Back On Track
Sue Knowles, Bridie Gallagher and Phoebe McEwen
Illustrated by Emmeline Pidgen
ISBN 978 1 78592 440 8
eISBN 978 1 78450 813 5

Education and Girls on the Autism Spectrum
Edited by Judith Hebron and Caroline Bond
ISBN 978 1 78592 460 6
eISBN 978 1 78450 837 1

M is for Autism
The Students of Limpsfield Grange School and Vicky Martin
ISBN 978 1 84905 684 7
eISBN 978 1 78450 198 3

M in the Middle
Secret Crushes, Mega-Colossal Anxiety and
the People's Republic of Autism
The Students of Limpsfield Grange School and Vicky Martin
ISBN 978 1 78592 034 9
eISBN 978 1 78450 286 7

THE ANXIETY WORKBOOK FOR SUPPORTING TEENS WHO LEARN DIFFERENTLY

A FRAMEWORK AND ACTIVITIES TO BUILD STRUCTURAL, SENSORY AND SOCIAL CERTAINTY

CLARE WARD AND JAMES GALPIN

FOREWORDS BY SARAH WILD AND
PROFESSOR LIZ PELLICANO

ILLUSTRATED BY CLARE WARD WITH ORLA LATHAM

Jessica Kingsley Publishers
London and Philadelphia

First published in Great Britain in 2021 by Jessica Kingsley Publishers
An Hachette Company

2

Copyright © Clare Ward and James Galpin 2021
Forewords copyright © Sarah Wild and Professor Liz Pellicano 2021
Front cover image source: Clare Ward

A CIP catalogue record for this title is available from the
British Library and the Library of Congress

ISBN 978 1 78775 396 9
eISBN 978 1 78775 397 6

Printed and bound by CPI Group (UK) Ltd, Croydon, CR0 4YY

Jessica Kingsley Publishers' policy is to use papers that are natural,
renewable and recyclable products and made from wood grown in
sustainable forests. The logging and manufacturing processes are expected
to conform to the environmental regulations of the country of origin.

Jessica Kingsley Publishers
Carmelite House
50 Victoria Embankment
London EC4Y 0DZ

www.jkp.com

CONTENTS

FOREWORD

I was delighted and really surprised to be asked to write a foreword for *The Anxiety Workbook for Supporting Teens Who Learn Differently*. I first met Clare at an open morning for professionals at Limpsfield Grange, and found her passion for supporting young people with special educational needs (SEN) inspiring. Clare was keen to find out more about what we did at Limpsfield Grange with our unique community of learners, and offered me lots of tips and resources over the years of correspondence. I was not at all surprised to learn that she and her collaborator Jamie had been asked to write a book.

This book is well timed and much needed. The central concept of Clare and Jamie's work – of identifying uncertainty as structural, sensory or social, then finding ways of reducing or managing the uncertainty – is really sensible and will resonate with teenagers, parents and professionals across the country. The book is very easy to use, with clear pointers to chapters for specific questions or scenarios, and I know this means readers will use it as a go-to tool when they are figuring out how to best support a teenager with special educational needs.

Over the past few months, our collective existence has become very uncertain; simple acts such as going to the supermarket or catching a train have been triggers for tsunamis of anxiety. As an educator, I love the cadence of the academic year, and only realised recently how disorientated I felt when all of those markers, sports days and end-of-year assemblies had been removed from my life. During the pandemic of 2020, one day started to feel very much like another, in so much as all days were unpredictable and frightening.

Unpredictable situations make us hypervigilant and mistrustful; they blindside us. I am hopeful that the pandemic will help all of us to understand how central certainty is to our sense of wellbeing – and will help us to better empathise with and support children and adults who find everything so unpredictable and uncertain that it colours every aspect of their life.

Sarah Wild, Headteacher of Limpsfield Grange School

FOREWORD

We are living in deeply uncertain times. As I write, the coronavirus is still wreaking havoc across the world. It has brought, and continues to bring, much uncertainty to all of our lives. People are not sure around when they can safely go outside, visit friends and loved ones, send children back to school, get on with finding a job, and doing those everyday things that give us pleasure.

These unsettling times are be felt even more intensely by those who are the subject of this wonderful book: young people who may learn differently. For the autistic children, young people and adults with whom I work, this has been an especially confusing and stressful period. Almost everything that gave some semblance of stability to their lives has been thrown up in the air: time at school, friendships with peers, even experiences in the outdoors.

There may just be a silver lining, however. For the fact that we have all shared the uncertainty of the Covid-19 pandemic might just help to provide a deeper understanding of how many autistic people live, most of the time. These are times of uncertainty for everyone, after all, and we shall do so much better if we learn to respond to it and make a new life together.

That spirit pervades this book, and that is the reason that I love it. Clare Ward and James Galpin begin, that is, from the understanding that uncertainty connects us all. We each need to make sense of it, respond to it and learn to thrive without ever wholly overcoming it. There are three more specific reasons that this work is so timely too.

First is its focus on teenagers. In the field of education, there are often loud calls on the importance of 'early intervention', which seeks to capitalise on learning during the very earliest years of a child's life, when there is a particularly dynamic period of brain growth and substantial neural plasticity. But this focus on 'the earli-er the better' means that slightly older young people all too often get overlooked. It is well established, however, that certain – and vitally important – parts of the brain take a longer time to develop and that the teenage years are crucial determinants of how adult life will go. The brain continues to be plastic and malleable throughout these teenage years, so there is great capacity for learning and so much that we need to get right.

Second is the focus on the needs of young people, rather than just on their diagnosis. While labels and diagnoses always have their place, and can often be empowering, they sometimes mask the importance of looking closer at the immense variety of experience, strengths and challenges that people face. In the text that follows here, there is none of that simplistic thinking. This is a book that takes people's differences seriously, encourages us all to take the time to know and respond to each person that we are called upon to work with and gives us direct guidance as to how we can do so.

Third, this is a book that moves on from the narrowly 'medical model' that all too often restricts the ambition of special education. According to that conventional model, difficulties with young people's learning, behaviour or social interactions are solely due to the young person themselves and their degree of 'impairment'. In this book, however, the physical and social environment in which the child lives and learns is revealed to play a crucial role. Clare and James' strategies and techniques encourage professionals to think about how their teaching style and the class dynamics they enable help or hinder each and every student as they seek to thrive.

None of us know how the Covid-19 pandemic will pan out next. There will be further changes that confront societies for other reasons too, whether emerging from the trouble with our economy, our climate or the technologies that are reshaping the world around us. Clare and James' book reminds us that even without all of this social change, a sense of uncertainty already pervades everyday life for millions of people. Their magnificent book shows us how we can respond in the best possible ways and help each other live fulfilling lives as a result.

Professor Liz Pellicano
Macquarie University, Sydney, Australia

ACKNOWLEDGEMENTS

This book would have been far less interesting without the help of a brilliant group of young people, who gave up their time, let us photograph them and talked to us about school. Some were initially reluctant; some couldn't wait to talk to us; and some managed to stay focused far longer than either of us thought possible. We thank you all, and though we changed your names (and sometimes your hair), you are the most important part of this book.

Particular thanks to the girls from Limpsfield Grange and Anja Melissa, whose writing and videos have informed and inspired us and our students. Anja's videos are available on her YouTube channel 'Asperger's Girl' and the girls' books *M is for Autism* and *M in the Middle* are available from Jessica Kingsley Publishers.

The idea for an actual book came from an out of the blue conversation with Amy Lankester-Owen at JKP when Clare was looking for new therapy ideas for young people with more than one identified learning difference (or no clear diagnosis at all). Many thanks to her for suggesting that we research and write one instead, and also to Claire Robinson and Isabel Martin for all their invaluable help along the way.

We would never have worked together if it hadn't been for the Bridge Outreach Service, and Bozena Marcyk (her Event Narratives were also the starting point for the thinking machine later in the book). Many of these ideas were formed as a result of conversations on the bus, while visiting various schools, for which we are indebted to Sarah Tyce, Claire Droney, Daniele Borghi, Menita Sekhon and Rosie Whur. Thank you for being an excellent team and for providing us with such rich opportunities for joint work, Italian food and committed karaoke.

The lesson-planning formats we used were supplied by Vanessa Russell and Jeanine Boulter – inspiring teachers, both. Thanks go to Jo Manuel from Special Yoga[1] for the stretches and the life-affirming work she does and Judy Courtney OT who provided the pressure exercises. Thanks also go to Manos Tsakiris for his comments on an earlier draft of Chapter 1.

---

1   https://specialyoga.org.uk

We are both part of Special Networks, a multidisciplinary group which provides simple, sustainable support for children, families and communities. Grateful thanks to Clare Alexander, Judy Courtney, Flossie Fairbairn, Elizabeth Gillies and Lottie Hart for your joint work, advice and encouragement.[2]

Most of the uncertainty glasses are by Lee at Bridges & Brows[3] and are available online or in his Shoreditch store (though they will not necessarily result in you seeing the world as more or less volatile).

Finally, a big thank you to our families – George, Rosie, Eliot, Orla, Gus, Alfie and Lulu – for not minding when we spend HOURS on our laptops or ask them if sentences like 'the uncertainty about the level of uncertainty that your existing perception of uncertainty may have can influence subsequent estimations of uncertainty' make sense.

2   For more on our work see www.specialnetworks.co.uk
3   www.bridgesandbrows.com

AUTHORS' PREFACE

THIS IS US

We come from different disciplines; Clare is a speech and language therapist with 30 years' experience and Jamie a developmental psychologist who specialises in applying research to practice. While our working lives have taken us along different pathways, we share the same fundamental passion for working with children and young people.

Clare began her working life as a teaching assistant in a school for children with specific learning difficulties and post-qualification worked as a speech and language therapist, social worker, NHS team manager, visual communication specialist, teacher and outreach worker with adults and children with a range of learning and physical differences and disabilities. Along the way, she also helped develop a series of special needs teacher training programmes and worked with mainstream teachers as part of an autism outreach support service, which is where she met Jamie.

She currently works mostly in secondary schools, though also directly with young people, to support social communication difficulties, as a member of Special Networks, a multidisciplinary group of professionals who provide simple, sustainable support to children, families and communities. Her work combines helping her students to develop greater self-awareness and tolerance of uncertainty with practical skill development and problem solving.

Clare is not an artist, she didn't even do Art GCSE, but she believes in the power of the visual. She hopes to show through these illustrations that with the right technology and some willing teenagers, anything is possible. Many thanks go to Orla Latham for her casting, styling, shoots and photos which were the basis of most of the drawings.

Jamie completed his undergraduate degree in Modern Languages where he attended a talk on child development. The interest that the talk sparked led him to complete a graduate conversion course to Psychology and then a Master's in Child Development. During his postgraduate studies, he worked as a teaching assistant supporting autistic students in mainstream schools. He also began working for an autism charity providing family support as well as working at and then running after-school and holiday clubs for autistic children and young people.

His interest in both research and practice within education led him to then complete a Master's in Research in Education and after that, a PhD in Developmental Psychology. On finishing his doctorate, he initially had to work simultaneously in a variety of positions, associate lecturer, researcher, as well as continuing to work in schools in order to combine his interest in both hands-on work, research and sharing knowledge. The opportunity to cover all three areas in one position arrived in the shape of a newly created role within a specialist teaching school. It was here that he first met Clare. He currently works for nasen (National Association for Special Educational Needs), researching practice-based evidence as well as designing and delivering training across all areas of SEND. He also continues to lecture part time at two universities.

We first worked together as part of a multidisciplinary outreach support service, where we supported teachers of children and young people with a diagnosis of autism, across an inner London borough. Our roles within this fantastic team gave us an opportunity to meet and work with a huge number of teachers, as well as parents, and appreciate some of the difficulties facing both autistic young people, their families and the people who work with them, as well as some of the issues surrounding diagnosis. This is something we continue to do in our work with Special Networks.

WHY WE WROTE THIS BOOK

We both continue to work mostly in schools, supporting students, teachers and parents and helping young people who may be struggling, both academically and socially. Over the years, we have been invited to provide training and support for a wide range of different issues and during this time we have noticed an increase in the number of diagnoses that teachers are expected to keep in mind, in both their planning and their day-to-day class management. Dyslexia, dyscalculia, developmental coordination disorder (formerly dyspraxia), developmental language disorder (formerly specific language impairment), dysgraphia, ADHD (attention deficit hyperactivity disorder), autism, attachment disorders, selective mutism, pathological demand avoidance, anxiety disorders, trauma, social (pragmatic) communication disorder and Tourette syndrome are frequently diagnosed by clinical and educational psychologists and specialist teachers in an attempt to help the child or young person, and the adults supporting them, understand what they might need in order to thrive in school.

Although some difficulties need discrete, specialist interventions, in our work we have never overtly focused on diagnoses; instead, we always look at need. We recognised that regardless of diagnosis, all the difficulties we were supporting students (as well as parents and teachers) with were underpinned by the same fundamental difficulty: uncertainty. This recognition in our practice has been echoed in wider research into mental health that has begun to explore what are known as transdiagnostic factors – difficulties that are experienced across diagnoses. One such factor that has been the subject of a lot of exploration is uncertainty.

The premise of this book and our practice is that all (special educational) needs are driven by a single factor – uncertainty.

The recent pandemic will have possibly helped us all better appreciate the fundamental idea which underpins this book, that as humans **the central difficulty we all face in our lives is uncertainty**. It will also have given us a greater recognition of how uncertain the world is. We always live in uncertain times, and while we may not be able to control events around us we can, by using some of the strategies in this book, help those who struggle become more resilient and tolerant of the day-to-day issues that uncertainty can bring.

On a visit to Limpsfield Grange (a specialist girls' school in Surrey), Clare and her colleague Sarah had the chance to spend some time with two of the students. We asked them questions about school, and how life had changed since they moved there. One student answered all of our questions quickly, while her friend ate her lunch very quietly beside her, her head down. The final question from Sarah was this: 'If you could say one thing to your teachers in your previous schools, what would it be?' The quieter student's head snapped up. She looked directly at us and said clearly, 'They should have "got" me.'

'They should have "got" me'

We put this book together in the hope that it might give teachers, parents, teaching assistants, therapists, counsellors, mentors, tutors and home educators a new way to think about support for the young people they live and work with – support for the students who have to deal with greater levels of uncertainty, who might be struggling at school socially or finding it hard to access academic work.

By focusing on the human universal of uncertainty, this book is an attempt to bridge the gap between young people who learn differently and their teachers, parents and carers. It's a presentation of a new theoretical framework for understanding behaviour: the 3S model of uncertainty, where we view uncertainty as occurring in three different interconnected arenas, each of which as a teacher or practitioner we can address for the student. The three areas are **Structure**, **Sensory** and **Social**. At the heart of our model is a recognition that all our struggles have the same fundamental cause, uncertainty. The book is also the distillation of many hours of clinical work and student interviews; interviews with young people who were keen to help the adults in their lives understand the reasons behind some of the things they do and work with them to find a way through the academic and social challenges of the secondary school years.

WHY A BOOK FOR TEENAGERS?

While childhood is generally a time when we can experience a great deal of uncertainty, we can use the learning this uncertainty brings to build up our model of the world and how it works.

The move from childhood to adolescence is a period of development associated with even greater levels of uncertainty and change.

It is a period of rapid physical and emotional development as well as hormonal change. It is also a period of increased academic expectations, where the combined pressure of schoolwork and exams is often associated with a decrease in the perceived ability to perform within the school context and a decrease in agency and self-esteem.

Social demands also increase during this time, with more complex peer relationships requiring more nuanced and refined social skills to manage complex hierarchical relationships within peer groups. In general, anxiety is greatest when a goal is important, and uncertainty is high. Adolescence is a period where our goals, implicitly or explicitly, have high stakes of importance – notably: achieving in school so as to ensure a positive outcome in life after school; and meeting social demands to ensure that we have a group of friends who can support us through this period. In short, there is a spike in uncertainty across all three areas of our model, Structure, Sensory and Social. Unsurprisingly, this time of change and uncertainty is associated with heightened levels of stress and anxiety. It is also associated with adolescents reporting lower levels of life satisfaction and a resulting increase in mental health difficulties.

Support for students during this time still often focuses on categorically defined difficulties, such as social anxiety or depression. These boxes we try to place students in imply a homogenous lump of symptoms and causes. But difficulties experienced during this period of change are more individual, transient and dynamic, shifting over time and context, so a dimensional, transdiagnostic approach based on our 3S model of uncertainty is therefore particularly useful for this group of students.

We have designed this framework, based on our combined years of experience, and the practical activities for supporting teens in this book, to be of immediate use to our readers who are working to support and empower teens with learning differences or special educational needs.

Ultimately, if '**Where's the uncertainty?**' is the first question we ask when working out how to support a student, that puts us on the right track to better addressing their needs.

All pages marked with ⤓ can be photocopied and downloaded at https://library.jkp.com/redeem using the code DQNMTMM

INTRODUCTION

Everyone, over the course of their journey through school, will at some point experience uncertainty. All students will naturally question their ability to take exams, manage friendships or deal with world events such as terror attacks or pandemics, so **the ideas in this book will benefit all students**. Some of the young people we work with have a specific diagnosis, many do not; some may be highly sociable, and others seem withdrawn, but all our students are different, surprising and brilliant in their own way. It is this natural variety and diversity of the minds we work with that makes schools (and the world) such a rich and diverse place to live and work in.

Although in the last few years we have worked mainly with teachers, we are also parents; between us we have five children who (at the time of writing) span the ages 3 to 18 and, like parents the world over, we became even more involved in our children's learning as the Covid-19 pandemic turned us all into makeshift home educators.

We hope that, as well as school-based educators, families and tutors will find this book useful as a way of better understanding behaviours we might find perplexing, and that some of the ideas in the practice sections are helpful at home. Whether we talk about 'the classroom' or 'home', 'students' or 'young people', we are always asking the same question: 'Where's the uncertainty?'

The recognition that the fundamental difficulty we all experience is uncertainty underpins our model of support, one on which we focus when we are identifying need. Understanding that uncertainty is the root of all the struggles a student is experiencing at school is only the first step to diagnosing need. There are a lot of things in the world which can cause uncertainty and, therefore, trying to isolate where exactly uncertainty is coming from could be an overwhelming process. Our **3S model** helps address this by focusing on the three areas where we feel uncertainty will lie: in the **Structure**, **Sensory** and **Social** realms.

Structure – we use this term to broadly refer to the way the world is organised, from the small scale (such as how an individual learning activity is set up), to the large scale (such as how school works). Chapter 3 covers this S.

Sensory – this refers to the way in which we process internal and external sensory information such as sights, sounds, smells, breathing rate, heartbeats, fullness, balance and body awareness. Chapter 4 covers this S.

Social – this is all about understanding the social world, ourselves and everyone else. Chapter 5 covers this S.

Difficulties in each of these areas can overlap and interplay with each other to compound uncertainty. In looking to answer the central question of '**Where's the uncertainty?**', we should always be looking at each of the 3S's (Structure, Sensory and Social) and exploring potential sources of uncertainty across each one. This will increase our chances of locating the correct cause of uncertainty by helping us to reduce any confirmation bias we might have, that is, we think it is a difficulty caused by Social uncertainty, for example, and so we then have a bias towards seeking out and interpreting information that confirms this to us (at the expense of other possible interpretations). It will also, over time, make us more aware of different potential sources of uncertainty and enable us to hone our skills as behaviour detectives so we can more effectively diagnose what the need might be.

This process of diagnosing need using the 3S model of uncertainty will enhance the support we are able to provide our students, allow us to experience greater empathy with them and therefore give us a greater sense of certainty over what the difficulties are that our students are trying to cope with. We continue, below, to explain in more detail why it is of such fundamental importance that we focus on diagnosing need, rather than seeking a diagnosis or 'label'.

NEEDING A DIAGNOSIS?

Diagnosis is part of the support journey for many students, and can open up access to useful, targeted and specialist interventions. It can also play an important role in self-discovery for young people, and many of our students have benefited from a greater understanding of why their brain seems to work differently. However, access to diagnosis is far from open, transparent or equal and many families spend months, sometimes years, waiting in 'the system' for an assessment. Added to this, the same child on a different day, with a different team, may present a different set of difficulties within the realm of special educational needs. We have worked with many young people who could (to our minds) have ticked all the boxes at some point. Once armed with a diagnosis, we believe it is then too easy for families and professionals to focus on 'the label' rather than the child, or to see the problems as purely located in the person with the diagnosis, and therefore not to make the necessary and often simple adjustments that can support and empower the student to thrive.

We do not, in this book (or indeed our professional lives), overly focus on specific diagnoses. Another reason for our approach is that we have noticed that school staff can become overwhelmed with an ever-increasing array of diagnostic acronyms they feel that they are expected to become experts in. Increasingly, therefore, we have worked with parents and teaching staff to support them to **diagnose need** as opposed to focusing on the **need for diagnosis**.

Another way of looking at this that we find helpful is to look at how SEN as a field has yo-yoed between various stages of what taxonomists describe as 'lumping' or 'splitting'. Unpacking this terminology, you can say that splitters highlight the differences between things, while lumpers look for the similarities. In the move towards more student-centred support, there has been a wider recognition of many different types of SEN. This greater awareness is welcome; however, it has resulted in a swing towards splitting – focusing on difference rather than commonality. This then in turn leads to a focus on identifying individual diagnoses (or multiple diagnoses for an individual) and then allocating students to specific, tailored interventions or differentiation – teaching to the label.

Within this process, the diagnosis can lose meaning for that individual. What that diagnosis means for this student, in this setting, at this time is not fully appreciated and we slip towards simply viewing a student as a diagnosis. The issue of what support we give a student is then focused simply on which diagnosis that student has, rather than on specific observable needs. The prevailing approach has become diagnose first, *then* put support in place.

We believe that this shift towards seeking a diagnosis first has increased the pressure on teachers to understand what is effectively an ever-growing forest of splinters, where teachers and other practitioners need to know how to support students with ADHD, social, emotional and mental health (SEMH) needs, dyslexia, an attachment disorder or multiple, sometimes bewildering combinations of these and many more labels.

If we simply look at students through the microscope of a diagnosis this can lead to the difficulties they are experiencing becoming pathologised; that is, we can start to see the younger person as psychologically abnormal, and therefore harder to empathise with. This can create a distance between us and our student; we may become alienated from our student, who, as a result of the emphasis on their diagnosis, is seen as extra-ordinary, outside the remit of standard teaching and needing specialist support or an alternative educational placement where their 'abnormal' behaviour can be better supported.

Furthermore, having to be an expert in so many different diagnoses creates **uncertainty** for teachers and other supporting adults, increasing our own doubt in our professional skills and ability. This can erode our professional confidence, and our sense of agency (our perceived ability to understand, manage and control a situation). It can leave us feeling helpless, believing we are not able to then provide effective support because there is 'something wrong' with the student that is outside our control.

The focus on the need for diagnosis can also create a perception that the source of the difficulty a student is facing is located within them, as opposed to being due to factors in their environment. At school this could mean that diagnosis overshadows the impact of the learning environment as a possible source of a student's difficulty. It oversimplifies the complex interaction between a student and their environment and means we might fail to diagnose the external sources of difficulty. The diagnosis gives us 'legitimate' bio-psychological 'proof' that the student is the sole problem, and not the physical, social and emotional environment over which we in fact have much greater influence.

In contrast, the emphasis we outline in this book, on diagnosing and addressing need, allows for a wider perspective on how to support any student and avoids simplified narratives to explain behaviours. So instead of thinking, **'They behaved like that because they have ADHD'**, we might ask **'For what difficulty is that behaviour a solution?'**

By not concentrating solely on the student, we shine light back on the setting, our teaching style and the class dynamic, allowing us to recognise the factors that might help as well as hinder a student in achieving their potential. This then allows us to take ownership in our endeavours to support students, and bring back our sense of agency – we can make a difference in these young people's lives.

DIAGNOSING NEED

There is a growing movement within psychiatric research to explore 'transdiagnostic factors', issues that appear across diagnoses that may underpin the different psychological difficulties young people can experience. This body of research has led to some researchers proposing that there is a single factor underlying all mental health difficulties. This body of work, though contested, has raised questions about the usefulness of our existing categorical diagnostic systems for learning difference – the 'little boxes' a diagnostic label can put us in. Clinical practitioners have reported that this approach is not particularly useful when it comes to selecting support for someone or giving an indication of their potential future outcomes. Some researchers have gone as far to suggest that categorical diagnostic systems are fundamentally broken.

An alternative approach to all this is a dimensional one, looking at difficulties along a sliding scale as opposed to discrete boxes. A dimensional approach focuses on the specific impact of difficulties for an individual and is driven by a recognition that:

> due to the rich individual differences in human personality and functioning, there may well be as many manifestations of psychopathology [mental health difficulties] as there are individuals to experience them. (Wright & Woods, 2020, p.6)

The same quote could equally apply to 'many manifestations' of need for support at school.

This may at first, then, seem overwhelming, as rather than having to get to know just four or five diagnoses, such as ADHD, autism, dyslexia, to understand our students, due to 'rich individual differences', there could be an infinite amount of needs to get to know! However, when we take a step back, we can recognise that this is what teachers do anyway – diagnose the needs of every student within the class because **all** students will vary and every class is full of variability.

Focusing on diagnosing need also allows for the recognition that there are students with a complex profile of difficulties who are often not receiving support because they have not met any specific diagnostic threshold. There is also well-documented evidence that a diagnosis can look very different, depending on the child. Broader research looking at the cognitive profiles (ways of thinking) of students with different diagnostic labels has also found that specific diagnoses, little boxes, fail to predict children's cognitive profiles, meaning they may not particularly help us to understand a child's strengths and difficulties any better.

CERTAINTY, THE FUNDAMENTAL NEED

The growing field of transdiagnostic research within psychiatry has explored universal areas to target for support. Anxiety has often been considered a fundamental difficulty, and within this uncertainty is the key component of anxiety that appears to be causing all the trouble. Uncertainty has even been proposed as a possible contender for the fundamental difficulty that underpins all mental health difficulties. We explore, particularly in Chapter 1, the research that underpins some of this thinking and tie it all together with current theories around how we think that provide the theoretical basis of this workbook, echoing what we have been doing in our practice for years.

This allows us to reconsider behaviours and difficulties which might currently be seen as psychologically abnormal, recognising them instead as being symptomatic of nothing more than universal human experience – uncertainty.

This leads us to a shift towards a dimensional, as opposed to categorical, system that diagnoses need. Such a system recognises that difficulties are not defined by causally homogenous 'disorders', but instead seen as the culmination of multiple, unique pathways. The 3S framework proposes that these pathways, while all unique in their origin and direction of travel, are all similar in that they are paved with **uncertainty**.

The way that uncertainty affects an individual will vary in the way it is expressed and the impact it can have cognitively (causing things like worry or disorganisation) and/or behaviourally (causing greater reassurance seeking or inaction). Fundamentally, however, uncertainty is something we all struggle with and, to varying degrees, try to resolve by seeking greater certainty. Some of us might seek certainty through avoidance – shutting down or withdrawing. Others might ruminate and get caught in negative thought loops, and others still might engage in negative certainty-seeking behaviours, such as aggression or substance abuse. The support we need to provide for students, therefore, is how to manage uncertainty and how, longer term, to increase our tolerance for it. As we go on to elaborate further in Chapter 1, this support is built around increasing the two things that help move us out of uncertainty: knowledge and/or agency.

By rethinking support in schools using the 3S model of uncertainty we outline in this workbook, we are not only trying to simplify the SEN landscape for school staff, but also to reinforce the value of one of the core skills of education professionals: understanding what students need in order to thrive.

We recognise that drawing everything back to a single human universal could move us back towards a 'lumping' approach as all students will have trouble with uncertainty. However, a transdiagnostic approach such as ours does not ignore observable differences or distinct diagnoses, but instead tries to emphasise student commonalities. Two individuals could be simultaneously similar or different depending on what we look at. An autistic student and a non-autistic student could appear similar in their enjoyment of swimming or different based on the amount of spoken language they use. There will also be variation among students in how much uncertainty impacts on their day-to-day school life, which will be determined by two factors: **how often they experience it** and **their capacity to manage it**. Different ways of thinking (which may or may not come with a diagnostic label) can point to the fact that we may experience a greater amount of uncertainty and/or have a reduced capacity to manage it.

We all struggle with uncertainty, but how often we experience it and our ability to manage it will differ, as a consequence of the different ways in which we experience the world.

Our 3S model that reconceptualises support needs, based on the common underlying factor of uncertainty, is more beneficial, meaningful and effective than a process which attempts to 'carve nature at its joints' and split individuals into increasingly distinct categories. Our unity is our diversity, and our diversity is our unity. While we may not all have a diagnosis of dyslexia, ADHD or autism, we have all been scared, confused, excited and uncertain. Recognising that the difficulties (and joys) our students experience are universally experienced by all humans allows us to better empathise with and understand what our students might be going through.

Knowing this can make the provision of support more intuitive. We can come up with strategies that all have the same aims: first, to **reduce uncertainty**, and second, to **increase the capacity to manage uncertainty**.

HOW TO USE THIS BOOK

This is a book you can read from cover to cover if you want to delve into the theoretical underpinnings of our approach. Alternatively, you can dip into the sections that you find most relevant to you at a given time, or with a particular class or student.

Below we therefore provide an overview of what's in the book, and what you'll find in each chapter. We show how they relate to one another, and we also provide a list of **quick links** that will allow you to jump straight to a section you may be particularly interested in.

The first chapter is all about theory and research; it provides the rationale for our 3S model and introduces some of the key concepts that we will call back to in subsequent chapters. We have also included a glossary at the end of the book, which provides a brief explanation of some of the key terms used throughout the book, most of which are introduced in Chapter 1. The second chapter looks at us, making us conscious of our attitudes and beliefs and how they might impact on our teaching approaches. We then address each of the three areas of possible uncertainty, the 3S's – Structure, Sensory and Social – in turn, in three separate longer chapters. Each of these chapters divides into two parts: **Theory** and **Practice** to make it easy for you to find hands-on activities and worksheets, while also understanding our reasons for suggesting you use them.

Although we have spilt the 3S's into distinct chapters (Chapters 3, 4 and 5, **Structure**, **Sensory** and **Social**), the location of any uncertainty may not always fall so neatly into these categories. Uncertainties may overlap and morph into one another, so we always look for the possible causes of uncertainty in **each** of the three key areas.

We work as a team of detectives alongside our students, identifying (with the people who know them best) where the difficulties might lie and planning which area we might target first for support. The odds are in our favour, however, as we know we are looking for **uncertainty** and it will be driven by one of the 3S's of Structure, Sensory or Social. In each of the 3S sections (Chapters 3, 4 and 5), we work through examples of different behaviours, looking at where the uncertainty might lie. We then provide you with a template that can be used to help answer the question '**Where's the uncertainty?**' for all the young people you live or work with.

CHAPTER OVERVIEW

Chapter 1 – Understanding Uncertainty

We begin by introducing a fascinating new theoretical framework that offers a unifying view on how our brains work and therefore how we **all** experience the world, learn and socialise. It provides the foundation for our simple, practical 3S framework of universal support: all behaviour can be better understood by asking '**Where's the uncertainty?**' and by using the 3S's of **Structure, Sensory, Social** to help answer that question.

This new way of thinking about difficulties, difference, diversity and ultimately unity will help reduce any of our own uncertainty as to why a student might be behaving in a particular way or struggling to manage as well as they could in different areas of their school world.

While this chapter forms the basis for the 3S way of thinking, and goes into it in depth, we also recap some of these ideas at the start of each of the three main chapters (with the practical activities) in the workbook. This means, if you are already thinking 'Uncertainty? Well that just makes sense!' and don't feel that you have the time right now to look at the theory up close – the 'why' – you can jump right into the subsequent chapters, looking at how we can put the theory into practice.

Chapter 2 – Understanding Our Own Uncertainty

This chapter looks at **us**, the adults, and how we can start by working on shifting our own, as well as our students', thought processes towards a more positive focus. We show how if we can understand 'behaviour difficulties' more as a 'search for certainty' this can help us manage our reactions to the behaviour and design better support. It also builds on the notion of 'diagnosing need' that is discussed in the introduction. We introduce here some ideas for helping our students develop a greater sense of perceived ability (agency) and ways to help them switch their (and our own) mindset to better embrace the challenge of searching for knowledge.

Chapter 2 also contains information on some of the different diagnostic labels that you might come across within an educational context.

Chapter 3 – Structure

This chapter looks at the first of our 3S's. We begin with the realm of Structure as it is one of the easiest and quickest ways for us to build some certainty for our students. It will inevitably take longer for us to support young people to develop more Sensory and Social certainty; however, we can make this process easier if the external world does not seem so chaotic. The chapter looks at universal ways to provide clearer structure for **all** our students. If we can set up our learning environments so that they are universally accessible we may find that the impact of the sensory and social uncertainties is greatly reduced.

This chapter and the activities and worksheets in it should be your starting point, regardless of the specific needs of the young person you have in mind. The ideas for building a more certain environment will be of benefit to every single student you will ever support.

Chapter 4 – Sensory

Our understanding of sensory information is central to our understanding of everything. As such the Sensory S is in the centre of our 3S's. This section begins by highlighting the influence of the Sensory realm on all other aspects of school life, including academic learning, and therefore how uncertainty in this area can be a huge barrier to students' ability to demonstrate their full potential in school.

We discuss some of the types of sensory support you may come across in schools, including sensory integration and sensory modulation. We look at the eight main senses to consider when looking at sensory uncertainty and we provide a particular focus on interoception.

The activities and worksheets in this section look at different ways to support students with sensory recognition, understanding and, therefore, regulation. We also place great emphasis on the ways we can support a better understanding of emotions by helping students develop their understanding of the sensory system that governs them.

Chapter 5 – Social

This chapter looks at the specific reasons why we can experience social uncertainty and what the implications might be. We discuss the central role that an understanding of ourselves has in our understanding of others and how we also appeal to broader social rules and norms to help us manage social uncertainty.

The activities and worksheets in this section focus on supporting students to better understand themselves and others. They do not focus on trying to make all of our students behave in a single homogenous manner. Instead they aim to support a common understanding that is central to any social connection.

QUICK LINKS

Would you like to find out more about why a student might behave the way they do?

Read the introduction in Chapter 1. Visit 'Flipping the narrative' in Chapter 2 for some alternative interpretations of commonly observed 'problem' behaviours. Focus on the 'The search for...' sections at the start of Chapters 3–5.

Are you interested in how the way we think affects the way we teach and learn?

Read Chapter 2, Understanding Our Own Uncertainty, to find out more about growth mindsets and how reconceptualising 'difficult' behaviour can help us reduce our own stress.

Are you looking for some quick adjustments you can make to your lessons or intervention groups to help everyone learn more effectively?

Chapter 3 contains lots of ideas on how to build in more structure and raise everyone's game.

Are you unsure how to help students with sensory-based difficulties?

Read Chapter 4 on the Sensory realm, which contains both theory and practical activities, most of which you can do with an individual or a whole class.

Would you like some new practical ideas for supporting students with social difficulties?

Chapter 5 on Social combines social skills practicality with some cognitive change techniques to support students in developing their social confidence.

Are you looking for a new evidence base for what you do?

Pay particular attention to the introduction to uncertainty in Chapter 1 and at the start of each chapter. You might also like to look more closely at some of the references and recommended reading at the end of each chapter.

FURTHER READING

Below is a list of journal articles that provide more information about the ideas discussed in this chapter. Many of these are elaborated on further in Chapter 1 and beyond.

Astle, D. E., Bathelt, J., CALM Team & Holmes, J. (2019). Remapping the cognitive and neural profiles of children who struggle at school. *Developmental Science, 22*(1), e12747.

Borsboom, D. (2017). A network theory of mental disorders. *World Psychiatry, 16*(1), 5–13.

Caspi, A., Houts, R. M., Belsky, D. W., Goldman-Mellor, S. J. *et al.* (2014). The p factor: One general psychopathology factor in the structure of psychiatric disorders? *Clinical Psychological Science, 2*(2), 119–137.

Honkasilta, J. (2017). Diagnosing the Need or in Need of a Diagnosis. Reconceptualizing Educational Need. In K. Scorgie & D. Sobsey (eds) *Working with Families for Inclusive Education: Navigating Identity, Opportunity and Belonging. International Perspectives on Inclusive Education* (pp. s.123–141). Bingley, West Yorkshire: Emerald Group Publishing.

Johnstone, L. & Boyle, M. (2018). The power threat meaning framework: An alternative nondiagnostic conceptual system. *Journal of Humanistic Psychology*, 0022167818793289.

Thomas, M. S. (2020). Developmental disorders: Few specific disorders and no specific brain regions. *Current Biology, 30*(7), R304–R306.

REFERENCE

Wright, A. G. & Woods, W. C. (2020). Personalized models of psychopathology. *Annual Review of Clinical Psychology, 16*, 49–74.

1

UNDERSTANDING UNCERTAINTY
GLASSES, PATHS AND DIALS

The aim of this book is to help anyone working with teenagers who may be struggling, academically or socially, by offering a new way of understanding behaviour and some new ideas for support.

Drawing on recent theories about how we think, see and feel, we will highlight the fact that all humans, including those teenagers who you had in mind when you bought this book, struggle with the same fundamental difficulty: **uncertainty**. Regardless of any specific diagnoses, we are all seeking to reduce and manage uncertainty. This chapter of the book will introduce you to the central, overarching theoretical concepts that underpin our 3S model of uncertainty. Some of the concepts may take a couple of readings to get to grips with, but each of the 3S chapters in the book reiterates some of the points made here, which will, we hope, make the ideas even clearer.

THIS CHAPTER AT A GLANCE

This chapter explains why uncertainty is a universal problem. We will look at how, from the point of view of our brain, the world is inherently ambiguous. The brain has no idea what's behind different sights, smells or sounds, so it must generate predictions, or guesses, about the causes. Our brain is a prediction machine, building models of the world based on inference. False predictions that do not explain what we are experiencing cause uncertainty. From a biological perspective, experiencing such errors is bad as they require energy to fix. The negative impact of errors reflects at a psychological level too, meaning uncertainty is the primary difficulty we face as humans. We are driven, therefore, to create the best models we can, to reduce errors in our predictions and, in turn, limit uncertainty. Everything we infer and do serves to minimise uncertainty and maximise the evidence for our models of the world. This means that all the behaviour difficulties humans display (including the teenagers we are supporting) are driven by the same fundamental aim: to create certainty out of uncertainty. So, the question we need to ask ourselves when a student is struggling in any area is:

'Where's the uncertainty?'

We then do what we can to bring about some certainty for them. As we will describe throughout the book, the three areas where the uncertainty will reside, and therefore where we can offer support are the 3S's – **Structure**, **Sensory**, **Social**.

UNCERTAINTY

The human experience is defined by uncertainty; it is 'written into the script of life' (Nowotny, 2015, p.1). Despite the inherent uncertainty of the world, we are constantly trying to wrestle some sort of certainty from it or at the very least trying to manage the uncertainty. We make plans, we save for a pension, we backup our files, we check the weather, we take out insurance, we Google it, we take a picture in case we forget, we get a second opinion. Having certainty about how the world works and our place in it allows us to feel comfortable in our knowledge of how things are but also, crucially, *how things will be*. It allows us to feel that we are in control (gives us a sense of agency) as we can predict what might happen and prepare for what is to come. We are rarely surprised by our everyday world.

Uncertainty, however, can lead to a perceived lack of control. It means we are unsure if we can achieve our goals, whether it be to manage a sensory experience (such as bungee jumping, or to simply engage in a social conversation), and/or work out what will happen as we try to achieve these goals.

Uncertainty is seen as innately threatening because it means that either we do not understand the current situation enough to bring some certainty to it (lack of knowledge), or we do not have the capacity (agency) to manage the situation and bring some certainty to it.

Either way, as far as the brain[1] is concerned, it means our very survival may be at stake. Recent ideas about how we think have highlighted the fundamental role that reducing uncertainty plays in action and cognition. It has been suggested that the goal of everything we do is to resolve uncertainty (Friston, 2018). The best way to achieve this goal is to be able to predict and prepare.

PREDICTING OUR WORLD

The relatively new idea of our brains functioning in the service of prediction cuts across all scientific domains that explore how we think. The story of predictive processing is helping to change our understanding of perception, language, social neuroscience, action and clinical psychology. It is a story that also makes logical sense. We are, like all organisms, biological entities and therefore resource rational: we seek to optimise our use of critical resources, which, for living creatures, are metabolic – energy is our most critical resource (Griffiths, Lieder & Goodman, 2015; Lieder & Griffiths, 2020). The brain uses energy in its main job of regulating our body to keep us alive (to predictively anticipate the bodily changes that I will need to regulate to maintain homeostasis[2]). For example, it helps us to run away from something that might be about to eat us, or, less dramatically, organises actions that lead us to stand up.

Our brain, dependent on energy like the rest of us, wants to be as efficient as possible. To effectively regulate us and keep us alive, it needs to make changes to our body *before* situations unfold (allostasis); we need to respond to predicted situations, not the situations themselves. So, to regulate efficiently, the brain must regulate predictively. It needs to coordinate our 'run away' response *before* we are eaten, as doing so afterwards would be a very ineffective way of staying alive. It needs to reorganise our blood pressure *before* we stand up otherwise we might faint, fall and bump our head. Our brains, therefore, need to anticipate possible outcomes, predict them and direct our behaviour based on these predictions.

Having good predictions not only makes it easier to stay alive, it is also very efficient. We do not need to rely on processing all the millions of pieces of information we are exposed to at any given moment to build an understanding of the world from the bottom-up. We can just focus on those bits of information that do

---

1   The brain makes little distinction between perceived threat and actual threat. As soon as the demands placed on us outweigh our perceived ability to meet those demands, we are under threat. That could be having to speak in front of a thousand people about a subject we know nothing about or survive a fight with a tiger. Even though in only one situation could we actually die our brain would still be perceiving a threat in both situations and trigger similar physiological responses such as increasing heart rate and dilating pupils.

2   This predictive regulation is called allostasis (Schulkin, 2011; Sterling, 2012, 2018; Sterling & Eyer, 1988), where a brain anticipates the needs of the body and attempts to satisfy those needs before they arise, minimising costly errors. For instance, we should be motivated to forage before essentials (e.g. water) run out of safe bounds (Sterling, 2012).

not match our predictions, the errors. To be super energy efficient in predictive regulation we need our predictions to be as accurate as they possibly can be. That way we need only process a small amount of information – the errors – and the fewer of these we experience the better. Prediction errors are costly in terms of wasted energy, not only because they could lead us to run away from something that will not actually eat us, but also because it requires energy to process them. As a resource rational organism, we want to reduce prediction errors as much as possible. We want to generate good predictions of the world, so we want good models of the world. This can help us minimise the amount of surprise, or uncertainty, that we experience.

The predictive processing story of cognition describes the growing understanding of how the brain builds models of the world and uses this alongside current sensory information to create the world that we experience.

A NOTE ON THE THEORY

Predictive processing (PP) is an elegantly simple but also highly complex idea. It encompasses a range of ideas that look to understand the idea of prediction in the brain, including the Bayesian brain hypothesis, predictive coding, active inference and the free energy principle. We are squashing elements of them altogether here and simplifying them to highlight the theoretical rationale for our 3S model – which might make some of the incredible folks that write brilliantly about these topics feel frustrated that the specifics of their work, including some very beautiful equations, are absent. To them we apologise! It is also important to note that what we discuss here is a tiny fraction of work that has been done looking at the PP story and some of the practical implications of it.

For those bits we do discuss, we have tried to stay as true to the underlying theoretical work as possible. However, we have also used poetic licence to try to bring it forward from theory into the realms of practice, where we operate, to consider some of the implications of these exciting developments in the story of cognition. So, it is important to remember that much of what we discuss is our poetic theory. For more information about the foundation for everything we are writing about here and to keep track of ongoing developments, the work of Karl Friston, Andy Clark, Lisa Feldman Barrett, Jakob Hohwy, Anil Seth, Manos Tsakiris, Aikaterini Fotopoulou and Nicholas Carleton is a good place to begin. We highlight some recommended further reading at the end of the chapter.

ONCE UPON A GUESS...THE STORY OF PREDICTIVE PROCESSING

> We are not cognitive couch potatoes idly awaiting the next 'input', so much as proactive predictavores – nature's own guessing machines forever trying to stay one step ahead by surfing the incoming waves of sensory stimulation. (Clark, 2015, p.52)

A long-standing model of how our brains work assumed that sensory information from the world ('bottom-up' influences) was the primary driver of perception and action. As sensory information was processed, the world was experienced. This was a very hands-off, passive conceptualisation of how we perceive the world. This supposed that the brain sat around waiting for sensory input and then jumped into action when it arrived, processing the input to determine our perception. It could be likened to moving around in a room with our eyes closed. The room would only come into existence, from our brain's perspective, when we opened our eyes and it perceived information. It would also be a very inefficient way of processing the world. It means we would need to spend energy scrutinising every piece of information we saw in order to interpret it. It would also mean that we would regularly be startled by pieces of information, unable to process what they were until we had brought it all into our brain and pieced it together. We could consider this conceptualisation of how we think to be a *reactive* way of processing the world.

The predictive processing (PP) story that describes how we think sees the brain as a prediction-making, inference machine. The brain generates predictions about potential future states, actions and outcomes based on models of the world that it has built.

This broadly speaking *proactive* conceptualisation makes a lot more sense. It is much more energy efficient to predict than to react. It explains why on our daily walk to work we are not constantly surprised by what we see – 'A car! Oh, a tree!' We have a strong prior **model** of what we expect to see, and we will only then focus on sensory input (information) that doesn't really fit in with that model – 'Oh a person riding an elephant!' We do not experience a great deal of uncertainty in our day-to-day life as a result of our models. If we do experience a lot of surprise and uncertainty it means that our models are not doing the best job at predicting our world. So how do we build these models and how do we ensure that they are a good fit?

A NOTE ON COSTS

The cost of cognition can be framed as the amount of information needed to update prior models to match current experience (Zenon, Solopchuk & Pezzulo, 2019). Only focusing on things we do not expect to 'see' as opposed to every single possible thing we 'see' is a very energy efficient way of doing things. Roughly speaking, this process is referred to in the PP family of ideas as predictive coding.

The major problem the brain has is that the information that it needs for building a model of the world is always going to be hidden. It can't hop out of our skull and look around. It must build models, or beliefs about the world, based on inference or educated guesses. The raw materials it uses to inform these guesses come from information received by our sensory systems. While this information is ambiguous (our brain can't jump out and tell exactly what is causing it), over time, sensory information can show repeatable patterns which can give us clues as to what is causing it and/ or where it is coming from.

Snowball fights in T-shirts

Sensory information is not always random 'noise' and can provide a 'signal' that helps us to identify an underlying cause of that information. It can have some statistical regularity. Repeated sensory experiences allow us to build models that generate predictions (generative models) about subsequent sensory activity. For example, every time it snows it is cold and this is a stable, repeatable pattern.

Experiencing snow and cold a few times can lead us to build a model of the world that predicts it to be cold when it snows. We have now built a prior model to add to our database of how the world works. This can be drawn on to help us when we experience uncertainty. It means if we find ourselves having a snowball fight in just jeans and a T-shirt, our brain now has a useful prior model available to it to help make a better guess as to why we might suddenly start shivering.

In this situation, we have moved out of our predictable, usual state – *not shivering* – and our brain needs to work out how to regulate us back to this certainty. In order to do this, it relies on two pieces of information: our prior models (beliefs) and our current sensory input (*shivering*). Very simply, what we experience, therefore, is what our brain calculates as the most likely cause of the current sensory input as a result of various possible beliefs (e.g. *being cold* or *being scared*). What we then experience is essentially a precision-weighted compromise between our beliefs and current sensory input. We weigh up the likelihood of sensory input A (*shivering*) being caused by belief B (*being cold*) or C (*being scared*) and then go with our best guess. This is why it can be considered a compromise, as there is always an outside chance it could be something else.

So, there are the two key pieces of information, classified in terms of a probability distribution, which are used as the compromise calculation[3] that decides how we experience the world:

1   The current sensory input[4] (*shivering*)

2   Prior models (beliefs) we hold about the possible causes of sensory input (*being cold* or *being scared*).

By seeing, feeling and so perceiving snow on the ground, we can draw on a prior model of the world (**snow = cold**) that means we would have a very strong expectation that it is cold. Our brain can then guess that there is a greater probability that **being cold, as opposed to being scared**, is causing our **shivering**. In our compromise calculation, we weight the prior model for being cold more heavily than the prior model for being scared. Our calculation and weighting of the different pieces of information in this instance has led to a good outcome. We experience a pretty accurate representation of the world. Our brain can now regulate us effectively; it can now predict, based on the ***being cold*** belief, what the best actions to take are. In this instance, we put on a coat, and this regulates us effectively and stops the

---

3   This calculation is thought to follow a process in line with Bayesian probability (Friston, 2009), which is why PP is spoken about alongside the 'Bayesian brain' hypothesis.

4   This is referred to as the likelihood in Bayesian terms. It is essentially how sensory input is represented internally.

loss of energy through shivering, returning us to homeostasis,[5] our 'home' state. We get back to certainty.

The snow, shivering and coat scenario above is an example of predictive processing functioning excellently. It illustrates how good prior models (it is important to stress that this is almost always plural), correctly applied, optimise our use of energy by bringing certainty to the cause of a change of state (e.g. shivering) and regulating us to be more efficient (putting on warm clothes). It also introduces the idea of the brain having more than one prior model available – in this instance **being cold** and **being scared**. Some of these models will be counterfactual, in that they will not accurately model what is happening in the world. We might not return to certainty as effectively if we misestimate the strength of our prior models or the current sensory input. For example, if we apply too much strength (weight) to our *being scared* model when we are cold, we might end up running and hiding in the snow. Doing this in just jeans and a T-shirt would result in the loss of more energy, not return us to homeostasis and not return us to certainty. This is an example of how *our* world can end up being very different to *the* world, how we can apply counterfactual models to a situation if we apply the wrong weight to our options when we are carrying out our compromise calculation.

Ideally, we want to build models that generate accurate predictions and we want to apply them accurately, giving them the correct amount of weight.

We want to avoid prediction errors, for example where we fail to predict that it will be cold because it is snowing, and we end up walking outside in just shorts and a T-shirt. This prediction error has an impact at a biological level; it moves us out of our 'home' state and therefore uses up energy to get us back there, in this case by shivering. It could also be seen to cost us at a psychological level because the error manifests itself as uncertainty – we move out of our certain state about how the world works. If we didn't expect to be shivering, our world is currently unexplained and therefore unpredictable. It then costs us, at the very least, a little bit of thinking power to try to get back to certainty. PP can, therefore. help us to better understand why uncertainty is such a fundamental problem from a psychological perspective.

---

5   Certainty from a biological perspective is called homeostasis. Our brain wants to regulate the environment to keep us in our 'home' state. A core body temperature of between 36.5 and 37.5°C in this example. It is always trying to bring us back here, because ultimately moving out of this might end up with us dying.

Predictive processing in summary

The broad application of the PP story states that every biological self-organising system is driven to reduce the amount of surprise (free energy) it experiences (Friston, 2013). Essentially, this means that we are driven by a fundamental, biological urge to avoid uncertainty. We do this by building good models and applying them accurately and by interpreting sensory input accurately. If we do not do this accurately it will result in a lot of uncertainty as a result of our failure to accurately predict the world, and impact on our ability to regulate ourselves effectively with the potential for catastrophic costs (we might end up dying of hypothermia). The PP story, therefore, also provides a theoretical rationale for the psychological impact of uncertainty that it is built out of an innate, overarching aim to avoid costly prediction errors. This helps to explain why uncertainty is not only thought to be the fundamental component of all anxiety (Carleton, Sharpe & Asmundson, 2007) but also the *possible* underlying cause of all psychological difficulties (Rosser, 2019).

In this book, we highlight the importance of recognising that any difficulties a student (or any human) is experiencing are a result of uncertainty. The remainder of this chapter looks at trying to understand how uncertainty can arise as a result of the PP process, highlighting that this is not because the PP machine itself (our brain) is 'faulty' but because it is operating with inputs, in terms of sensory inputs and prior beliefs, that may not be as good as they could be.

We will look at how uncertainty comes about due to one or all of the following: lack of a prior model that is a good enough fit; applying too much or too little strength (weight) to our prior model or applying too much or too little strength (weight) to the sensory input.

We also reiterate throughout how we can help to address this by supporting our students to gain more knowledge (build better models) and increase their agency (the perceived ability to do things, like effectively manage uncertainty and build good models!).

PERFECT MODELS IN AN IMPERFECT WORLD

A simple way to avoid uncertainty and the associated psychological distress and biological cost would be to build perfect prior models that flawlessly predict our world. Unfortunately, this is impossible.

As mentioned earlier, our brain cannot directly access the world. There is an inherent ambiguity in sensory input and its possible worldly causes. That loud bang could have been a firework, a gunshot, a car backfiring or a balloon bursting. Our sensory processing systems are also limited. We cannot process every single piece of information we are exposed to because we simply do not have the computing power. This means the ideal of perfect models is never going to be a reality. So, models will always be imperfect and inevitably lead to prediction errors for two reasons:

1   **The models we build are never going to be exact replicas of the world**. As a result of the limitations of our senses (that provide building blocks for models), models must be a pragmatic simplification and so are inevitably partly wrong (Clark, 2015).

2   **The world is a noisy, uncertain and always changing place**. It is important to recognise, therefore, that our models are not strictly binary in that they either exactly fit or do not fit the world. They exist on a spectrum of good fit to poorer fit, which means we will inevitably experience prediction errors and will all have to manage uncertainty when the predictions generated by our prior model/s do not immediately account for the sensory information we are receiving. However, over time we tend to end up with models that are good enough for us in our particular environment because we can adapt and update them. We learn (which also means we can be taught!) to adapt to *our* world – not necessarily *the* world.

A NOTE ON PRIOR MODELS

We often illustrate our examples with just one or two priors. Our generative model of the world is one that can generate multiple predictions or guesses, and it is going to be useful to have a few to call on (due to the noisy, changing world we live in). We will usually have some prior models that are stronger than others, if correctly weighted, depending on the context we find ourselves in.

If we hear a bang as a car drives past on a sunny June day, we could predict it to be a balloon popping, a firework, a gunshot or a car backfiring. The car back firing would be the strongest prior and the one we would bring to this situation and give most weight. If, however, we heard a loud bang at night on 5 November in the UK, the firework belief would be the best one to bring.

DECISION MAKING UNDER UNCERTAINTY: LEARNING

Prediction errors, though inevitable, are what we are fundamentally striving to avoid due to our innate desire for certainty. But prediction errors are not all bad. They can provide us with a learning opportunity.

Errors can give us an indication that our prior model is not fitting as well as it could and needs changing. However, a prediction error signalling that a prior model is a poor fit does not necessarily mean it's time to change or drop that model (Fletcher & Frith, 2009). Updating our prior models or making new ones comes at a cognitive (and therefore metabolic) cost, so we should only do it when we need to, otherwise it would be a waste of energy. The important thing we need to figure out is which prediction errors we use to update our models and which we should just ignore as part of the random chaos of the world. Are the potential causes of a surprising event (an error) useful to know? Should we just ignore it? Is it worth the energy of updating our model or looking for more information to reinforce our existing model? Our decision will be influenced by the amount of precision we apply to our prior models and the current sensory input. Let us look at how precision works with some examples of the calculation that our brain goes through to make sense of an ambiguous situation that we have not predicted (a prediction error).

A NOTE ON WHY WE MIGHT LIKE SURPRISES

If our aim is to reduce uncertainty, why might we seek uncertainty/errors sometimes – try new things? Well, we need surprises in order to learn. The uncertainty they cause can help us update our models so that they might be better fits for the world. This could lead to a longer-term reduction in the amount of surprises we experience – greater certainty about our world. But constantly seeking out surprises will mean we are spending a lot of energy and we are resource rationale, so we want to be very parsimonious in our use of it. So we have a balancing act to carry out: if we do not explore enough, we might be missing out on valuable information that might mean we build better models that cause fewer errors and therefore save energy in the long run. But if we explore too much unnecessarily (i.e. our models are already good enough fits we do not need more information) we are wasting energy.

This is referred to as the explore-exploit dilemma. Do we exploit the certainty our prior models currently provide, for example always go to the same restaurant and order the same dish? Or do we explore an uncertainty – try a new restaurant? Do we try to make new friends or stick with the ones we have? Do we go to that party or stay at home as usual? Do we try to learn something new or stick with what we know? How precise we perceive our models to be and how confident we are in our ability to gather more evidence for them will influence how much exploring and exploiting we do – how we take a calculated risk.

The monster in the bedroom

As mentioned earlier, the brain combines two pieces of information, our prior model and the current sensory input, to determine our experience. The compromise calculation it carries out helps us to make decisions under uncertainty. It is important to point out that all this back and forth between prior models and current sensory input takes place outside our conscious awareness. However, it is easier to understand this process and consider the practical implications as if it occurs consciously.

We have invented a person called Jordan, whose prior experience and knowledge we can control, so we can manipulate the prior model/current sensory input calculation their brain carries out and show how by changing the precision of each we can change Jordan's world. We are going to run through a simple example that illustrates how Jordan uses the PP process to resolve a perceptual (visual) uncertainty, how they come to visually interpret (see) something that may initially seem ambiguous. In the following 'strange silhouette' example, we are going to give Jordan two prior models to draw on: that what they are seeing is *a monster* or that it is a *pile of clothes*. One of these is clearly a highly counterfactual prior model in terms of the world (we are all almost certain monsters do not exist…). By manipulating the precision Jordan applies to the current sensory input and their prior models we are going to show how a brilliantly functioning PP system can, among other things, make Jordan's world a place where monsters exist.

Imagine Jordan wakes up in a bedroom in the middle of the night and catches a glimpse of a strange silhouette on the chair next to them. This quick visual impression provides current sensory input. Their prior model is based on context (their bedroom) and memory. This glimpse of visual information briefly creates some uncertainty – what is that strange silhouette? Jordan now needs to resolve this uncertainty. If Jordan had a really strong prior model, they would perhaps not even register the strange silhouette as an error and simply see the chair, but we are not going to let them handle this situation that easily. Instead we are going to make Jordan uncertain. We will have them register this prediction error and have their brain look to resolve it by combining their prior models with the current sensory input (strange silhouette) to try to bring certainty to what they are perceiving. We will manipulate the precision we give each of these two elements to demonstrate how we can change Jordan's reality.

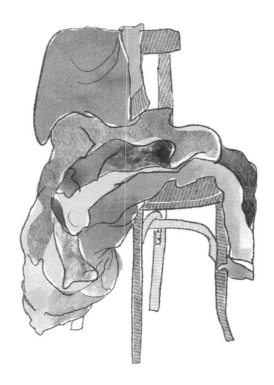

Precision

Precision is different from accuracy: a prediction can be precise but inaccurate, imprecise but accurate, or indeed any other combination. We can think of precision in terms of the strength of the conviction we have in something. The higher the strength of the precision, the more certain we are of the information. Precision, in terms of our prior model, can be thought of as the strength of the expectation it gives us (we are almost completely certain that in this situation we should see a chair with clothes on it). The more precise our prior model, the stronger and more influential it is in determining what we experience. Precision in sensory data is a function of its reliability – unambiguous, clear sensory data will be given high precision (e.g. if it is daytime, and we have our glasses on, we are fairly sure this visual information is coming in loud and clear, so it has high precision). The more precision current sensory input has, the stronger and more influential it is in determining what we experience; it holds more sway in our compromise calculation. We can think of precision as being a set of strength dials that we can turn up or down, increasing or decreasing the influence of our priors or current sensory input. When we are struggling to manage errors or generate a good enough model it is often going to be due to a **misestimation of precision** – we have set at least one of the dials too high or too low.

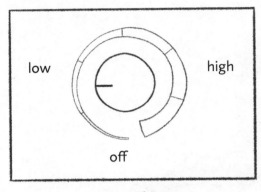 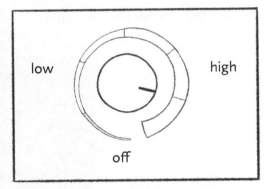

current input   **priors**

The relative strength (precision) we give to our prior model and the current sensory data when processing information, particularly a prediction error, will influence:

- **If we learn**. This will depend on whether we even register a prediction error (if we're not processing it, we aren't going to learn) and, if so, whether we feel it truly indicates that our prior model needs changing (it's a signal), or if the error is just random noise.

- **What we learn**. If we do look to resolve a prediction error, how much sway do we give to current sensory input and our prior models in the compromise calculation that determines what we end up perceiving.

Ultimately, therefore, precision will determine if we learn and what it is we learn. In our strange silhouette example, as we are not giving Jordan a super strong prior model, we are going to make them register the error, 'What is that strange silhouette?', and so we have addressed the first point above, by registering the error Jordan will have to 'learn'. Jordan (and anyone resolving uncertainty) now has three possible learning paths they can travel down:

1 **Register the error and update their prior model/s** to now account for (and include) this unexplained sensory information (*perceptual learning*).

2 **Register the error as a random event** by viewing the strange silhouette as statistical noise, dismiss the error as meaningless and don't update the model.

3 **Register the error but look for more evidence that supports the prior model** (active inference – *active learning*).

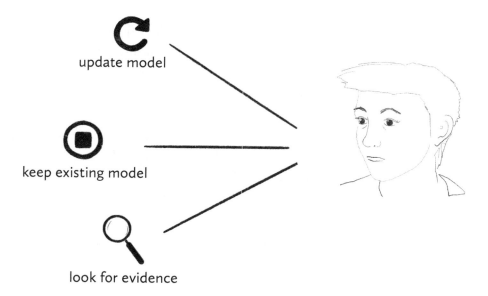

update model

keep existing model

look for evidence

The learning outcomes of the three paths could be very different and have significant consequences. If the 'new' model or updated belief about the world (posterior) that results from Jordan learning, through following path 1, 2 or 3, is not a good fit, they will find themselves experiencing ongoing uncertainty. Their new model will continue to result in errors as it will not accurately align with future sensory input. It is important therefore that we follow the best path. We will look at what factors influence the path we take later on. First let's demonstrate the impact of each taking each path, specifically looking at how following paths 1 and 2 could lead to us generating better fitting models, before then looking at how it could also lead to poorer fitting models, before looking at path 3. On the face of it, path 3, double checking, looks as if it should always be the best bet, a no-brainer. However, as we explore below, it is a little more complex than that.

Path 1 better fitting model = less uncertainty

To follow path 1 and update their model, to one in which monsters can exist, could be a good idea, if it is an unfamiliar bedroom. In this situation, their prior model would not be great as they have not experienced this room much before. So updating the model of *this bedroom* would be useful. It means when they wake up again, having fallen back asleep (albeit in the presence of a monster!), the sensory input (silhouette) will match with their updated model: this bedroom has a monster in it. No visual uncertainty.

Path 1 poorer fitting model = more uncertainty

Equally, they could follow path 1 but over-generalise and not just change their model to 'what this bedroom looks like' but 'what the world now looks like – it has monsters in it'. Doing this would perhaps resolve the short-term uncertainty (what am I seeing?), but over-fitting a model based on a single sample would lead to a very volatile world. Jordan would expect to regularly see monsters, and this would be unlikely, so they would therefore have a new prediction error – no monsters! Another less fantastical example might be if Jordan updated their model for what rain sounds like based on the specific sound rain made one day as a result of falling heavily onto a corrugated roof. That would be their new 'rain sound', that is, what they would expect to hear if it were raining. They would then be surprised at the sound of rain the next day when it was falling lightly onto the grass. Their model would be overly precise, too specific. They would be trying to fit precise models to an imprecise world, and their world would end up being a very uncertain place, filled with errors (uncertainty) and constant updating.

Path 2 better fitting model = less uncertainty

If Jordan follows path 2 and it turns out that the strange silhouette was nothing they needed to pay too much attention to, a random anomaly, then ignoring it and sticking with their existing model would be a good choice to take. They would not have created an updated belief based on a random piece of information. It is similar to when we trip up while walking, and we would not update our model of our ability to walk. We would put it down to a random, one-off occurrence.

Path 2 poorer fitting model = more uncertainty

If, however, they took path 2 when encountering an error and failed to update their model, they risk an under-fitting model. For example, let's give Jordan a prior model of the world in which the brakes for their car always worked (as they had never failed). If one day their brakes were *a little less responsive*, an error, following path 2 would not be a good idea. Sticking with their prior model *brakes never fail* and dismissing the *a little less responsive* sensory input as 'noise' would lead to an under-fitting model. Brakes can sometimes fail and so the model should have been updated. Not updating the model would lead to Jordan not having the brakes checked and could then result in a serious accident.

Path 3 better fitting model = less uncertainty

Following path 3, seeking more information, could result in Jordan reinforcing their prior model and making it stronger. So, by turning on the light, for example, they can receive more evidence (in the form of more precise sensory data) that confirms their prior model. Instinctively, this might seem like the most sensible option – always double check. Often it is the best plan. It is not as simple as saying always take path 3 to resolve uncertainty though.

Path 3 – complications

Wasting energy

Path 3 will cost us energy, so we should not take it if it is unnecessary (this is where the explore-exploit dilemma comes in). If our prior model is good enough then taking this path would be a waste of energy. So, if we have mistakenly given our model low precision when it should have been higher, we are wasting energy by exploring when we should be exploiting.

Prerequisites

So, if our prior model is not as good as it could be, it would almost always make sense to take this path. But this path may not be as easily accessible for everyone. Taking this path means we have confidence in our ability to find more evidence and resolve uncertainty in this way. Our confidence in this would be determined by a broader, overarching belief (a hyper-prior) in our ability (our agency). If Jordan had a low sense of agency (maybe referred to in school as having 'low self-esteem' or 'lacking self-confidence'), path 3 would not be considered as often as it should be, as Jordan would not have the prerequisite confidence to help push them down this route.

Second guessing

Ironically, however, if Jordan had been someone who had been constantly taking path 3 previously, even when they did not need to, it could be the cause of their current low sense of agency and the barrier to them now taking this path. Constant checking can undermine the confidence we have in our prior models. For example, we might double check a calculation we do in our heads on our phones. Even if the checking confirms we were correct, the safety-seeking behaviour of checking implied that we were not certain of our ability (otherwise why would we have wasted the energy on checking?). It has eroded the confidence we have in our prior model (*we are good at maths*). The more we check, the more we chip away at specific prior models (*we are good at maths*) but also that hyper-prior (*our prior models are good, we live in a world of certainty*).

This type of behaviour might shed light on the negative impact of not letting students take enough risks (not necessarily double checking) and how this can lead to learned helplessness. There is a body of work that is looking at the extent to which increased connectedness (having the answer to everything – 'certainty' – in the palm of our hands through our smartphones) is leading us all to experience greater anxiety (uncertainty) as a result of constantly taking path 3, 'I'll just quickly Google it to double check', when we do not need to (Carleton *et al.*, 2019).

We can be uncertain about everything we try to predict. For example, perceptual uncertainty is uncertainty about what we are experiencing (a monster or not a monster?). Outcome uncertainty is uncertainty about what the implications or outcomes of this experience might be (will we get eaten?). Action uncertainty describes the uncertainty around what actions we might need to take (do we stay put, run away or fight?). (Motor) planning uncertainty is uncertainty about how to carry out those actions (how would we go about fighting a monster? Which route would we take to run away?). Lastly and importantly, agentic uncertainty describes uncertainty around our perceived ability (can we successfully fight a monster? Are we faster than a monster?). Various areas of uncertainty build on each other (FeldmanHall & Shenhav, 2019) to generate deeper uncertainty. This can create a domino effect: perceptual uncertainty leading to outcome uncertainty on to action uncertainty and (motor) planning uncertainty and so on.

What this essentially means is that we can easily descend into an uncertainty spiral. As educators supporting people who are struggling, we can try to reduce the impact of some of those uncertainties by increasing certainty around **Structure** (see Chapter 3). We can, for example, try to bring some certainty to what someone might be experiencing (e.g. a maths lesson) by presenting what the outcomes of that experience will be (learning about long division), what actions are needed to achieve those outcomes (practise the method), how to carry out those actions (by modelling how to do it and setting the task out clearly) and increase their agentic certainty (by giving them control – choices over which specific questions to answer). We can also look to support longer-term confidence in our understanding of our body and the signals it gives us (interoception, see Chapters 4 and 5) as the body can provide an anchor in this uncertain world.

Giving Jordan a precise push down each path

By manipulating the precision of the prior model and current sensory input we can impact which learning route Jordan takes and what they learn from it. The panels below help illustrate the influence precision can have on shifting our best guess either over towards our prior model or the current sensory input. As mentioned earlier, we are also going to show how we can make Jordan's world one that is very different from but not less 'real' than the world. Differences in how precision is applied help us to understand how individual brains model the external world differently even though the process of modelling is similar in us all. It will, we hope, help us to better understand how someone can perceive the world so differently from us; not because there is anything fundamentally wrong with their modelling system, but because their estimates of precision might be very different. Their dials are set to different levels.

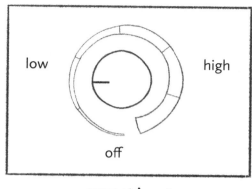

current input

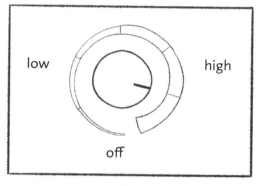

priors

Back to the monster in the bedroom

To recap, the situation for Jordan is this: Jordan wakes up in a bedroom in the middle of the night and catches a glimpse of a strange silhouette on the chair next to them. We have looked at the impact of following different paths (1, 2 and 3). We will now go on to show how the precision we apply to our two compromise calculation variables (current sensory input and prior model) impacts on which path we take and subsequently what our world is like.

The following four examples (panels 1, 2, 3 and 4) show how changing the precision dials on different inputs impacts on the learning path Jordan takes and what it is they learn and ultimately then perceive the strange silhouette to be.

The dials represent how much weight Jordan is giving their current input (what they are seeing, feeling and perceiving) compared to their prior models (what they believe about the world).

The graphs look at how this combination of input and prior models will determine Jordan's thinking, shifting the probability either towards monster or chair, and therefore determining their best guess: whether they are more likely to see a pile of clothes, a monster or whether they get up and turn the light on.

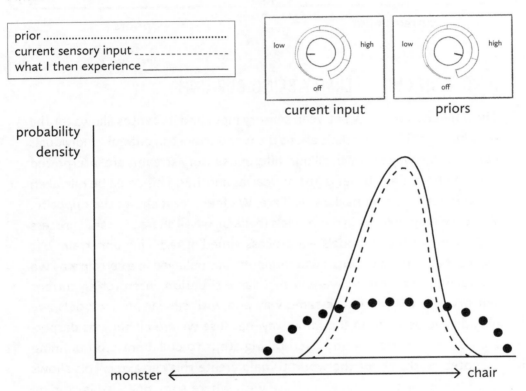

Panel 1

Let's turn down the precision strength for Jordan's prior model of the bedroom (the flatter dotted line in the graph). We will make the space unfamiliar to them by having them arrive at night to stay at their auntie's house for the first ever time. We will make it even less likely for them to have a precise prior for this room by having them sharing the room with their younger cousin, so they had to creep into this unfamiliar bedroom when it was dark so as not to wake them. However, we are going to turn up the precision on the sensory input (the pointier dashed line in the graph) by having their cousin wake up, turn on the light and leave it on while Jordan was asleep. The graph then shows that the best guess (the peak of the probability density) is more likely to be falling at the chair end of the graph.

So, Jordan wakes up in the night and sees the room, and the pile of clothes, for the first time. For a split second, they wonder what they are looking at. As it is an unfamiliar room Jordan updates their model of where they are in line with the precise ('it is light, so I trust my eyes') current sensory input.

This scenario illustrates what happens when a low precision prior (because of the unfamiliar room) for *pile of clothes* is combined with high precision sensory evidence (because the light is on) for a *pile of clothes*. Jordan will perceive a pile of clothes on a chair. Their certainty, or precision, of this is strong as a result of clear sensory data signalling a *pile of clothes*. We have pushed Jordan down path 1. It has resulted in an accurate interpretation and Jordan's updated model will be a great fit when they wake up in that room again later that morning.

Jordan's learning: path 1 – they have resolved the uncertainty by updating their model of this room.

In unfamiliar environments, it usually makes sense to turn down the precision on our prior models. Although, as discussed earlier, if we update too readily, applying too much precision to sensory input based on a limited number of examples, we could build models that are not based on statistical regularities but on random 'noise'. This will lead to models that over-fit our world. Let's change Jordan's world by doing this to them in panel 2.

PANEL 2

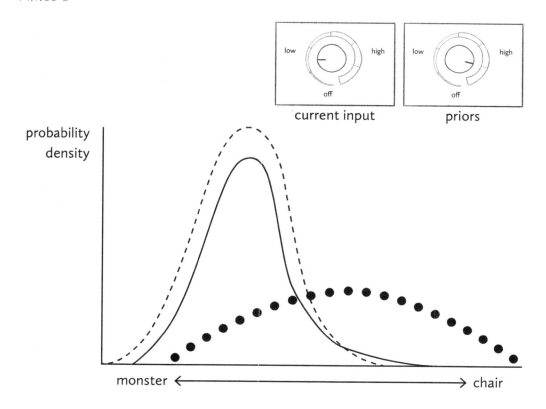

Panel 2

We will keep Jordan in the same unfamiliar setting and so keep the precision strength for the prior model, the *pile of clothes*, turned down (flatter dotted line). So, the space is still unfamiliar to them, but let's also say that, unbeknownst to Jordan, in this scenario their younger cousin was dressed as a monster for a party earlier that day and left their costume on the chair next to Jordan's bed. Once Jordan is asleep, their auntie opens the bedroom door, leaves it slightly ajar and puts the light on in the hallway. So, the room has a little light shining in. When Jordan wakes up, they see a strange silhouette. In this scenario, we have slightly turned up the precision on the sensory input by having the half-light and a just a single costume with a vaguely discernible outline on the chair as opposed to just a pile of clothes. Again, the higher precision sensory data combined with the lower precision prior model of the bedroom means we have pushed Jordan down path 1. This time, however, they will perceive a monster, due to the relative strength of the sensory data signalling *a monster* over a prior model (*this specific bedroom*). This data then holds more sway, pulling Jordan to the *monster* prior model and, therefore, perceiving a monster.

We have shown in this panel how Jordan can have a counterfactual experience. They perceive a monster despite the reality being that monsters do not exist. This shows more broadly how we experience reality not as it is but how we perceive it to be – we see *our* world by guessing *the* world.

Jordan's learning: path 1 – they have resolved the uncertainty by creating a newer model of the world, one where monsters exist. However, we have, in this model, made Jordan misestimate the level of precision the sensory data was providing (it was a costume, not an actual monster!). The current input dial should have been turned down lower as the room was still quite dark, so they should not have had so much confidence in the accuracy of the sensory data, as it was not as precise as their dial suggested. In this scenario, they should have taken path 3.

In panels 1 and 2 we have turned the precision strength down on the prior models, and shown how when this is the case we can be more heavily influenced by the current sensory data for which we turned up the precision, for good (panel 1) or for bad (panel 2). However, priors are not always this weak, and sensory evidence is not always perceived as being so unambiguous.

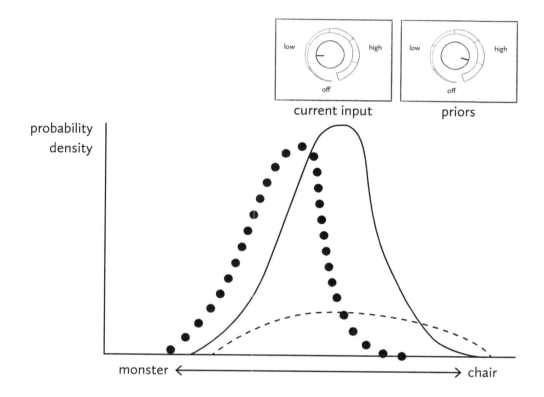

Panel 3

In this panel, we'll give Jordan strong precision for their prior model. Let's place them in their own bedroom, which always has a pile of their clothes on the chair next to their bed. We will keep it dark though, so the sensory input is going to have low precision (flatter dashed line). When this precise prior model (*pile of clothes*) is combined with relatively weak sensory input (it is dark so our visual information is not going be as clear), the prior model should (and in this case does) have a very strong influence on what we experience – it pulls our perception towards the chair. Here Jordan will wake up and almost instantly see a pile of clothes on the chair.

This panel illustrates that even though Jordan is getting imprecise visual signals (current sensory input) because it's dark, their confidence in the strange silhouette being a *pile of clothes* is boosted by their strong prior model. In familiar, stable environments we will all tend to have the precision for our prior models turned up pretty high. Our prior models in these environments hardly ever result in errors as we are very familiar with these environments and they are therefore considered with a high level of certainty even in the face of uncertain, counterfactual sensory input. In these environments, we would usually also turn down the precision dial for current sensory inputs (or even turn it off completely!), almost always dismissing any errors as random noise. This is often the most effective setting to have for our dials. We rarely waste energy pursuing path 3 or needlessly updating our model following path 1. However, as mentioned earlier, there is always the chance it could lead to models that under-fit. As our sensory dial is so low (or prior dial so high), we may dismiss sensory input as just 'noise' when it could have been a 'signal'.

Jordan's learning: path 2 – they have resolved their uncertainty by dismissing the current sensory input as just 'noise' and sticking with their prior model.

PANEL 4

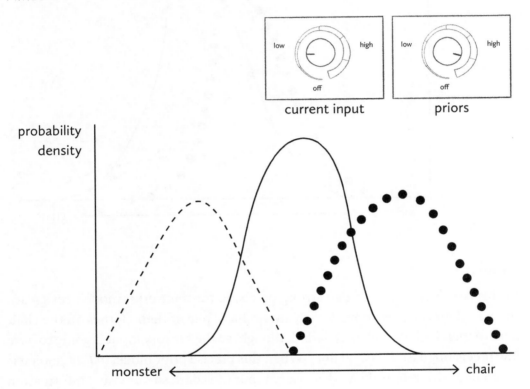

Panel 4

This final panel shows how a lack of strong prior expectations combined with ambiguous sensory data (i.e. low precision on both dials) can change our experience to a less certain middle ground. In this scenario, we have put Jordan in the unfamiliar bedroom at their auntie's house (that they entered in darkness, as in panel 1) and made it dark. They once again awake to see a strange silhouette. In this scenario, the low precision sensory input combined with the equally low precision prior model pushes them towards a middle ground: they are neither confident that it is a *pile of clothes* or a *monster*. Jordan lingers in the middle ground of uncertainty. This is not a good place to be. We might experience something similar if we were lost in an unfamiliar forest in the middle of the night. In this scenario, the situation should be pushing Jordan down path 3 – this would be the best path to follow. They should use their agency to look for more evidence to confirm one of their priors (*monster* or *pile of clothes*) and move out of uncertainty. Let's say in this case they turn on the light. This would then turn the precision dial right up on current sensory input and push them towards perceiving a *pile of clothes*.

Jordan's learning: path 3 – they have resolved the uncertainty by searching for more evidence to support their priors.

Any time we take path 3 we are doing so because we have a little bit of confidence in the prior model that we are looking to confirm. It is an 'optimistic' path to take. We are looking to enact a self-fulfilling prophecy: 'I think the cause of the strange silhouette is *a pile of clothes*, so I will look for evidence that confirms it is a pile of clothes.'

As we noted earlier when looking at the consequences of the paths Jordan could take, path 3 should seem like the best path to always take, 'better to be safe than sorry'. We noted the possible long-term impact of always taking path 3 not only in terms of possible wasted energy but also in how it can erode the precision (our confidence in) of all our prior models, our hyper-prior about our prior models. This could then lead to a negative spiral which would result in us never using path 3 again. If we do not feel we have a prior model with at least a little precision to call on, we will never take path 3 as this would be a waste of energy. There is no prophecy to fulfil.

Equally, if we identify this situation as one that cannot be resolved by seeking more evidence (see unexpected uncertainty below), we will not follow path 3 as this would be a waste of energy. Instead, we should choose path 1 and update our model of the world to one in which this uncertain *monster/pile of clothes/something* middle ground exists. This introduces the last factor that will determine how we manage and perceive uncertainty (errors) – the level of uncertainty we attribute to the situation/environment as a whole.

A NOTE ON SELF-FULFILLING PROPHECIES

> We perceive our surroundings – and ourselves within them – not as they are, but as is useful for us to do so. Each of us navigates the buzzing, blooming profusion of our individual worlds by following a probabilistic thread of self-fulfilling perceptual prophecies. (Seth, 2017)

Ultimately, our brain will choose to take the course of action that it estimates will cause the most ongoing certainty and therefore will most support our prior models. This has important implications. If we have a limited set of beliefs that brings us certainty, for example due to a limited belief in our ability (agency), we can regularly skew towards a limited set of prior models, or even just one single prior model, and find ourselves stuck in a self-fulfilling prophecy loop.

If Jordan has built up a single prior model of their self-worth (*I am a terrible person*), then any time they experience any uncertainty they are going to try to find a way back to the certainty of that model. This is a self-fulfilling prophecy.

Jordan might receive an error as a result of a teacher giving them some praise. To resolve this error and move out of uncertainty, Jordan will then look for evidence to support their prior model (*I am a terrible person*). For example, they could swear and try to hit the teacher. To us, this doesn't seem like the best course of action for Jordan given the problems it will lead to. However, for Jordan, this behaviour is a solution to their problem of uncertainty triggered by the teacher's praise. The sensory input Jordan receives from the swearing and hitting (*teacher upset, Jordan suspended from school*) confirms and increases the strength (precision) of their prior model for the future. They can then return to the sanctuary of certainty (*I am a terrible person*). Problem solved.

The teacher will also experience uncertainty in this scenario. They might have two possible priors about why Jordan lashed out (*bad kid/disordered*). So, they may normalise Jordan's behaviour and interpret it as being because Jordan is a *bad kid*. Or they may pathologise it and deduce that Jordan did it because they have *a disorder*. What we hope to do with this book is to give that teacher an incredibly precise hyper-prior in which the precision strength dial is turned up to 11: **all behaviour can be better understood by reconceptualising it through uncertainty and the 3S's.**

WHAT *WE* HAVE LEARNED SO FAR!

We experience a prediction error (uncertainty) when the current sensory input does not fit with our prior model. When calculating its best guess as to what it is experiencing (and therefore what might cause the error), our brain needs to take into account the precision strength of both our model and the current sensory input. The relative strength of each determines what we experience. Typically, we want models with a high level of precision. If we are confident in them, we can surf over the inevitable waves of uncertainty around current sensory input with little negative impact. But sometimes we might miss a signal. So, we need to work out which uncertainties (errors) in current sensory input we should pay attention to and use to update our models (learn from). When do we turn down the precision we attach to our models and when do we turn up the precision on current sensory input? Our learning rate will be significantly influenced by how we frame the wider context, the level of uncertainty we attribute the situation/ environment as a whole. We illustrate these levels of uncertainty using the image of the **learning glasses** we are seeing the situation through.

OUR LEARNING GLASSES

As the panels earlier illustrate, after we process a prediction error, we use the precision applied to this specific error (based on where the dials for current sensory input and the prior model are set to) to determine our learning path. However, these levels of precision are themselves influenced by the more general level of uncertainty associated with the environment which will impact on our learning rate (how quickly we learn) and which path we take.

There are three broader levels of uncertainty we associate with any given environment that we are going to introduce. As these frame the specific error we are processing, we illustrate their influence by imagining them as glasses that we are wearing, each with a different type of uncertainty lens in them.

Temporary or estimation uncertainty

Wearing our temporary uncertainty glasses leads us to look at errors occurring simply as a by-product of trying something new, exploring. Say Jordan is in a maths lesson learning how to multiply fractions for the first time. They can't and don't know how to do it *yet*, as they will not have a precise prior model. In trying to master this skill we would want Jordan to be wearing their temporary uncertainty glasses. The uncertainty is temporary because it should be removed by experience. When Jordan tries to apply what they have been taught to multiply some fractions and it goes wrong (an error), if they are wearing these glasses they should have slightly turned down the precision on their (possible) prior models (*I am terrible at maths/I am stupid/I know everything*). With each attempt to complete a calculation they should slightly turn up the precision on the sensory input (right or wrong answer) and pay more attention to it.

In wearing these glasses, Jordan will be more open to the fact that they might be *terrible at maths*, but also recognise a degree of ambiguity in the sensory data of their first attempt: it is not necessarily a 'signal'; it could just be 'noise'. By turning down our priors and being ready to adjust the precision of the sensory input, we slightly increase our learning rate but not to the extent that we immediately update our prior models based on one error and head off down path 1. Nor will we ignore the error and stick with our current model and head off down path 2. We will operate somewhere in between.

We want to create a classroom learning environment (see Chapter 2) where our students are most likely to wear their temporary uncertainty glasses when embarking on learning exercises where practice can bring greater certainty. Wearing their temporary uncertainty glasses means they are aware that there will be errors when learning new things. By predicting errors, we limit the impact they have on our sense of uncertainty and recognise that there is a high probability these errors will be learning opportunities: 'signals', not 'noise'. Wearing these glasses means students will more likely head down path 3, looking for more information to help them build better models. These better models will then help them bring more certainty to their world as well as developing their hyper-prior regarding their models and their ability to search for evidence. It will help to increase their agency.

A NOTE ON A GROWTH MINDSET

Framing new challenges with temporary uncertainty could be seen as being akin to having a growth mindset. It allows us to recognise that ability is not fixed but changes as a result of effort. Supporting teenagers to develop a growth mindset might make them better at estimating temporary uncertainty, leading to better learning, better fitting models and less uncertainty.

Expected (or irreducible) uncertainty

Wearing our expected uncertainty glasses leads us to look at errors occurring based on probability, as opposed to deterministically (which is more how we viewed them in temporary uncertainty) (Pulcu & Browning, 2019). For example, when the weather report says it is going to rain, there is a strong probability it might rain, but also a slight chance it will not. There is a level of expected uncertainty. The relationship between the weather report and actual weather is not fixed, so it is not always the case that it will rain when the weather report says so. Expected uncertainty increases as the probability of an observation (the weather report) causing a hidden process (it rains) becomes lower, for example a seven-day forecast. It also decreases as the probability increases, for example the weather reporter is reporting on the weather live from outside our house and we can see they are being rained on!

For humans, social interactions and the building of models about our social world are almost always more effective if we are wearing our expected uncertainty glasses. Remember that our brain does not have direct access to the causes of sensory input; it has to infer this information. It does this based on statistical regularities. People, unfortunately, are not perfectly regular in the statistics they give us. Some people can be for most of the time, but nobody will be all the time. There will be errors. These errors may not necessarily provide a good learning opportunity as we can never build a highly precise model when it comes to human behaviour.

For example, there is a low level of expected uncertainty (a high chance) that when someone is sad, they are going to cry. There is a high probability they will (expected), but also a chance they will not (uncertainty). We could observe someone crying a thousand times because they are sad but there is still a chance they might not cry the next time. What complicates things further is that we gather data to build our model of *people* from multiple sources. All of these folks are different, and all bring their own degree of expected uncertainty. Some people may only cry once for every thousand times they are sad, others may cry 999 times.

Wearing our expected uncertainty glasses will cause us to lower our learning rate and look to pay more attention to an average across multiple occasions of sensory input to form models that better predict its cause. This will leave us typically taking path 2 or most probably path 3. Importantly, however, unlike with our temporary uncertainty glasses, wearing these ones will help us see there is a limit to how effective path 3 is. Gathering more data (path 3) might change the probability associated with an event but it can never completely reduce the uncertainty and so will reach a point where we have to stop exploring and exploit the 'good enough' model we have. We can watch people cry a thousand times but the model we build from this data will never be correct all the time. Uncertainty in predicting humans is 'irreducible' – there will always be a bit left, we need to accept and use a model that is 'good enough'.

Unexpected uncertainty

Wearing our unexpected uncertainty glasses leads us to look at errors occurring as a result of the highly unpredictable nature of the thing we are trying to predict and model (Pulcu & Browning, 2019). We should wear our unexpected uncertainty glasses when we are in a highly volatile environment, where the things we have models for (or are in the process of modelling) are always going to be changing.

For example, we should definitely take them with us on a big night out. Imagine we are in a dark, crowded nightclub. We have never been here before and so our prior model has low precision. We are trying to get from the dancefloor to the bar and in between are hundreds of drunken (unpredictable) people all moving around. The only lighting comes from strobe lights, that flash on and off. We only have these flashes of sensory data to work with. By wearing our expected uncertainty glasses, we know our model is quickly going to be a poor fit, it will go out of date fast as people move, the environment is highly volatile. We can build a model of the nightclub and a clear route to the bar quickly based on the strobe flash, but by the time the next strobe flash comes on everybody will have danced about and moved so the route will no longer be clear. The thing we are learning about – the clearest route to the bar – is constantly changing. Wearing these glasses brings an element of certainty to chaos. We know we cannot build models that will help us make any precise predictions, so we strap ourselves in and roll with it running down path 1, recognising that our model is only as good as the last bit of sensory input. We therefore have our precision for our prior models turned down and precision for current sensory input turned right up – we are alive to all the world's noise as this noise is the best signal we have.

Wearing these glasses when we are not in a chaotic environment, however, leaves us full of uncertainty. Wearing these glasses at the wrong time, misestimating uncertainty, can leave us trapped in an uncertainty loop, failing to notice statistical regularities that will, if we take paths 2 or 3, help us bring some certainty to our models and turn down the volume on all the world's noise. We would be able to build some precise priors and would not then need to be wasting our energy on heading down paths 2 or 3. We could relax along path 1.

Unexpected uncertainty glasses are the learning glasses that we would want our students to be wearing the least when they are at school. We do not want them to see school with all its Sensory, Social and Structural complexity as a highly volatile environment – there are statistical regularities, and they can build good models. Students experiencing chronic anxiety have most likely put these glasses on and never taken them off, stuck in an uncertainty loop. We need to help them take them off and wear the other two pairs of glasses.

Misestimation of uncertainty and the uncertainty loop

Misestimation of uncertainty (the wrong glasses) and precision (the dial turned to the wrong strength) leads to constantly experiencing poorly fitting models. This in turn leads us to experience uncertainty more frequently and reduces our capacity to manage it. Our prior models have been shown to be a poor fit through a series of errors, so we do not have confidence in them giving us the information we need to help us manage the uncertain situation – the precision for our hyper-prior for our models is low. This leads to a greater focus on single instances of current sensory data, leading us to building more poorly fitting models, which lead to prediction errors, and so the loop begins again. The constant uncertainty causes greater perception of volatility, keeping the unexpected uncertainty glasses pressed firmly on and leaving us spiralling down into a mess of uncertainty and stress. We can break this uncertainty loop for our students by helping them to wear the right glasses in the right situations and helping them to adjust the strength of their precision dials.

In general, the temporary uncertainty and expected uncertainty glasses are the most appropriate for students at school. We are trying at the very least to reduce their use of their unexpected uncertainty glasses, and for some situations stop them using them at all. The remaining chapters in this book look at ways of supporting students to (1) wear the right glasses and (2) turn their dials to the best settings to build the best fitting models they can.

All of this is framed in the broader context of recognising everything we are trying to do: first, reduce uncertainty, and second, increase our students' capacity to handle uncertainty across each of the 3S's.

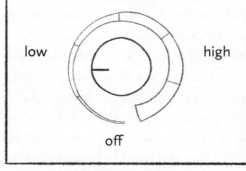

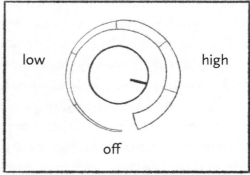

| **current input** | **priors** |

THE 3S MODEL OF UNCERTAINTY

As we described at the start of this chapter, we see uncertainty as a fundamental difficulty we all experience. The examples above illustrate the importance of prior models and sensory input on our certainty regarding the world. More specifically, the role that the precision or certainty that each holds is what will define the frequency with which we experience uncertainty, and our capacity to manage it. In recognising this universal difficulty, we can understand that all of the difficulties experienced by our students boil down to uncertainty. The three areas that this uncertainty is coming from make up our 3S model.

Structure

The importance of prior models, our beliefs about how the world works, is reflected in the S for Structure. We begin with Structure as it is one of the easiest and quickest ways for us to build some certainty for our students. Our models are our world. For some of our students, their precision for their prior models might not be set at the best level it could be for a given situation, either turned down too low or turned up too high. The prior models themselves might not be the best fit for a situation they find themselves in. They might have over-fitting models or under-fitting models. They might not have a large enough range of models to call on. Imprecise models mean we inhabit an imprecise world. Our prior models of how the world works hold our world together, and support our reality. It is therefore the first of our 3S's.

Sensory

The importance of sensory input is reflected in the S for Sensory. For some of our students, their precision around this might not be set at the best level it could be for a given situation, either turned down too low or turned up too high. Some students might have a specific sensory impairment, such as a hearing impairment. Others might just experience sensory differences as a result of natural human variation, including different ways of seeing the world that may or may not come with a diagnostic label. As sensory information forms both the raw data for understanding the world and the signal that we are experiencing prediction error differences in sensory precision, it can lead to both short-term and longer-term uncertainty and trap students in an uncertainty loop. Our understanding of sensory information is central to our understanding of everything. As such the Sensory S is the central S in our 3S framework.

Social

Unlike Sensory or Structure, Social is not explicitly analogous to current sensory input or prior models but it is fundamental. The world is inherently social, filled with people. We need to be able to predict what people might do in order to make our world predictable; if we cannot do this accurately, our world becomes filled with uncertainty. To make others predictable, we need a model of their model, we need to be able to *think through others' minds* (Veissière *et al.*, 2019). As in the earlier note on our diversity being our unity, we all will build models that are specific to our experiences.

To perfectly predict other people, to have social certainty, we would need a model of every person we encounter. Next time you are on a busy street, look around and consider how many models you might need. We might manage to build a few, a lot even, but this brings its own problem. The more plausible predictions we can generate about another person, the less precision any one specific one might hold. As we discussed earlier, low precision models can lead to higher precision sensory input and before long we are wearing our unexpected uncertainty glasses and following path 1 to an uncertainty loop. This can have incredibly negative consequences on our ability to regulate in our world, reducing our capacity to interact socially, effectively making it impossible to exist in *the* world. Everything we do is trying to build up to being confident social beings; as such it is the final S in our 3S framework.

A FINAL NOTE ON KNOWLEDGE AND AGENCY

> My unease is not the fear of something bad, but of **something out of my control**. Situations I am not in charge of and **events I can't predict** confuse me, whether they are negative or positive. (James, 2017, p.1)

This quote highlights two of the key components that help us to create certainty by illustrating how their absence leads to uncertainty:

1   A perceived sense of control (agency).

2   Knowledge (which enables us to make more accurate predictions).

Carleton (2012) has also described the same two ways we can move out of uncertainty: knowledge and/or agency. A person with enough knowledge (in the PP story this would be people with good enough prior models) or agency when encountering uncertainty (and therefore a threat) experiences either the certainty of calm, because there is no threat, or the certainty of fear, because the threat is being realised. However, the person would not experience uncertainty (anxiety) about what they were encountering – it would either almost certainly be a *pile of clothes* or it would almost certainly be a *monster*.

These two factors are, therefore, fundamental to the support we put in place for students.

The remaining chapters of this book look not only at helping us to reconceptualise behaviour through the 3S model of uncertainty but also at how our support can:

- reduce the amount of uncertainty we and the learning environment create for the young people we support

- create ways in which we can help them access more knowledge to build better prior models and help give them a greater sense of agency.

As better prior models make The World more predictable, they make us feel we have more ability to exert control over it: knowledge and agency therefore operate in a virtuous circle.

We hope this chapter has given you a more accurate model with which to understand your students and you now have a greater sense of agency around how to provide even better support for all the young people you live or work with (and any other humans you might encounter).

CHAPTER SUMMARY

▶ The predictive processing story of cognition suggests we see the world by guessing the world.

▶ We arrive at our best guess by weighing up the relative strength of (1) the current sensory information we are receiving and (2) our prior beliefs about what might cause this sensory input.

▶ What we want to build are models that accurately predict what sensory information (internal and external) we can expect to experience in any given situation.

▶ A prediction error can occur when we experience sensory information that we have not predicted – this leads to uncertainty, something that from both a biological and psychological perspective we do not want.

▶ There are three options (paths) we can take to resolve a prediction error: (1) ignore the sensory input, (2) change our model, (3) change (increase) the sensory input we are getting.

▶ Each of these 'learning' paths has pros and cons and it is important we choose the correct one to avoid further uncertainty down the line.

▶ The precision, or weight, we give to the current sensory input and our prior beliefs influences if and what we learn from an error, that is, which path we take, and therefore what best guess we will end up experiencing (our world).

▶ Setting our precision dial to the 'wrong' setting will lead to the wrong path and more uncertainty down the line.

▶ Our precision dials and therefore our best guesses are influenced by how uncertain we feel the situation to be, what learning glasses we are wearing.

▶ Wearing the incorrect glasses and turning our precision dials to the 'wrong' setting will lead to greater uncertainty in the long term (and often in the shorter term too) across the 3S's.

▶ We can help to move our students out of uncertainty, wear the best learning glasses and reset their dials by increasing their knowledge and agency.

The remaining chapters in the book will build on and develop some of the fundamental ideas discussed here, hopefully further clarifying the theory behind our practice.

FURTHER READING

Carleton, R. N. (2016). Fear of the unknown: One fear to rule them all? *Journal of Anxiety Disorders, 41*, 5–21.

Clark, A. (2018). A nice surprise? Predictive processing and the active pursuit of novelty. *Phenomenology and the Cognitive Sciences, 17*(3), 521–534.

Clark, A. (2020). Beyond desire? Agency, choice, and the predictive mind. *Australasian Journal of Philosophy, 98*(1), 1–15.

Colombo, M., Irvine, E. & Stapleton, M. (eds). (2019). *Andy Clark and His Critics*. New York, NY: Oxford University Press.

Feldman Barrett, L. (2017). *How Emotions Are Made: The Secret Life of the Brain*. Boston, MA & New York, NY: Houghton Mifflin Harcourt.

Feldman Barrett, L. (2017). The theory of constructed emotion: An active inference account of interoception and categorization. *Social Cognitive and Affective Neuroscience, 12*(1), 1–23.

Friston, K. (2010). The free-energy principle: A unified brain theory? *Nature Reviews Neuroscience, 11*(2), 127–138.

Friston, K. (2019). A free energy principle for a particular physics. *arXiv preprint arXiv:1906.10184*.

Hohwy, J. (2013). *The Predictive Mind*. New York, NY: Oxford University Press.

Schulkin, J. (2011). Social allostasis: Anticipatory regulation of the internal milieu. *Frontiers in Evolutionary Neuroscience, 2*(111), 1–15.

Seth, A. K. (2018). Consciousness: The last 50 years (and the next). *Brain and Neuroscience Advances, 2*, 2398212818816019.

Seth, A. K. (2019). From unconscious inference to the beholder's share: Predictive perception and human experience. *European Review, 27*(3), 378–410.

Seth, A. K. & Tsakiris, M. (2018). Being a beast machine: The somatic basis of selfhood. *Trends in Cognitive Sciences, 22*(11), 969–981.

Sterling, P. (2012). Allostasis: A model of predictive regulation. *Physiology & Behavior, 106*(1), 5–15.

Sterling, P. (2018). Point of view: Predictive regulation and human design. *Elife, 7*, e36133.

Sterling, P. & Eyer, J. (1988). Allostasis: A New Paradigm to Explain Arousal Pathology. In S. Fisher & J. Reason (eds) *Handbook of Life Stress, Cognition and Health* (pp.629–649). New York, NY: Wiley.

Tsakiris, M. & De Preester, H. (eds). (2018). *The Interoceptive Mind: From Homeostasis to Awareness*. Oxford: Oxford University Press.

REFERENCES

Carleton, R. N. (2012). The intolerance of uncertainty construct in the context of anxiety disorders: Theoretical and practical perspectives. *Expert Review of Neurotherapeutics, 12*(8), 937–947.

Carleton, R. N., Sharpe, D. & Asmundson, G. J. (2007). Anxiety sensitivity and intolerance of uncertainty: Requisites of the fundamental fears? *Behaviour Research and Therapy, 45*(10), 2307–2316.

Carleton, R. N., Desgagné, G., Krakauer, R. & Hong, R. Y. (2019). Increasing intolerance of uncertainty over time: The potential influence of increasing connectivity. *Cognitive Behaviour Therapy, 48*(2), 121–136.

Clark, A. (2015). *Surfing Uncertainty: Prediction, Action, and the Embodied Mind*. Oxford: Oxford University Press.

FeldmanHall, O. & Shenhav, A. (2019). Resolving uncertainty in a social world. *Nature Human Behaviour, 3*(5), 426–435.

Fletcher, P. C. & Frith, C. D. (2009). Perceiving is believing: A Bayesian approach to explaining the positive symptoms of schizophrenia. *Nature Reviews Neuroscience, 10*(1), 48–58.

Friston, K. (2009). The free-energy principle: A rough guide to the brain? *Trends in Cognitive Sciences, 13*(7), 293–301.

Friston, K. (2013). Life as we know it. *Journal of the Royal Society Interface, 10*(86), 20130475.

Friston, K. J. (2018). Active inference and cognitive consistency. *Psychological Inquiry, 29*(2), 67–73.

Griffiths, T. L., Lieder, F. & Goodman, N. D. (2015). Rational use of cognitive resources: Levels of analysis between the computational and the algorithmic. *Topics in Cognitive Science, 7*(2), 217–229.

James, L. (2017). *Odd Girl Out: An Autistic Woman in a Neurotypical World.* London: Bluebird.

Lieder, F. & Griffiths, T. L. (2020). Resource-rational analysis: Understanding human cognition as the optimal use of limited computational resources. *Behavioral and Brain Sciences, 43*, e1.

Nowotny, H. (2015). *The Cunning of Uncertainty.* Hoboken, NJ: John Wiley & Sons.

Pulcu, E. & Browning, M. (2019). The misestimation of uncertainty in affective disorders. *Trends in Cognitive Sciences, 23*(10), 865–875.

Rosser, B. A. (2019). Intolerance of uncertainty as a transdiagnostic mechanism of psychological difficulties: A systematic review of evidence pertaining to causality and temporal precedence. *Cognitive Therapy and Research, 43*(2), 438–463.

Seth, A. N. (2017). Nothing to be afraid of. Retrieved from https://granta.com/nothing-to-be-afraid-of.

Veissière, S. P., Constant, A., Ramstead, M. J., Friston, K. J. & Kirmayer, L. J. (2019). Thinking through other minds: A variational approach to cognition and culture. *Behavioral and Brain Sciences, 43*, 1–97.

Zenon, A., Solopchuk, O. & Pezzulo, G. (2019). An information-theoretic perspective on the costs of cognition. *Neuropsychologia, 123*, 5–18.

2

UNDERSTANDING OUR OWN UNCERTAINTY

ATTITUDES, AWARENESS AND APPRECIATION

This chapter is primarily about us – the teachers, parents, carers, support staff, therapists, tutors and other students who are part of a young person's day-to-day environment. We look at how we are the starting point in addressing uncertainty. However, we also need to ensure that we are addressing our own uncertainties, while being prepared to manage those which will inevitably arise as we challenge the ways of thinking and teaching that will have provided us with certainty up until now.

Are we open to all possible changes? Do we appreciate difference? Does the terminology we use reflect an understanding that we are all different, and celebrate this? Are we prepared to change the way we think and act? The following pages contain information, questionnaires and checklists to help us examine our own attitudes in preparation for building a more accepting (and certain) environment for our students. We will look at:

▶ **Growth and fixed mindsets:** questionnaires for teachers (and students)

▶ **Understanding our triggers:** what are they and how can we break any negative cycles?

▶ **Flipping the narrative:** looking at 'difficult' behaviour in terms of uncertainty

▶ **Terminology and the words we use and why it matters:** neurodiversity and terminology used around difference

▶ **Peer awareness and celebrating neurodiversity:** opening up the conversation in schools and families, why we need to talk about 'difference'.

▶ **Building awareness and appreciation:** practical ideas for schools.

The biggest change of mindset that we are hoping for with this book is a rethinking of behaviour in the light of **uncertainty**. Whenever we, our students or indeed any other human are struggling or behaving in a way that we find unhelpful or unexpected we need to be asking:

'Where's the uncertainty?'

GROWTH AND FIXED MINDSETS

'The growth mindset allows people to value what they're doing regardless of the outcome' (Dweck, 2016, p.48). Genuine belief in the possibility of change is fundamental for teachers and students. Yet all too often we meet teachers who feel that the restrictions of the education environment deny them this belief. The many differing needs of their students, time spent on behaviour management, inaccessible resources, assessment schedules, lack of time for pastoral care and lack of understanding from senior leaders all feature regularly in our discussions about support. We are encouraged to build resilience, challenge, measure and produce results, yet often the constraints of the timetable and curriculum make us uncertain of our abilities to bring about lasting change in learning and attitudes.

The concept of fixed versus growth mindsets is no doubt a familiar one. While not the panacea it can often be misrepresented as, it provides a neat framework for challenging our ways of thinking. Carole Dweck (2016) in *Mindset: The New Psychology of Success* sets out clear reasons why we need to foster the belief in our students that nothing in terms of our abilities is set in stone and help them appreciate the real value of effort and setbacks. But what about us? What do we believe about the changes we can make, if we are truly honest with ourselves? And how do we handle our own uncertainty and setbacks? If you're interested, have a look at the questions below. Make a note of your answers and turn the page to see the results. Be ruthless in your honesty and try not to second guess the answers.

MINDSET QUIZ FOR TEACHERS

Having the awareness of whether we have a fixed or growth mindset is often enough to help us hold more positive and flexible beliefs about ourselves and the work we do. It can also help us give ourselves less of a hard time when things quite don't go to plan. Be honest in your answers.

1 Do you, or others you know, have a natural ability for teaching?

    a) Yes, I think that some people are born to be teachers.

    b) No, I think good teaching develops with time and experience.

2 How often do you run a lesson exactly as you planned it?

    a) Most of the time – I've had plenty of experience with my planning/subject.

    b) Sometimes – depends on my students.

    c) Rarely – there are always unexpected changes I need to make. Sometimes students just don't get it and I need to think again.

3 How do you organise your teaching to match students' ability?

    a) I have to plan lots of independent work which students can engage with at different levels and change my teaching groups almost weekly to reflect students' changing needs.

    b) I have ability groupings which remain pretty constant over the term. I know my students' limits.

4 Which of these do you prioritise in assessing student learning?

    a) Competence as measured by correct answers and achieving the learning objective.

    b) The processes used – for example, the strategies tried, focus and effort.

5 What do you do when a student makes a mistake or experiences difficulty?

    a) I quickly support them with prompts and strategies, so they don't get discouraged.

    b) I give them the answer if they start to get embarrassed.

    c) I encourage them to keep puzzling or struggling, and to try other strategies or talk to friends.

    d) I recognise the opportunity to use the mistake or difficulty as a learning point for the whole class and bring it to their attention.

6   How do you feel when a student has trouble learning something?

a)   I feel incompetent. I feel I am not a good teacher.

b)   I feel challenged. I know I need to increase my understanding about this student, this difficulty and the topic I am teaching in order to improve my teaching.

c)   I feel exasperated. I blame the previous year's teacher, or the parents.

d)   I feel resigned. I will take them back down a level.

7   What is your response when a colleague offers to come and observe your lesson?

a)   Great! An opportunity for some constructive feedback. I think I will ask them to focus on something specific.

b)   No thanks. I'm scared I'll get negative feedback.

c)   No thanks. I don't have any problems.

d)   Here's a chance to prove myself as a good teacher. I'll teach that lesson on probability as I know that is pretty easy for the students, so I'm unlikely to experience any problems.

8   How do you respond to challenges in your career?

a)   I feel anxious and shy away from them.

b)   I feel excited and embrace the opportunity.

9   When students don't pay attention or don't follow your directions, do you:

a)   Feel incompetent and defensive?

b)   Blame the students or the curriculum requirements?

c)   Wonder whether students have understood what you are teaching or what you could do to improve students' motivation?

10   When a colleague makes suggestions for your teaching, do you:

a)   Feel criticised and angry?

b)   Feel defeated and look for an excuse?

c)   Listen with interest, and ask questions?

d)   Seek the next opportunity to try these out?

11 How do you feel when it seems as if a colleague is better than you at something?

a) I feel jealous, but console myself that there are other things I can do better than him/her.

b) I feel threatened and think about how I can prove myself to be competent.

c) I feel eager to learn and wonder if this teacher might engage in a mentoring relationship with me.

12 How do you feel about collaborative teaching?

a) I'd rather go it alone. I have enough teaching ability to carry me forward.

b) I have got my teaching all organised and working well. I don't want to have to adjust anything.

c) I'd jump at the chance. I think what I could learn about teaching and my students from watching someone else teach them.

The answers are on the following page.

Do you have mostly a growth or fixed mindset at this point? Carrying out some of the following activities with our students can help us to develop our own growth mindsets, as well as giving them some useful life skills.

FLIP IT – FIXED AND GROWTH MINDSETS

An activity to teach turning fixed mindset thoughts into a growth mindset alternative.

Why

According to Dweck's research, students who have growth mindsets achieve at a higher level than their fixed mindset peers. They also experience less anxiety.

You will need some blank pieces of paper, large enough to hold a sentence.

How

→ **Find a good moment.** This might link to something you are covering in non-subject time (personal, social, health and economic education/form time/tutorial, etc.) as it has implications for good mental health. You could use it at the start of the year, or as a subject for a debating activity.

→ **Explain the activity.** Show a short film about growth and fixed mindsets (there are lots online) and explain how learning to find opportunity in adversity can help us to achieve and reduce anxiety. Cut up the cards on the next two pages.

- Version one: print out and cut up the cards and choose a fixed mindset statement. Ask students to match it to an appropriate growth mindset card.

- Version two: print out and cut up several copies of the fixed mindset statements only. Ask students to flip them over (literally) and write a growth mindset alternative on the back.

- Version three: Give out plain cards and ask each student to write a fixed mindset statement on it. They then swap with their neighbour, flip the card and write the growth mindset alternative.

→ **Conclude** by explaining that if we can be aware of our fixed/negative thoughts and learn to flip them in our head, we will find it easier to learn new things and are likely to feel more positive.

Answers to mindset quiz for educators:

1 a) Fixed mindset; b) Growth mindset

2 a) b) Fixed mindset; c) Growth mindset

3 a) Growth mindset; b) Fixed mindset

4 a) Fixed mindset; b) Growth mindset

5 a) b) Fixed mindset; c) Growth mindset; d) Fixed mindset

6 a) Fixed mindset; b) Growth mindset; c) d) Fixed mindset

7 a) Growth mindset; b) c) d) Fixed mindset

8 a) Fixed mindset; b) Growth mindset

9 a) b) Fixed mindset; c) Growth mindset

10 a) b) Fixed mindset; c) d) Growth mindset

11 a) b) Fixed mindset; c) Growth mindset

12 a) b) Fixed mindset; c) Growth mindset

Fixed mindset thought cards

These are some examples of fixed mindset cards. You may prefer to write your own sentences, using views that your students may have expressed (or look some up online). These ideas fall into the broad categories of **failure**, **challenge**, **effort**, **criticism** and **other people's success**.

I can't do this.	I'm really bad at this and I don't care enough to try.
I'm not going to try this question, it's too hard.	I know I'll get it wrong.
Why should I bother to try? It won't change anything.	My teacher doesn't like me, that's why he's saying I'm wrong.
They are all better than me at football. There's no point in me playing.	I can never keep my stuff organised.
I tried it last week and it didn't work.	It's not really my thing.

Growth mindset thought cards

Suggested growth mindset alternatives to the cards previously. There will be lots of different answers, so these should be considered examples only.

I find it difficult to do this now. If I practice, I can get better at it.	This skill isn't really a priority for me at the moment.
It would feel better to be able to do this easily, but at least I'm learning.	I might not get it right the first time. It might feel bad, but I will learn something from it.
If I don't try, I won't learn anything, and it will be just as hard next time.	I should learn from this. What can I do differently next time?
I wish I was that good, but if I play with them, I might get better.	I haven't kept my stuff organised up till now. I can try a new way.
Maybe if I keep trying, it will work out.	I might like it one day.

MY MINDSET - STUDENT QUESTIONNAIRE

A questionnaire to find out whether your students have mostly growth or fixed mindsets. Are they ready to embrace a challenge or shy away from it?

Why

According to Dweck's research, students who have growth mindsets achieve at a higher level than their fixed mindset peers. Understanding how students think can also help us understand how they feel and behave.

How

→ **Explain the activity**. Run through some examples of fixed and growth mindsets (see previous flip card activity). Explain how research shows that having a growth mindset helps students achieve higher grades. It's a questionnaire to find out what kind of mindset we have.

→ **Allow time for completion**. This is best done individually. Check that everyone understands the task and model the first answer. 'So if I think number 1 is true, I mark it with a T.'

→ **Go through the answers one by one and as a group**. Go through the answers one by one and as a group. If you think a fixed statement is true you score one F. If you think a growth statement is true you score a T. Ignore all other answers. Ask students to mark on their sheet whether they have a mostly fixed or growth mindset at this point.

→ **Take time to debate**. Alternatively, use each statement as a debate topic, encouraging students to argue why they feel a certain way. Decide on the answer at the end of each debate.

→ **Collect the sheets**. Knowing which of your students has more of a fixed or growth mindset may help you understand their behaviour when faced with a difficult task. Using the vocabulary of 'fixed and growth mindset' can help students develop greater awareness of the thoughts they have.

Answers:

1	Fixed	5	Fixed
2	Growth	6	Growth
3	Fixed	7	Fixed
4	Growth	8	Growth

WHAT KIND OF MINDSET DO I HAVE (AT THE MOMENT)?

Do you think these statements are true or false?

1 You're born with a certain amount of intelligence and it isn't something that can be changed.

2 Intelligence can increase or decrease depending on whether or not you spend time exercising your mind.

3 You can learn new things but you can't change your underlying level of intelligence.

4 Learning new things can increase your underlying intelligence.

5 Talent is something you're born with, not something you can develop.

6 If you practise something for long enough, you can develop a talent for it.

7 People who are good at a particular skill were born with a higher level of natural ability.

8 People who are good at a particular skill have spent a lot of time practising that skill, regardless of natural ability.

How did you do? (Tick which one applies to you)

☐ I have a mostly growth mindset.

☐ I have a mostly fixed mindset (at the moment).

Don't worry if you have 'mostly fixed' thoughts at this stage.

Knowing this can help you notice when you are having a fixed thought and turn it into a growth thought.

TEACHING FOR MASTERY AND GROWTH – A SKILL CELEBRATION

So how can we encourage a growth mindset in our students? Consider this list when evaluating your teaching strategies. Many will be familiar to you and you will be using them regularly. There may be some new ideas in there too.

Mark them with a ✓ (Yes, I use all of these) or a ★ (I would like to do this more often).

STRATEGY	[TICK/ STAR HERE]
Share ownership – give students choices about how and what they learn, teach self-regulation while acknowledging difficult feelings, involve students in creating classroom rules and practice.	
Show respect – foster a mutually supportive, caring and respectful atmosphere, convey respect for students and create situations where all students feel comfortable and capable to participate actively.	
Encourage engagement – present topics through tasks that students find interesting/engaging/emotionally charged. Encourage active debate and engagement rather than rote learning. Relate activities to students' lives and goals whenever possible.	
Show recognition – make your students who struggle academically feel 'seen'. Celebrate personal and social successes inside and outside the classroom, as well as academic achievement. Provide a choice of extrinsic rewards (points, ticks, early finish, a week off homework, biscuits, stickers, etc.) when students are not motivated to learn by the task itself (and plan to fade these). Show students how their *efforts* (rather than any natural ability) led to their success.	
Promote interaction – provide frequent structured opportunities for students to interact, teach the skills students need to interact with peers, promote a mutually caring, respectful and supportive atmosphere (see Chapter 4 for more on this).	
Time – allow plenty of time to gain true mastery of key skills through repetition and revision, let students' interests dictate activities (whenever possible), include opportunities for independent learning and student-led teaching.	
Evaluation – make evaluation criteria clear, minimise competition for marks, give written concrete suggestions on how to improve, teach students how to self-evaluate, valuing effort and self-regulation alongside academic success.	

UNDERSTANDING OUR TRIGGERS

I can cope with most things — I've been teaching a while now - but if I'm working with a student who repeatedly says how boring a lesson is, it can make me feel really mad and frustrated. (Kofi, Key Stage 4 teacher)

We've all been there. We know from our own work, as well as from observation and discussions with other teachers, that there are some classroom behaviours that can cause us to experience 'uncomfortable' feelings. It's not uncommon for our students to make us feel anxious, frustrated, despairing and even angry as we work hard to create a calm yet stimulating working environment. It makes us uncertain of our ability.

We might not be able to change these behaviours, or (in the short term) the instant reactions they cause, but we can change what we do and how we think about them. A questioning approach to our experiences, taking a step back and interrogating them, can create a change in our emotions. This is based on breaking down how our thoughts, feelings and actions interact and is a useful model for dealing with common difficulties we might be experiencing in the classroom. Using this technique alongside an understanding that all negative thoughts and behaviours are borne out of **uncertainty** can help us better understand and manage difficult situations experienced by our students and/or ourselves.

Let's take the example raised by the Key Stage 4 teacher above.

The behaviour

Leo is a creative, popular and able student with variable attention. He will often not undertake an activity as instructed, instead throwing himself on to the desk, rolling his eyes and saying how boring an activity is. Due to his status in the class, this can affect other students' attention. His teacher, Kofi, has tried talking to him about the behaviour as he suspects there may be a learning or attention issue behind it, but Leo has not engaged in any form of discussion, maintaining that he 'just finds it all really boring'.

The feeling

Kofi is aware of feeling an intense spike of frustration/anger in himself when this happens.

The thoughts

Kofi experiences uncertainty. He thinks, 'Leo's finding this boring. Although I've spent a long time trying to make this engaging, it's not worked. He's going to convince all the other students that it's not worth doing. He's trying to undermine my authority; I feel insecure in my role when he does this and worry that it will make me lose control of the class.'

The action

Kofi seeks some certainty; he normalises the behaviour, 'Leo is just a disruptive/ rude/bad kid', which enables him to explain away why he is not enjoying the lesson. This reduces his uncertainty in his ability to plan an engaging lesson. Kofi also looks for some structural certainty and gives Leo a formal sanction in line with the school's behaviour policy. Leo then looks to manage the uncertainty of being in trouble by seeking more control (agency) and so usually disengages for the rest of the lesson and sits slumped in his chair with his arms folded.

Kofi knows that this particular behaviour/consequence loop gives him trouble and would like to change the well-trodden path of events, so he works on changing his thoughts and actions and reconceptualising the behaviour as **the search for certainty as a result of uncertainty in one of the 3S's**.

The new thoughts

'This is not about me. Why is this behaviour more preferable to Leo than paying attention to my class? What is he struggling with? **Where's the uncertainty?** Leo is finding this task difficult and needs more scaffolding (structural uncertainty), or he's finding it hard to maintain his focus (sensory uncertainty).' Kofi has now diagnosed potential needs as a result of uncertainty. This means he can take more constructive action; he can try to meet those needs. He also now has some agency, some control. Kofi can make changes.

The new actions

Kofi knows that increasing a student's sense of agency and knowledge can reduce uncertainty. So he asks students to take on more 'teaching' – for example, giving them sections of a lesson to read, digest and then present to the class from the teacher's desk. This gives them a greater sense of control (agency). He makes sure that Leo is often involved as a 'teacher', asking him to draw diagrams on the whiteboard (he is an excellent illustrator) or make up examples. He also works with the class to draw up a collaborative set of rules for all students (including Leo) around movement breaks. This means students who may experience sensory uncertainty can regulate themselves and it also allows students who have a need for structural and social certainty to know when and why others might be moving around.

The new feelings

Leo still occasionally demonstrates the behaviour, but Kofi now feels interested (rather than feeling angry and anxious) as he has greater certainty around why Leo might be struggling and is able to keep retuning to the same question every time Leo is not engaged: **'where's the uncertainty?'**

UNDERSTANDING OUR TRIGGERS

What are your triggers? What thoughts, feelings and actions usually follow? Where's your uncertainty?

TRIGGER BEHAVIOUR	THOUGHTS	FEELINGS	ACTIONS
For example, student repeatedly calling out.	They are doing it on purpose/ they don't respect me/we won't get through the work/ they are doing it to 'get attention'.	Anxious/annoyed/ frustrated.	Raised voice/ loss of control/ sanction.

What would you like to happen? How can you reduce the uncertainty for everyone?

TRIGGER BEHAVIOUR	THOUGHTS	FEELINGS	ACTIONS
For example, student repeatedly calling out.	They are looking for structural/ sensory/social certainty.	Calm/in control.	Structure: feedback in groups – only spokesperson speaks, in turn. Sensory: more group work to allow for planned auditory stimulation (noise). Social: notice and quietly praise any small positive behaviour – help them feel 'seen'.

Sometimes simply being aware of our own uncertainty and its impact on our thoughts and feelings can help us deal with situations in a different way. It can be helpful to fill these charts out with a colleague, mentor or supervisor.

WHAT HAPPENS NOW

TRIGGER BEHAVIOUR	THOUGHTS	FEELINGS	ACTIONS

WHAT I WOULD LIKE TO HAPPEN

TRIGGER BEHAVIOUR	THOUGHTS	FEELINGS	ACTIONS

FLIPPING THE NARRATIVE

The way we interpret our students' behaviour can change how we think and feel, as well as impact on the student–teacher relationship and subsequent academic outcomes. Learning how to 'flip' our thoughts, reframing behaviour around uncertainty, can improve the school day for us all.

FIXED MINDSET	GROWTH MINDSET
Aggressive	Exaggerated need for control due to uncertainty. Easily triggered *fight* response to stress, perceived danger or threat – high anxiety.
Anti-social	Socially selective. Seeking the certainty of avoiding social interaction due to this type of uncertainty.
Attention seeking	Connection-seeking, reassurance-seeking, social or structural uncertainty.
Disobedient/ defiant	Never defiant! Exaggerated need for control – their control, as they do not want ours, they want their own. Experiencing high uncertainty; searching for certainty.
Dramatic	Overwhelmed, low interoceptive awareness (sensory uncertainty), difficulties regulating, social uncertainty.
Hyperactive	Passionate, curious, adventurous, enthusiastic, eager, energetic, sensory seeking, finds it hard to self-regulate, sensory uncertainty.
Impulsive	Spontaneous, honest, intuitive, brave, fun, inventive, sensory uncertainty.
Inflexible	Exaggerated need for control, single channel attention, high uncertainty makes change and transitions stressful.
Intense	Hyper-focused, deep thinker.
Lack of attention to detail	Big picture thinker, innovative thinker.
Lack of focus/ daydreamer	Experiences high uncertainty and anxiety, 'escapes' into vivid daydreams where they have control, hyper-focused on something else, deep imaginative thinker.

cont.

FIXED MINDSET	GROWTH MINDSET
Lazy	Uncertainty creates withdrawal, anxiety and a fixed mindset: 'I can't so I won't.'
Loud	Excited, anxious, sensory uncertainty.
Oversensitive	Extreme empathy, sensory uncertainty, low interoceptive awareness makes 'big' emotions confusing, may have deep emotional connection with people and animals, extreme sensory/emotional uncertainty, intense body signals.
Perfectionist	Uncertain and possibly anxious, needs completion and 'correctness' for certainty.
Rude	Direct, social uncertainty and exaggerated need for control, structural uncertainty: uncertain of social rules, impulsive.
Self-obsessed/ uncaring	Structural uncertainty: uncertain of social rules, social and sensory uncertainty, exaggerated need for control.
Slow to start	Flexible and creative thinker, struggles to see only one way or direction, overthinker, uncertain how to begin – structural uncertainty.

TERMINOLOGY: THE WORDS WE USE AND WHY IT MATTERS

Every now and then, Clare runs a course called 'Visual Communication' for educators in special schools and at the start of the session she holds up a banana and asks the group what it is.

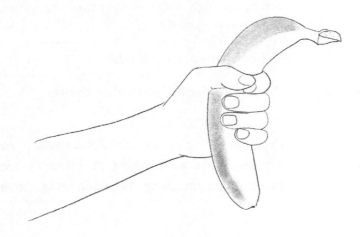

Eventually someone risks it and says quietly 'a banana?', to which the answer is 'No, it's a soft fruit grown in tropical countries which has a curved shape and a generally yellow skin – SOME people call it a banana but that's not what it actually **is**.'

Language is a culturally determined shorthand, which means we can talk about things when they are absent, or in order to describe abstract concepts. The words we use often then take on their own significance, especially when they describe attributes which differ from the cultural norm. Think about the words that predominantly Caucasian cultures use to describe people of other ethnicities and how this has changed over the years. The way we describe people who think differently has changed too and will no doubt continue to do so. It's why it's important to make sure that we listen to the lived experience of all and that these attempts at understanding are reflected in the words we choose.

The list that follows will no doubt date this book but, for now, here are some pointers.

Neurodiversity

The idea that **everyone** processes their thoughts in a different way. There is no single correct 'normal' way of thinking. It's also the idea that differences attached to a diagnostic label like autism and ADHD are the result of normal, natural variations in all humans, rather than an illness or disability – differences, not deficits. It's a noun, for example *'Our aim is to develop a greater understanding of neurodiversity.'* Recognising and embracing neurodiversity is fundamental to the 3S approach to understanding behaviour. It builds greater empathy and understanding – we are all the same because we are all different, our unity is our diversity and our diversity is our unity. Some argue that an acceptance of neurodiversity may one day lead to an end for a need for the specific diagnoses listed below – that people will simply be known by their name and not their diagnosis. The debates around this are beyond the scope of this book. However, there are many, many books and articles that explore this as well as broader ideas of what it means to be 'normal'. We have listed some that might be of interest in the further reading section at the end of this chapter.

> Diagnosis has a necessary place in every evaluation, but never tells the whole story. We must not reify our labels, but recognize they are a collection of 'temporarily useful diagnostic constructs', not a catalogue of 'real' diseases. (Frances, 2013, p.73)

As you will have read in the Authors' Preface and then the Introduction, diagnoses are not necessarily very good indicators of support needs. We also need to ensure that we avoid the single biggest danger with diagnostic labels, and that is a loss of meaning. If a student has a specific diagnosis we have to consider **meaning** for that individual, for example what does the diagnosis mean for that specific student, living in their specific community at their specific age? However, while we come from a place of diagnosing need, rather than needing a diagnosis, we recognise that diagnosis can have a place (often for resource reasons) and it is important to understand the words people use to describe certain types of behaviours. Below we describe some of the labels you might come across.

Autism

Autism assessments look for two broad types of behaviours and use them in conjunction with detailed case histories to decide on a diagnosis. The descriptions of these two areas are detailed below and are adapted from the *Diagnostic and Statistical Manual of Mental Disorders, fifth edition (DSM-5)*, which, along with the *International Classification of Diseases, 11th revision*, is currently used to diagnose mental health difficulties as well as what some consider to simply be different ways of thinking.

- Differences in social communication in a variety of contexts: turn-taking, social interaction, understanding non-verbal communication, making and maintaining relationships.

- Restricted, repetitive patterns of behaviour, interests or activities: repetition of words/movements, desire for sameness, intense interests/fixations, sensory hyper- or hypo-sensitivity (see Chapter 4 for more on sensory differences).

Autistic person/person with autism

How should we refer to people who have received a diagnosis of autism? This depends on who you are, where you are and what you believe. Many people in the UK autism community prefer the identity-first language of 'autistic person' to 'person with autism' (Kenny *et al.*, 2016). We will mainly be using 'autistic person' throughout this book; however, we have also included some autism-first language, so as to respect the views of a range of people. Some individuals with an autism diagnosis feel that 'autistic people' leads to their whole identity being defined by a stereotype, whereas some people feel that 'person with autism' suggests that they might need an extra seat when booking travel or a seat at the cinema. Below we very briefly try to summarise the reasoning behind our use of both person-first and identity-first language.

Person-first language has been long seen as the 'correct' language to use when talking about difference and it represented an important cultural shift away from derogatory and dehumanising language. More recently, however, the person-first approach has been questioned in line with the broader recognition of neurodiversity and the idea of difference, not deficit. This perspective sees autism as an expression of natural human variation (difference), rather than pathology (deficit). Many self-advocates with autism argue that autism should therefore be valued and celebrated as a central part of one's identity. The current argument for the use of more identity-first language rests on both this idea that autism is part of someone's identity and also that the use of person-first language might perpetuate stigmatising views (Gernsbacher, 2017). This is because desirable attributes are normally expressed through adjectives preceding nouns (e.g. 'a smart child'), and alternative semantic constructions often suggesting undesirable attributes or a more pathologised perspective (e.g. 'a child with depression').

In order to respect the views of autistic self-advocates and the broader neurodiversity movement, and in recognition of the current debate around terminology, we ensure that we include identity-first language in the book. We also ensure that we include person-first language too as we know that there are some within the autism community who are often not represented in the self-advocacy movement, including minimally verbal individuals, as well as others from the broader autism community who may prefer the use of person-first language. Ultimately, as we non-autistic individuals understand it, the common goal that both person-first and identity-first language have is that they aim to de-pathologise autism and inspire respect. This too is our aim. As such, we take the conscious decision to use a mixture of both types of language so as to reflect and respect, as best we can, the preferences of people throughout the autism community and advance the message of 'difference, not deficit'.

Asperger syndrome and high-functioning autism

At the time of writing there is considerable debate about the removal of the Asperger's diagnosis from the latest versions of the diagnostic manuals. Many people identify strongly with these labels, yet others feel it splits the community into more and less 'able'. The terms high and low functioning are also used less. They can lead to people having their ability or their needs underestimated – often what looks like 'high functioning' reflects 'extreme masking', with an increased later risk of mental health difficulties. Many autistic individuals labelled as 'low functioning' have low expectations placed on them and may also then be incorrectly labelled as having an intellectual disability (Mottron, 2017). These labels fail to capture the spiky profile that all people have – there are some areas where we might be low functioning (particle physics, for example) and others where we might be high functioning (baking cinnamon buns), and there may also be times when we are all low functioning (4.15am on a Monday morning?). Increasingly, education settings are referring to individuals who have higher or lower **support needs**. This puts the focus back on the environment, and what the needs are that are not currently being met.

Specific learning difficulties (SpLD)

This is the umbrella term for particular difficulties with reading (dyslexia), writing (dysgraphia) and maths (dyscalculia). A diagnosis is made by a qualified practitioner, usually a specialist teacher or educational psychologist, using standardised tests. Specialist interventions focus on fluency of word reading to allow for comprehension, improved motor planning and conceptual thinking.

ADHD/ADD

The *DSM-5* uses the term attention deficit hyperactivity disorder only, to describe differences in attention, impulse control and the need for activity; the term attention deficit disorder (ADD) is no longer used. However, you can be diagnosed with three different types of ADHD:

▸ **Inattentive:** where someone experiences difficulties with inattention/easy distractibility but isn't hyperactive or impulsive.

▸ **Hyperactive/impulsive:** when a person has difficulties with hyperactivity and impulsivity but not inattention.

▸ **Combined:** when someone has a combination of inattention, hyperactivity and impulsivity.

Developmental coordination disorder (DCD)/dyspraxia

DCD is the current term for people who experience differences in their movement, coordination and motor planning. It can cause clumsiness, difficulties with maths, organisational abilities and hand–eye coordination in both gross and fine motor skills. It used to be called dyspraxia. Specialist interventions are carried out by occupational therapists.

Sensory processing disorder (SPD)

SPD does not exist in any diagnostic manual; however, it is often used to highlight the needs of people who appear to experience differences in the way they process sensory information. For example, before sensory differences were recognised as part of the diagnostic criteria for autism, a lot of autistic young people were also given the SPD label to draw attention to their needs for support in this area. SPD largely affects how people tolerate and process information about light, touch, sounds and information from their own bodies.

Developmental language disorder (DLD)

This is the current term for people with a persistent type of speech, language and communication need that cannot be better explained by another diagnosis (e.g. autism). Specialist interventions are carried out by speech and language therapists, and often focus on the development of vocabulary.

It is worth pointing out that if someone receives any one of these diagnoses, they have a 60 per cent chance of receiving another, and a 30 per cent chance of ticking more than two boxes.

The work we do, and the framework we use, is not limited by labels. We work transdiagnostically, applying the same principles to every individual in every home, classroom or learning environment. Part of the 'flip' in mindset we are hoping to achieve with this framework is one shifting from a **need for diagnosis** back to **diagnosing need**, so the activities in this workbook are appropriate for everyone, with and without a diagnosis. See the next section for ways in which we work with the whole school to try and improve the school experience for everyone.

PEER AWARENESS AND CELEBRATING NEURODIVERSITY

I was bullied a lot for not fitting in. When I tried to fit in the bullying got worse because apparently I 'wasn't doing it right'. While the bullying was severe, the school never did anything about it. I think it might have helped some people not pick on me if the school had stepped in and explained that everyone is different and it's not okay to pick on people while also not singling me out. (Anja Melissa)

The desire to fit in, for any pre-teen or teenager, creates all kinds of uncertainty, much of it social. 'Do I look right/walk right/dress right/speak right? Are they mocking me? Where will I sit on the bus? Who will I get into a pair with? Am I tall/small enough? Do they like me? Is my hair okay? Did she just 'air' me? Did that come out right? Am I weird?' For students who struggle with social uncertainty, this can be significantly amplified. And then there's social media…

Social media is for many young people a largely positive force. Some report a sense of 'belonging' that they struggle to find in school, a chance to find other people who share their passions or a platform for sharing a skill. However, we also know that for some it amplifies the uncertainty and means that students continue with this 'second guessing' both in and outside school hours. This can be exhausting and affects everybody's ability to tolerate uncertainty. Chapter 5 offers some practical ideas for helping students deal with this social uncertainty by increasing awareness of themselves and other people, but this is usually carried out as part of a whole-school strategy to raise awareness and appreciation of difference.

The response to intervention approach

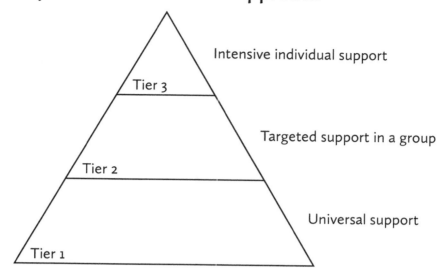

This widely used approach to interventions relies on the premise that 80–85 per cent of students benefit when universal, school-wide supports are put in place, in Tier 1. In this support context, we recommend to schools that **everyone** learns about neuro-difference as part of a Tier 1 support, at the same time as identified students have access to more specific small group/one-to-one strategies as part of Tiers 2 and 3.

Families help here too. Due to the genetic factors associated with neurodiversity, there may be several people in any one family who have had to work harder than most to manage the often one-size-fits-all environment of secondary school. Talking about these experiences and perhaps how 'outside-the-box' thinking can be a benefit in the workplace and life after school can help build certainty, especially when it comes to the ultimate (and often unspoken) uncertain thought of 'What might my future bring?'

BUILDING AWARENESS AND APPRECIATION

Every school has a different way of having these conversations, but here are some ideas:

▶ Use the sessions allocated to personal development to develop students' understanding of difference, be it physical, sensory, religious or neurological.

▶ Study the neuroscience behind different ways of thinking and offer experiential activities that give insight into some of the difficulties experienced by people who might have a diagnosis of, for example, dyslexia, autism or ADHD.

▶ Encourage students to undertake projects on different aspects of neurodiversity as part of an extended project qualification, art project or writing assignment.

- Look for national events that celebrate difference. Lots of UK schools put on events for 'Neurodiversity Celebration Week' – a week of celebrating the achievements of people who think differently.

- Invite speakers who represent all types of neurodiversity to talk to students about the successes they've had in life after school as well as some of the difficulties they have had. You could ask them to highlight the importance of being understood by those around them and maybe choose three things that they did which helped them manage school.

- Find online role models that promote a positive and open approach to neurodiversity. Look for people who reflect the population that you work with, whether this is because of their age or cultural background.

- Read some of the many first-person accounts written by people who think differently as part of a book group or recommend them as part of a year group reading list.

- Celebrate the growing list of young people who think differently who are making a difference – Greta Thunberg (climate change), Siena Castellon (neurodiversity), Loyle Carner (ADHD), to name a few – to promote some of the positives of neurodivergent thinking. Watch TED talks about neurodiversity, and show your students the list of millionaires with dyslexia!

FURTHER READING

Instagram/Twitter

One of the benefits of social media is the proliferation of writing and drawing by many different kinds of minds. We are constantly being challenged to 'flip the narrative' – to consider behaviours that make us feel uncomfortable as an expression of uncertainty (and a search for certainty). We are indebted to the many social media contributors who currently help us understand the world from so many different perspectives. Here are some of our current favourite accounts (in no particular order):

@rossgreene @melissa_anja @neurodiversityworks @thefutureisnd @myunsecretdiary @geniuswithin @notjustclumsy @dldandme @autismacademy @tourettesawareness @adhd_is_me @happy_nd_lady @brianmendler @incredibletwentynineteen @limpsfieldgrangeschool @autismacademy @dld.andme19 @adhdfoundation @additudemag @qlmentoring @themighty @loylecarner @bethevans @tourettics.unite @ausomecork @sootmegs @lianafinck and of course... @specialnetworks

Publications

Armstrong, T. (2015). The myth of the normal brain: Embracing neurodiversity. *AMA Journal of Ethics, 17*(4), 348–352.

Burman, E. (2016). *Deconstructing Developmental Psychology*. London: Taylor & Francis.

Chapman, R. (2019). Neurodiversity and its Discontents: Autism, Schizophrenia, and the Social Model. In S. Tekin & R. Bluhm (eds) *The Bloomsbury Companion to the Philosophy of Psychiatry* (pp.371–389). London: Bloomsbury.

den Houting, J. (2019). Neurodiversity: An insider's perspective. *Autism, 23*(2), 271–273.

Dweck, C. (2017). *Mindset: Changing the Way You Think to Fulfil Your Potential – Updated Edition*. New York, NY: Robinson.

Honeybourne, V. (2017). *A Practical Guide to Happiness in Children and Teens on the Autism Spectrum: A Positive Psychology Approach*. London: Jessica Kingsley Publishers.

Kirby, P. (2019). Gift from the gods? Dyslexia, popular culture and the ethics of representation. *Disability & Society, 34*(12), 1–22.

Milton, D. (2019). Difference Versus Disability: Implications of Characterisation of Autism for Education and Support. In R. Jordan, J. M. Roberts & K. Hume (eds) *The Sage Handbook of Autism and Education* (pp.3–11). London: Sage.

Pripas-Kapit, S. (2020). Historicizing Jim Sinclair's 'Don't Mourn for Us': A Cultural and Intellectual History of Neurodiversity's First Manifesto. In S. K. Kapp (ed.) *Autistic Community and the Neurodiversity Movement* (pp.23–39). Singapore: Palgrave Macmillan.

Rosqvist, H. B., Chown, N. & Stenning, A. (2020). *Neurodiversity Studies: A New Critical Paradigm*. London: Routledge.

REFERENCES

Dweck, C. S. (2016). *Mindset: The New Psychology of Success*. New York, NY: Ballantine Books.

Frances, A. (2013). *Saving Normal: An Insider's Revolt against Out-of-Control Psychiatric Diagnosis, DSM-5, Big Pharma, and the Medicalization of Ordinary Life*. New York, NY: HarperCollins.

Gernsbacher, M. A. (2017). Editorial perspective: The use of person-first language in scholarly writing may accentuate stigma. *Journal of Child Psychology and Psychiatry, 58*(7), 859–861.

Kenny, L., Hattersley, C., Molins, B., Buckley, C., Povey, C. & Pellicano, E. (2016). Which terms should be used to describe autism? Perspectives from the UK autism community. *Autism, 20*(4), 442–462.

Mottron, L. (2017). Should we change targets and methods of early intervention in autism, in favor of a strengths-based education? *European Child & Adolescent Psychiatry, 26*(7), 815–825.

3

STRUCTURE

ACTIVITIES TO SUPPORT STRUCTURAL CERTAINTY

This chapter is all about **structural certainty** and how a few simple changes can help young people feel less anxious and more engaged.

The activities include questionnaires and checklists to help find out how your students like to learn and what you are already doing that supports them to manage their structural uncertainty.

Introduction

Theory

▸ Modelling the world

▸ Structural uncertainty and the need for control

▸ The Universal Design for Learning framework

▸ Research evidence for UDL – the story so far...

Practice

▸ The search for structural certainty

    • What does it look like, what could it mean?

    • Using the 3S framework to understand behaviour

▸ Using the UDL framework in lessons

    • How I learn – questionnaire for students

    • How this class learns – summary sheet

    • How I design lessons – questionnaire for teachers

▸ Lesson design

    • Inclusion on demand or by design?

    • Other resources

▸ Building structural certainty

    • Structure through representation

    • Structure through action and expression

    • Structure through engagement

If you only have five minutes

References

INTRODUCTION

This book is about supporting students to manage anxiety by building certainty. In this chapter, we look at the first of the 3S's, Structure, and how we can understand and support uncertainty in this area, making sure that we are not, accidentally, creating an environment that creates uncertainty in our students. The failure of an environment to accommodate a person's needs creates problems for that person, it can disable them (Oliver, 1996, as cited in den Houting, 2019). As Bowe (2000) points out, this recognition matters, because it means if we can change the learning environment, even in small ways, we can reduce the difficulties our students may experience. These students may already be dealing with high levels of anxiety, we do not want to bring more uncertainty to their lives.

> I had to know what was going to be in a lesson. I'd stay up really late learning the work so I when I was in the classroom I could focus on the social stuff. It worked in some lessons but there were some where I had no idea what was going on and my anxiety used to get so bad that I sometimes had to just leave the room. I'm better now, but I still like to know what we're doing before we do it. (Aliya, Year 13)

We all need and rely on structure. Most of us have some kind of morning routine which takes the anxiety out of getting to work on time. It makes our morning more predictable and reduces stress. Some of us can tolerate small changes (e.g. brushing our teeth after the shower instead of before), some of us would struggle if anything changed at all and some of us prefer to get through the morning events in a different order each time.

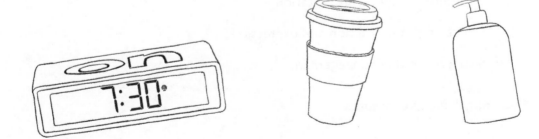

We use calendars, to-do lists, alarms, reminders and routines; we arrange things in alphabetical order, colour order, height order and order of priority. We might collect things and get great pleasure out of putting them in order, or getting a 'set'. We all have different needs when it comes to our work or home environment; some of us can't begin to concentrate in a messy work space, whereas others crave the vibrancy of a more creative, anything-but-tidy space.

We also rely on some simple repetitive social structures – those formulaic conversations we might have on a Monday morning at work:

'How are you?' *'Good, you?'* 'Yeah, I'm good. How was your weekend?' *'It was okay – quite quiet. Yours?'* 'Had a few friends over yesterday, yeah it was good.' *'Nice. See you later.'* 'Yeah, see you later.'

Our students are no different; they too need the certainty of structure. We begin here as it can often be the most effective way to provide immediate support.

THEORY

MODELLING THE WORLD

As we discussed in Chapter 1, the predictive processing (PP) story of how our brains work is that they essentially operate as **prediction-making machines**. Instead of reactively responding to the world, our brain looks to predict our world and it does this through the use of **internal models**, approximations of the world that generate predictions which we use to bring some certainty to what is, from our brain's point of view, a world of hidden causes.

These models provide the fundamental structure that we use to navigate our environment and stay alive within it. They help us to bring some form of order to the blooming, buzzing complexity of the noisy, vibrant, unpredictable planet we inhabit. The accuracy of our models (how well they 'fit') is directly related to the amount of uncertainty we experience in the world. The better fitting they are, the less uncertainty we experience.

The more volatile our perception of the world we are experiencing, the more it can lead us to build poorly fitting models. This can create an uncertainty loop. Our poorly fitting models lead to poor predictions, which leads us to experience our world as deeply unpredictable. As we will discuss in our subsequent chapters, Sensory and Social are two areas where our students may be particularly prone to experience the world as a volatile place. When they see the world in this way, through their unexpected uncertainty glasses, they may feel adrift on a chaotic stormy sea, buffeted from uncertainty to uncertainty. Structural certainty we receive from the external environment can provide a port in this storm. It can provide refuge and safety from where they can learn more effectively and build better models.

Within school, students can have difficulties in a lesson for a number of different reasons, all which are driven by the anxiety they can feel as a result of structure, sensory or social uncertainty. Structure is one of the quickest and easiest ways to help reduce a student's uncertainty. In terms of the 3S framework and support we can put in place, we can think of **structural** uncertainty as an **external uncertainty**, one experienced in our physical environment.

Unlike our students' internal models that govern sensory and social uncertainty which we do not have immediate, direct access too, the external learning environment is something over which we have a lot of control. If this external learning environment is also filled with uncertainty it can compound the impact of the sensory and social uncertainty a student might experience.

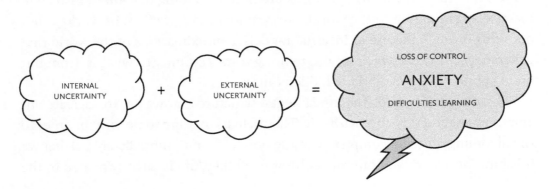

If, however, the learning environment, the world we have built around our students, is solid, predictable and filled with certainty, they will be better placed to manage other forms of uncertainty. They can learn to surf the inevitable waves of sensory and social uncertainty more easily if they do not see the sea as quite so stormy.

INTERNAL UNCERTAINTY + EXTERNAL CERTAINTY = SELF CONTROL LEARNING SELF BELIEF

Some students will experience greater uncertainty than others, and all students have days when they are more anxious than usual – but that's okay. If we design lessons that prepare for this, that are built on an understanding that all students will show variability, they can all access greater certainty as they need it. We build in certainty to **all** our lessons as it will help all our students, even those students who may not seem like they need it, so it is ready and waiting for the day when they do.

Imposing my own routines and rituals

One thing that we should remember when looking at building structural certainty is that certainty-seeking behaviours often arise due to an **exaggerated need for control**. This can often come in the form of control of the physical environment, as a student may be trying to find one area that can be made predictable.

Some students create certainty by increasing their sensory-based behaviours. We might notice these as an increase in fidgeting, moving and noise-making in the classroom as they try to increase the predictive accuracy of their models. If a student does not know what is going on in the class (or anticipates they won't understand what they need to do next or how to do it), they can bring some certainty to their experience through humming while flicking a pen repeatedly against the desk as they know what their body and brain feel like when they do this. These sorts of behaviours, often referred to as 'low-level behaviours', need to be recognised as part of a search for certainty as a student tries to negotiate an uncertain situation. They should flag to us that a student might be experiencing some anxiety and is trying to manage it.

More broadly, when we are looking at behaviour in class that we may see as undesirable or disruptive, if we ask ourselves, '**Why is this behaviour more**

preferable to the student than the behaviour I would like them to display?', the answer will always be, '**Because the behaviour they are displaying brings them more certainty**'. So once again we need to think, 'Where's the uncertainty?' When it comes to structural uncertainty this is likely to be around 'What is happening now?', 'What is happening next?' and 'What is expected of me?'

Structure helps us all better prepare for change (transition), big or small. It could be simply moving from one activity in class (reading a passage of a text) to another (answering a question) or moving to a new classroom. It helps us have certainty over 'What is happening now?', 'What is happening next?' and 'What is expected of me?' Without it we will experience uncertainty. It is worth keeping in mind the fact that:

Every time we move from what we are currently doing to a new activity, we are moving from certainty to uncertainty.

If we don't create a clearly structured, predictable environment our students may be unable to transition from one activity to the next. They may appear 'defiant' (remember none of our students should ever be labelled as defiant; it is an exaggerated need for control due to uncertainty), pretend not to hear so that a specific action or event can be completed or carry out a routine that may be part of their '**internal timetable**'.

For some of our students, these internal timetables may be more entrenched because they have had to manage for many years in a learning environment that, to them, had an unclear structure; they may have imposed their own routines and rituals in order to bring some certainty. The fact that such a timetable does not exist somewhere, for us to clearly see, makes it hard for us as adults working to support them, for three reasons.

First of all, if they have imposed their own routine and rituals on the world (their internal timetable) to try to bring some certainty and something does not conform to this structure, they may go into crisis and be overwhelmed by uncertainty. The world is no longer operating as predicted. However, as their expected structure only existed in their head, it makes it hard for us to know what went wrong. We have to try to guess what **should** have happened that didn't, as well as the perceived implications on the rest of the structure or their day. Typically, one thing in a routine not happening can cause a domino effect on everything else; this can make it seem like someone's whole world is crashing down. It makes it hard to reassure our students if we do not know what we are trying to reassure them about.

Second, a student might have imposed a routine or ritual, to try to create certainty, which leads to much greater difficulties in the longer term. This routine or ritual not only fails to manage their anxiety but can also enhance it and therefore make it more difficult for us to provide support. An example of this might be always needing to leave the classroom last. The student has imposed this ritual so as to manage the uncertainty associated with transitioning to a new environment. However, this strategy brings with it a secondary anxiety: 'Will I be allowed to leave the classroom last?' What is worse is that this strategy has a lot of variables at play which are outside the student's control, for example the teacher might ask the student to leave first, other students might not let that student leave last, the teacher might stay behind to complete some work. This will exacerbate the anxiety the student was already feeling as a result of the initial transition. These types of behaviours are sometimes referred to as insistence of sameness behaviours – insisting on things being the same. These sorts of behaviours will not help our students in the long run.

Third, once a student has imposed their own routines and rituals, whatever they may be, it will be hard for us to support them to move away from these as we would essentially be saying to them, 'So, you know this one thing that provides you with structural certainty? We are going to take that away now and do this other, unfamiliar, uncertain thing.' Doing this would require the student to have a huge amount of trust in us and confidence in their own ability (agency) to manage this change.

This is why we put clear structures in place, so our students do not have to. They do not need to hold the world together; we can show them that there are firm structures that can provide external support. Once we have these structures in place we can support students to manage changes to them, to manage structural uncertainty. Many of the activities towards the end of this chapter look to teach our students how to do this, but we do this in a planned way, we structure uncertainty!

Finally, before we look at structural uncertainty in more detail, we need to draw attention to a key point. While Structure represents the first of our 3S's behaviours that we may identify as resulting from uncertainty in this area may have come about due to a primary reason in one of the other areas. As we stated in the Introduction, this is why when we are asking **'Where's the uncertainty?'** we need to look at all 3S's. The passage below illustrates this point.

Many children who grow up with a highly selective diet may have initially been driven by sensory uncertainty affecting certain foods, creating difficulties with certain textures or tastes. For example, someone not liking the sound, feel, smell or taste of crunchy foods or strong flavours would mainly eat mashed potato. At school, every lunchtime, as school and their parents wanted to ensure they were eating, they ate mashed potatoes. While their sensory uncertainty might have reduced as they grew up, to be able to better modulate (manage the precision of) sensory signals, the selective diet could have remained. This is because it could now be driven by structural uncertainty. It had become part of the routines or rituals they imposed on the external world to make sense of it; in this case, lunchtime equals mashed potatoes. It provided structural certainty.

For the remainder of this chapter we look at how we can make the day-to-day school environment more certain for our students, and how the way we organise classrooms and plan lessons can reduce structural uncertainty, and positively impact learning and behaviour. A large focus on how we can support all our students is through the use of the **Universal Design for Learning** (UDL). When students are engaged and can choose from a variety of learning activities, have multiple ways in which those learning activities are represented and multiple ways they can show their knowledge and understanding, they can maximise their strengths and minimise their weaknesses (Scanlon & Baker, 2012). Engagement with school, regardless of all the other variables associated with a student (including home life), has been shown to be a key factor in increasing student wellbeing (Patalay & Fitzsimons, 2016). The support described in this section aims to engage students' existing knowledge and give them strategies to manage knowledge gaps and ultimately gain a greater sense of control – agency – so as to reduce uncertainty around structure.

STRUCTURAL UNCERTAINTY AND THE NEED FOR CONTROL

The need for control has been counted among the most basic human needs (Fiske, 2002; Pittman and Zeigler, 2007). Researchers across clinical, personality and social psychology agree with the equally common-sense notion that **people are motivated to feel in control of their lives** (Presson & Benassi, 1996; Skinner, 1996), and, again unsurprisingly, that **people often dislike perceived uncertainty and chaos** (Pennebaker & Stone, 2004).

As detailed in Chapter 1, the fundamental difficulty for all people is uncertainty, and therefore the main barrier to learning in school will also be uncertainty. Counteracting uncertainty and maintaining a sense of control most often requires a combination of seeing the self in control (agency) and also seeing the external world as orderly and predictable (having knowledge about the world) (Landau, Kay & Whitson, 2015).

Having sufficient knowledge and understanding of the world and therefore seeing it as orderly and predictable can be more explicitly defined as having 'simple, clear and coherent interpretations of the social and physical environment (Structure, Sensory, Social)' (Landau *et al.*, 2015, p.694). So, to move out of a state of uncertainty, a person requires:

▶ sufficient knowledge and understanding of the world and how it works (including **specifically relating to the situation causing anxiety**)

and/or

- **agency – the sense that we have the ability to control, manage or influence our world** (Carleton, 2012).

For example, we might be experiencing anxiety due to uncertainty about the causes of strange noises we can hear outside the front door at night (a prediction error). We can:

- avoid the uncertainty all together if we have the knowledge and understanding that our partner is coming home late, has left their keys at the office and had a couple of drinks – use **knowledge** to explain away the uncertainty (see path 1 in Chapter 1)

and/or

- control the situation by getting a torch and opening the door, feeling that we have the ability to manage whatever we might encounter – use **agency** to control and remove the uncertainty (see path 3 in Chapter 1).

Many of our students who are struggling may well have knowledge that either does not fit well enough to help explain away the uncertainty or they are not applying enough precision to that knowledge (see precision in Chapter 1). Or/and they may have a reduced sense of agency. In this situation, we need to provide greater levels of external certainty and make the world more certain.

In a school environment, if we are unsure whether work will be presented in a way that we can access, we are unable to predict the impact of our own actions. Will we be able to complete the task? How will we be perceived by our classmates? What action might the teacher take? So, naturally when a student's agency is low or threatened, they may seek to cope by searching for a safe structure in the world around them (Whitson & Galinsky, 2008). As mentioned above, they will be desperately seeking certainty by imposing their own routines and rituals on the world. In the learning environment, a clear framework can instead provide some of this certainty. Universal Design for Learning provides an excellent guide for how we can set up our learning environment to build on the strengths and address the needs of all our students, providing them with more agency and certainty.

If our students know that the learning environment has been set up in a way that will suit how they think and learn, and that there will be learning ramps where they need them, then they have sufficient **knowledge** regarding the situation. It is predictable and certain, insofar as they know it will be suited to their needs, and they will also have a sense of control over the situation as it is predictable. This can lay the foundation on which **agency** and certainty can then be built (or rebuilt). Read on for how we can build external, structural certainty through UDL.

THE UNIVERSAL DESIGN FOR LEARNING FRAMEWORK

UDL is just good teaching. We've been doing it for years but now it has a name and a guideline to follow, but it is what really good teachers have always been doing. That's kind of what I tell people when they ask what it is? (Teacher cited in Lowrey *et al.*, 2017, p.235)

Universal Design for Learning (UDL) emerged from Universal Design (UD), developed in the fields of architecture and industrial design (Edyburn, 2010). UD highlighted the benefits of creating environments that are accessible to all from the outset rather than having to retrofit them later with myriad specific adaptations. UD was added as a core part of the United Nations Convention on the Rights of Persons with Disabilities (CRPD) and defined in Article 2 as the design of 'products, environments, programmes and services [are] to be usable by all people, to the greatest extent possible, without the need adaptation or specialized design' – inclusion by design (United Nations, 2006, p.4).

The UDL framework, developed by the Center for Applied Special Technology (CAST), recognises that flexibility and individualisation of options within the way we teach are critical to student success because no single strategy meets the needs of every student. It challenges us to recognise rigid, homogenous, one-size-fits-all teaching methods and curricula as disabling.

Central to the framework set out by CAST is that we design learning environments, curricula and teaching methods to be flexible so that they fit the strengths and preferences of all students, regardless of specific needs, rather than expecting students to adapt to uncompromising curricula, teaching methods and teachers (!) (Edyburn, 2010; Hitchcock & Stahl, 2003; Lieberman, Lytle & Clarcq, 2008; Rose & Meyer, 2002). In doing so, we create learning environments and lessons that better reflect the inevitable variability in the students we teach. It recognises that

'If you can't learn the way we teach, we'll teach the way you learn.'

By following the three fundamental principles of UDL providing, from the outset, multiple, flexible methods of **representation**, **expression** and **engagement**, we give all students equal opportunities to learn (CAST, 2011; Rose & Meyer, 2002).

UDL and the brain

CAST looks to align the three fundamental principles of UDL with research around three interconnected brain networks (Rose & Meyer, 2002; Rose & Strangman, 2007):

1   The recognition network deals with **what we learn (representation)** as well as how we collect facts and classify what we hear, see and read. It helps us identify and make sense of information and patterns. This network is the 'what' of learning.

2   The strategic network deals with **how we learn (expression)**. This network plans and performs tasks. What's more, how we organise and express our ideas is a strategic task. It enables us to act on information.

3   The affective network deals with **why we learn (engagement)**. It covers how students get engaged and stay motivated as well as how they are challenged, excited or interested, all of which are affective dimensions. It enables students to make emotional connections to information (Meyer, Rose & Gordon, 2014).

While there is some debate around the role neuroscience can play in education (Bowers, 2016; Thomas, Ansari & Knowland, 2019), UDL's principles often echo what many practitioners feel 'makes sense'. Practitioners and researchers acknowledge the intuitive potential benefit of UDL on the basis of its basic principle of *proactively* applying flexible instructional design (Coyne, Kame'enui & Carnine, 2011; Orkwis, 2003), designing the environment with integrated learning ramps.

There is an extensive summary of the research that underpins the rationale for each of the checkpoints available on the CAST website,[1] but read on for a summary.

RESEARCH EVIDENCE FOR UDL – THE STORY SO FAR...

UDL has been characterised as a major positive shift in education (Edyburn & Gardner, 2009), and research supporting its benefits continues to grow (Mangiatordi & Serenelli, 2013). Dymond and colleagues (2006) describe how, in their study, the UDL framework and guidelines were used to redesign a science curriculum to provide more ways to engage students, more ways of representing information to students and more ways students could demonstrate their understanding. The new design led to a reported increase in student engagement and participation and overall enjoyment.

A group of researchers in the US (Lieber *et al.*, 2008) showed how a school had used UDL principles on their curricula design to support young students in literacy, maths and social skills. On standardised measures in these areas students showed significant gains. While this is a clear positive, it is important to note that the precise impact of the specific UDL elements is difficult to determine.

---

1   https://udlguidelines.cast.org/more/research-evidence

Spencer (2011) highlighted the three key benefits to the implementation of UDL. First, incorporating many techniques (i.e. multiple means) into lessons increases accessibility for all students thereby, creating a learning atmosphere of engagement and confidence. Second, maximizing students' individual learning strengths creates independent learners. Finally, behaviours that challenge can be reduced if student learning needs are met. Further supporting this last point, researchers have reported that addressing academic and behavioural needs simultaneously may improve academic outcomes (Bradley, Doolittle & Bartolotta, 2008; Gable *et al.*, 2002; McIntosh *et al.*, 2006). This highlights the point that the provision of emotional (and therefore behavioural) support and academic support is not a zero-sum game. Despite this, schools often still see it as an either/or and will usually prioritise academic outcomes over and above supporting students to manage their emotions and therefore behaviour. Adopting the UDL framework will allow schools to address academic and behaviour needs simultaneously, with the guidelines for engagement particularly relevant for students experiencing greater levels of uncertainty.

An increase in engagement is especially critical for improving the academic outcomes of students with socio-emotional needs, and as such practitioners should pay particular attention to these guidelines (Cook, Rao & Collins, 2017).

Behaviours that can be viewed as problematic decrease when learners have choices (agency) and activities that incorporate their interests (familiar knowledge) (Jolivette *et al.*, 2001).

Reducing uncertainty in the learning environment – Lesson design

Why do I like Mr G? Because he draws pictures to explain things. Also, because he's calm and on the first day he let us choose where to sit, and because it worked he let us stay there. (Eve, Year 10)

Universal Design for Learning can provide the foundation on to which we can build more external (and therefore ultimately internal) certainty. It can also provide us, as educators, with certainty as it has a very clear framework for how to use it. We use it to help us plan lessons and we like it because it flows from the basic understanding that: 'barriers to learning...arise in learners' interactions with inflexible education goals, materials, methods and assessments' (CAST, 2014).

UDL allows us to be inclusive by design. When we are planning our teaching, choosing activities, structuring lessons and giving or receiving feedback, it's easier to build in support for students with all types of learning differences **from the start**, rather than trying to make individual adjustments once we discover more about the inevitable variability in all our students. This is because, as Frank Bowe (1999, as cited in Ostroff, 2001), a non-traditional learner and researcher, says, 'most teachers cannot individualise instruction for so many diverse learners. What they can do is present material in multiple ways.'

Let's look again at how the UDL approaches lesson design in practice. It focuses on three main areas where we can make adjustments and increase certainty:

1   **How teachers create interest and motivation**, so having multiple means of engagement: relating learning to real life, referencing student interests, offering choices, offering flexibility, individual/paired/group work and so on.

2   **How teachers present information**, so having multiple means of representation: use of video, audio, text, graphics, objects, emojis, movement, dual or single channel input.

3   **How students communicate with teachers and each other** to demonstrate their learning, so multiple means of action and expression: speaking, writing, drawing, multimedia presentations, speech recognition software, voice recording, quizzes, 3-D models, drama, role play and so on.

Lots of this will be familiar to you; using different techniques to present new ideas and concepts is common good practice and in the last few years we have seen many more teachers using technology to gather feedback.

We feel it is the first of these, engagement, that is the most fundamental and has the greatest potential to change the way students learn as we can create a greater sense of being in control (agency), which can, in the longer term, boost internal certainty as:

engagement   feeling of control   certainty

The practice section outlined in this chapter includes questionnaires that will help find out how your students like to learn, a structure to summarise all this information, and a chance to look at what you are doing in your lessons that help all your students.

CARLA'S LISTS

Carla is an able student who finds some lessons really difficult. She is (in her own words) 'hyper-organised', which is her way of dealing with the uncertainty she experiences in school. She has lists on the back of her door to remind her which books she needs in school on which days, she always gets up the minute her alarm sounds and has a strict morning routine. She likes to get everywhere early. In her 'dream world' she says she would have access to all the lesson plans for each term at the start so she could understand how everything fits together and track progress through the term. Some lessons are great but some are really hard. Carla lists these as her top five 'stresses':

1   A teacher arrives late and seems distracted.

2   I don't know what's going to happen in the lesson.

3   The teacher takes too many questions and isn't clear about whether you need to put your hand up first.

4   Vague feedback; things like 'good work' so I don't know WHAT I did well.

5   Too much listening, not enough to look at, like when a teacher just reads or leaves the class to watch slides without a commentary.

And her best lessons?

1   A clear beginning – they say what we are going to do in the lesson.

2   Mixture of whiteboard/video/reading from the text/discussion.

3   You get some kind of choice so you can use a mind map/bullet points/ drawing in your book if you want and there's time for this.

4   The teacher sticks to hand up/call out/choosing people to give answers.

5   Same ending each time – homework and what's in the next lesson.

Carla is not alone; notice the variety that she needs within her structure, too. This need for a sense of agency within a framework comes up time and time again in our conversations with various students.

Antoni: 'I mainly like PE because there's not a teacher telling me constantly what to do and I have more freedom in the lesson.'

Eve: 'We should be able to look how we like – everyone would be happier that way and I know I work better on non-uniform days.'

Luke: 'If someone tells me to "stop talking" I kind of have to finish it off.'

Malika: 'I like to take my time and finish things properly. I have to use colour.'

Antoni: 'The best lessons are the ones where you get to do your own thing. They let us listen to music on headphones, it's quiet, you can ask for help if you need it, and they don't ask you questions otherwise. It's you in your own mindset.'

Molly: 'It's just so much better if lessons are really clear and organised and we can see the whole thing: like all the PowerPoints or worksheets for that topic. Booklets are the best, I know what we're doing and nothing will surprise me.'

As always, the central question to keep in mind, in this case when planning a lesson or activity, is **'Where's the uncertainty?'** These are suggested structures, and as with all strategies to reduce uncertainty they centre around increasing students' knowledge and agency (and therefore helping them to find better fitting models of the world and reduce prediction errors which lead to uncertainty!). There may well be questions you want to add or ignore, but by the end of this chapter you should have options for some new ideas you might like to try to reduce uncertainty around structure before finding out more about the other two types of uncertainty that lead to unexpected behaviour and barriers to learning: sensory and social.

PRACTICE

THE SEARCH FOR STRUCTURAL CERTAINTY

What does it look like, what could it mean?

This chart considers behaviours that may be accounted for by the Structure part of the 3S framework and works like this.

Each line contains:

▸ a commonly observed behaviour which may indicate a search for structural certainty, or which suggests a need for structural support

▸ the possible cause of this behaviour, as the student seeks certainty

▸ ideas that might help a student deal with the uncertainty – by creating more structural certainty and increasing their sense of agency.

You can download the 3S worksheet below this chart to create your own record of observable behaviours, in terms of sensory, social and structure. This worksheet is repeated in each of the 3S chapters.

The interpretations below are not the only suggestions for understanding these behaviours. Many of them repeat in the Sensory and Social sections of the book, with a different analysis. As always, we should look at all 3S's when trying to locate where the uncertainty is. However, as this chapter is focusing on Structure, we will simply look at this as a possible cause of the behaviour in the examples below. It will nevertheless be clear how the other two S's may also be having an impact.

WHAT IT MIGHT LOOK LIKE	WHERE'S THE STRUCTURAL UNCERTAINTY?	IDEAS FOR STRUCTURAL CERTAINTY
Rarely contributing in class.	Uncertainty predicting **how** to contribute creating anxiety and withdrawal. *'Is it a "hands-up" question? How come **he** called out and the teacher let him answer?'*	**Clearly signal how students are to respond to each question BEFORE asking a question.** **Regular use of pairs work – discuss, agree, feedback.**
Frequent calling out in class, despite reminders.	Impulse control and uncertainty predicting and/or remembering feedback structures. *'I've got no idea how to contribute so I'm just going to call out – that way I'll have to be heard.'*	**Consider using a visual system – raising different coloured cards or objects to signal different types of feedback BEFORE asking a question: hands up/first to call out/written/pairs work and feedback/group work and feedback.** **'Okay, this is a yellow, a "hands-up" question...'**
Criticising peers in class for rule breaking or perceived unexpected behaviour.	Uncertainty caused by inconsistency of rules and resulting prediction errors. *'She was late, that's against the rules, why is it not okay to say that out loud?'* *'That behaviour got a mark yesterday, why is this teacher not doing the same? Why are the rules different every time?'*	**Be as consistent as possible as a staff team – make time to review behaviour case studies and compare management techniques.** **Use the 'Thinking machine' structure (see Chapter 5) to analyse both perspectives as well as positive and negative outcomes of this behaviour.**

Difficulties remembering equipment.	Uncertainty remembering and predicting what equipment is needed for different days/lessons. *'It's all a blur, what I need for different lessons. I lose everything all the time; it's stressful but that's just how I am...'*	**Encourage students to use sectioned zip-up pencil cases – one side for arts subjects and one side for science. Add laminated labels to help student be certain about what should be in each.** **Consider using clear, A4 plastic zip folders, colour coded for days of the week – each contains stationery and other equipment for that day.** **Help students at start of each week to check case/folders. Gradually fade support to develop independence.** **Support students to create their own large, colour-coded wall chart for home. Parents can support and gradually fade this support.**
Difficulties getting started in class/with homework, may repeatedly ask questions.	Uncertain of the specifics of the task and therefore their ability to complete the task. *'I think I know what's needed, but maybe I've got it wrong.'* *'What if I get it wrong?'* *(Also see perfectionism below.)*	**Be very clear about what students *are* and *are not* expected to do for every task. Make this information available as a grid (or other visual) on a screen/whiteboard/flipchart for the duration of the task, in class or available online for homework.**

cont.

WHAT IT MIGHT LOOK LIKE	WHERE'S THE STRUCTURAL UNCERTAINTY?	IDEAS FOR STRUCTURAL CERTAINTY
Daydreaming.	Uncertain of lesson structure and role in session, lack of agency. So seeking certainty in daydreaming. *'I feel unfocused and detached from this lesson. I'm not sure what my role in this is. My daydreams give me a feeling of certainty as I am in control of them.'*	**Be very clear about expectations for participation (and structure) at start of lesson.**
Demanding key roles in lessons/ projects/ performances/ family events.	Uncertain of status in group. May also be unsure of process behind role allocation. *'I need to feel seen. Will I ever get a turn? Is the teacher sharing these out? Is it FAIR? Where are the rules?'*	**Be explicit about how roles are chosen and allocated. If possible, use a printed rota sheet to explain to students how decisions are made or when their turn will be.** **Increase levels of positive feedback and encouragement.**
Monopolising the conversation, talking over peers/ teachers.	Uncertain of status and social communication structures – particularly turn-taking. *'I find it hard to join in, I can't get my timing right. I'm just going to say it. I need to be heard.'*	**Establish the rules of engagement as a group/ class. How do we feel if one person talks more than others all the time? How can we manage this?**

Need to 'have the last word' and win arguments.	Unsure of status/role and rules of engagement causing 'need for control' and sense of agency. *'If I am the last person speaking, I will have "won". I will feel more certain. I find it hard to tolerate "losing" feelings and would rather get in trouble than back down.'*	**In the moment: avoid calling attention to rudeness in wider group. Remember that for us adults, having the second to last word is acceptable. Explain to the student the behaviour you would have liked to see and move on confidently.** **Away from the class: if this persists, use the 'Thinking machine' structure (Chapter 5) to analyse and look at both perspectives, as well as positive and negative consequences of this behaviour.**
Perfectionism and reluctance to admit mistakes/ defeat/not knowing something.	Uncertainty predicting social responses from teachers and peers creating anxiety and search for certainty in perfectionism and catastrophising. *'If I get everything right, I will feel certain of myself and my abilities.'* *'If I get one thing wrong, then everything will be wrong.'*	**Model tolerance of mistake making/winning/losing for all. Be explicit on learning opportunities that comes from each.** **Look for opportunities to practise winning and losing in class – use the 'Thinking machine' to analyse thoughts and feelings if needed.**
Unusually sensitive to feedback.	Uncertainty predicting exactly WHAT is being assessed for any one task. *'Is there more that I need to do, other than get the answer right? What else is there I need to think about?'*	**Try using a structured feedback grid (see the end of the chapter) to make feedback explicit. Divide comments/grades into achievement/effort/ presentation, etc.** **Provide regular specific praise whenever possible.**

cont.

WHAT IT MIGHT LOOK LIKE	WHERE'S THE STRUCTURAL UNCERTAINTY?	IDEAS FOR STRUCTURAL CERTAINTY
Finds break times/ weekends/ holidays difficult, may seem more uncertain than during lessons/ weekdays/ term time. **May regularly get into arguments at these times or withdraw to private spaces (e.g. toilets).**	Uncertainty predicting behaviour of others and expected behaviours of self during unstructured times. *'I can't tolerate the uncertainty. I don't know what to do with myself and feel surrounded by unpredictable behaviour.'*	**Identify other students with similar difficulties and any jobs that need doing in the library/office/pastoral department/reception/art/ PE department (depending on students) and create informal teams.** **Fade adult scaffolding once friendships appear established and encourage students to return to social spaces.** **Try to keep to a flexible structure for everyone during non-school times at home.**
Difficulties with inference and following plots in book/ film/video.	Uncertainty predicting what information to use to support inference. *'I know I'm supposed to be looking for clues, but I don't know where to look.'*	**Make sure students have written synopsis and character summaries before watching something.** **Offer structured worksheets when reading or listening to stories/ watching film/plays to guide observations.** **Prompt students to look for specific inferential information: facial expressions/body language/movement/tone of voice/eye pointing/ reactions of others/physical environment, etc.**

Difficulties with certain team sports (though may be 'sporty'), often has disagreements, especially during competitive games.	Uncertainty tolerating unstructured and unpredictable events. 'I didn't know she was signalling to me to move into the space and then she got annoyed with me.' 'They never pass to me, so when they do I just try and keep the ball as long as possible.'	Individually: use the 'Thinking machine' structure to help understand other perspective. Suggest team sports with less emphasis on understanding social cues (running/athletics/rowing/track cycling, etc.) or those that 'drill' whole-group participation (dance, yoga, cheerleading, etc.)
Overuse of non-social gaming (where players do not communicate with each other).	Low tolerance of uncertainty in unstructured social times, creating anxiety and search for certainty through structured solo games. Uses gaming as comfort behaviour – it provides certainty. 'I can't handle social situations, but I feel isolated. If I game all the time, it's easy for me to forget about everything.'	Look for new opportunities to develop social certainty in school, within and across year groups. Design lunch/after-school clubs around activities that your student enjoys (see below) and encourage participation. Assign roles supporting younger students in activities your student enjoys. For example: film-making, trampolining, electronic music making, game design, skateboarding, coding, cooking, singing, drumming, running, comics, animation, etc. Consider a peer mentor in school.

Using the 3S framework to understand behaviour

The next page contains our 3S analysis sheet completed to look at some support ideas for the **Structural** aspects of Jordan's behaviour at lunchtime only. This worksheet repeats at the same point in the Social and Sensory chapters, with a different analysis.

On the following page, there is a blank version for you to use to help you interpret your student's behaviour using a Sensory, Social and Structural approach.

3S ANALYSIS

Name of student: Jordan   Year group: 10   Date: 10 Jan
Adult(s) completing checklist: SB, CA

WHAT'S THE BEHAVIOUR?	WHERE'S THE SENSORY, SOCIAL AND STRUCTURAL UNCERTAINTY?	IDEAS FOR CERTAINTY?
Avoids lunch — spends time in bathroom or sits at back of classroom. Talks about feeling ill.	Sensory: Unable to manage the high levels of sensory input in the environment, seems too volatile. Social: Uncertain of who to sit with in the canteen. Structure: Uncertain of managing unstructured times (lunch).	Structure: Talk to Jordan about what they like to do in their spare time. Design a lunch club/group that allows for this activity. Break lunch into three sections and timetable activities for each one, e.g. eating, walking, check-in with staff, lunch club, exercise.
	Sensory: Social: Structure:	
	Sensory: Social: Structure:	

3S ANALYSIS

Name of student: Year group: Date:

Adult(s) completing checklist:

WHAT DOES IT LOOK LIKE?	WHERE'S THE SENSORY, SOCIAL AND STRUCTURAL UNCERTAINTY?	IDEAS FOR CERTAINTY?
	Sensory: Social: Structure:	
	Sensory: Social: Structure:	
	Sensory: Social: Structure:	

USING THE UDL FRAMEWORK IN LESSONS

The next few pages give you a step-by-step process to help work out what adaptations for **engagement**, **representation** and **action and expression** will be useful in your current classroom.

Step 1: Find out how your students like to learn with the 'How I learn' questionnaire.

Step 2: Summarise the information on the 'How this class learns' template (or make a mind map, poster or spreadsheet).

Step 3: Fill in the 'How I design lessons' questionnaire and think about how you teach for inclusion.

Step 4: Have a look at the 'Lesson design' template and samples and the recommended reading at the end of this chapter.

HOW I LEARN – QUESTIONNAIRE FOR STUDENTS

A questionnaire to find out how your students prefer to learn.

Why

> When I first approached my school with a diagnosis, my student advisor suggested I fill out a student profile with what my diagnosis was and how that affected my time at school. It also included things about me I thought my teachers should know and any requirements I might have or things they should possibly take into account. I think this would be helpful information to have on a student who is neurodivergent as it gives you the information you need in one PowerPoint or word document. It also allows for a smoother school experience for both teachers and students involved as there is less of a clash. (Anja Melissa)

Teenagers who are finding it difficult to manage the classroom environment may not appear anxious but can be getting into trouble more than other students. The students we interview often know what they need to help them stay calm and work, but when they are asked if they've ever told a teacher all this, they usually haven't.

This type of information gathering can increase a sense of agency (and certainty) for all students as well as providing us with useful practical information. Their ideas may not be that practical, or financially viable, but they can tell us a great deal about how a student thinks and feels in our lessons.

How

→ **Find a good moment**. It's best done at the beginning of a school year or term but could also be done if you suddenly find yourself with a new class, a student who is struggling or you just want to try a new approach.

→ **Explain the activity**. It's a questionnaire to find out how all students like to learn and what they are interested in. It will be seen by you and maybe by some of their other teachers.

→ **Read each question with examples** (add your own if necessary) and allow time for full answers. Work through the questions as a group. Make sure everyone knows what to do. Use a visualiser if you have one and show a sample answer for the first question.

→ **Fill in a questionnaire as a worked example**. Complete it based on how you learn in activities for continuing professional development.

→ **Talk about the answers**. Allow students to share their answers with the group, find out who makes animations in their spare time, who likes it when the teacher reads out loud, who would rather draw their feedback, and so on.

→ **Collect the sheets**. Keep them safe, as they may be useful in the future, especially if a student is struggling in another lesson. They are also useful for meetings where staff have behaviour concerns about a student you teach.

Next steps

→ If you like, fill in a 'How we learn' worksheet summarising what you have learned about the class.

→ Share what you know. Tell teachers of other classes what you are doing, talk about it in a staff meeting.

HOW I LEARN – EXAMPLE

This questionnaire is to find out about how you like to learn.

Name: AH   Class: 10B   Date: 15 January

WHAT DO YOU ENJOY IN SCHOOL?

e.g.– drama – humanities – science – sport – maths – getting involved in clubs – music – coding – art – school plays – working with other people – being organised – being on time – being sociable – being helpful – being positive – something else?

I enjoy clubs, maths, science and am great at being on time.

WHAT DO YOU ENJOY OUT OF SCHOOL?

e.g. swimming – running – football – skating – making things – making music – gaming – drawing – making people laugh – organising my friends – making new friends – going to new places – relaxing – looking after animals – coding – animation – juggling – solving a Rubik's cube – volunteering – speaking another language – something else?

Gaming.

HOW DO YOU PREFER TO LEARN NEW INFORMATION IN A LESSON?

e.g. video – using equipment – photos/pictures – diagrams – independent computer work – listening to the teacher – drama/role play – practical demonstrations – PowerPoint – filling in worksheets – reading handouts – school trips – visiting speakers – mind maps – something else?

I like PowerPoint, independent computer work and worksheets.

WHERE DO YOU LEARN BEST?

e.g. in a pair – in a small group – on my own – as a whole class – with my friends – at the back – in the middle – at the front – near the teacher – away from my friends – near the window – away from the window – on a computer – somewhere else?

I like working in a pair if it's someone I know.

HOW DO YOU LIKE TO ANSWER QUESTIONS IN LESSONS?

e.g. put my hand up – discuss in a pair or group and one person gives the answer – in writing on paper/post-its – in whole class discussion – on a whiteboard – red, amber, green cards in planner – on the main whiteboard – using actions (thumbs up, thumbs down) – in writing – another way?

I like writing – on a whiteboard or post-its.

HOW DO YOU LIKE TO ASK FOR HELP?

e.g. put my hand up – see the teacher after the lesson – use an agreed signal (e.g. red card in planner) – ask a friend – go up to the teacher's desk in the lesson – email the teacher later – I don't ask for help – anything else?

I like to ask someone I know or I don't ask.

IF YOU COULD DESIGN A LESSON – WHAT WOULD IT BE LIKE? WHERE WOULD IT BE? HOW WOULD YOU GET THE INFORMATION? HOW WOULD YOU ASK OR ANSWER QUESTIONS? WHAT WOULD YOU LEARN? WHAT ELSE?

I would give everyone a networked laptop or iPad and they could write their answers on it so the teacher could see. If there were not enough computers I would let us choose who to work with and share. Or use whiteboards more.

IS THERE ANYTHING ELSE YOU WOULD LIKE YOUR TEACHERS TO KNOW ABOUT HOW YOU LEARN? YOU CAN WRITE OR DRAW FOR THIS BIT.

I don't like talking in front of the big group, I like to talk to people I know and they can say the answer for me. I really like it when Miss H gets us to use the cards in our planners and she can see if I'm amber and can come round and say, 'How are you getting on?'

I only really like science and maths. I wish I didn't have to do English.

HOW I LEARN

Name: Class: Date:

WHAT DO YOU ENJOY IN SCHOOL?

e.g. – drama – humanities – science – sport – maths – getting involved in clubs – music – coding – art – school plays – working with other people – being organised – being on time – being sociable – being helpful – being positive – something else?

WHAT DO YOU ENJOY OUT OF SCHOOL?

e.g. swimming – running – football – skating – making things – making music – gaming – drawing – making people laugh – organising my friends – making new friends – going to new places – relaxing – looking after animals – coding – animation – juggling – solving a Rubik's cube – volunteering – speaking another language – something else?

HOW DO YOU PREFER TO LEARN NEW INFORMATION IN A LESSON?

e.g. video – using equipment – photos/pictures – diagrams – independent computer work – listening to the teacher – drama/role play – practical demonstrations – PowerPoint – filling in worksheets – reading handouts – school trips – visiting speakers – mind maps – something else?

WHERE DO YOU LEARN BEST?

e.g. in a pair – in a small group – on my own – as a whole class – with my friends – at the back – in the middle – at the front – near the teacher – away from my friends – near the window – away from the window – on a computer – somewhere else?

HOW DO YOU LIKE TO ANSWER QUESTIONS IN LESSONS?

e.g. put my hand up – discuss in a pair or group and one person gives the answer – in writing on paper/post-its – in whole class discussion – on a whiteboard – red, amber, green cards in planner – on the main whiteboard – using actions (thumbs up, thumbs down) – in writing – another way?

HOW DO YOU LIKE TO ASK FOR HELP?

e.g. put my hand up – see the teacher after the lesson – use an agreed signal (e.g. red card in planner) – ask a friend – go up to the teacher's desk in the lesson – email the teacher later – I don't ask for help – anything else?

IF YOU COULD DESIGN A LESSON – WHAT WOULD IT BE LIKE? WHERE WOULD IT BE? HOW WOULD YOU GET THE INFORMATION? HOW WOULD YOU ASK OR ANSWER QUESTIONS? WHAT WOULD YOU LEARN? WHAT ELSE?

IS THERE ANYTHING ELSE YOU WOULD LIKE YOUR TEACHERS TO KNOW ABOUT HOW YOU LEARN? YOU CAN WRITE OR DRAW FOR THIS BIT.

HOW THIS CLASS LEARNS – SUMMARY SHEET

A summary of all the information you've gathered about your students, by using the How I learn questionnaire.

Why

Because it's hard to look at lots of different sheets at once.

This information will be useful for you when you are planning lessons, as you will be reminded quickly and easily what interests and learning preferences you have in the class.

The summary sheet will be useful for sharing information with colleagues or for any changes in teaching arrangements later on in the year.

How

→ **Use this template** or make a spreadsheet, draw a mind map, make a grid, create a map, use photos... Do whatever you like to bring all this information together. There's a completed example below.

→ **Use initials only to identify specific student preferences**, or keep it completely anonymous and use numbers (the example following uses a combination of this).

→ **Keep it safe, but look at it often**.

Next steps

→ Share the information with other teachers of this class.

→ Fill in the 'How I design lessons' questionnaire that follows this summary sheet.

HOW THIS CLASS LEARNS – SUMMARY SHEET EXAMPLE

Class: 10s   Date: 10 October   Teacher: LP

What do they enjoy in school?

Drama: JG RW, science: RAG IQ IO KQ, maths: EC, art: RP OL AU, English: LY

sport: BC DB, humanities: EL AA WA, school plays: NG, French: RH CA, music: RA, orchestra: OS, clubs: AH, helping: CA, being organised: AO EL RA OS, 'Nothing': 4

What do they enjoy out of school?

Skateboarding: AA RP, making electronic music: RA, playing instrument: OS NG, BMX: AU, football: EL IQ YM BC, basketball: KQ WA, fashion: ST LY, volunteering: NG, KR, being with my friends: JG DB RW JP, dance: OL, relaxing: PF, swimming: RH, making people laugh: YD, coding: AH

Presentation preferences

Video: 27, audio (being read to): 20, PowerPoint: 28, drama/role play: 6, mind maps: 15, bullet points/grids: 27, worksheets: 20, drawing: 12, demonstration: 23, large photos on whiteboard: 2

Groupings

Pairs: 28, small groups: 18, individual work: 20, whole class discussion: 19

With friends: 20, away from friends: 9

Answering questions

Hand up: 25, group feedback: 22, mini whiteboard: 20, RAG cards: 15, 3 don't like it when teachers call on students who haven't put their hands up

Asking for help

Hand up: 15, asking neighbour: 13 (but some worried about getting into trouble for talking), using red/amber/green cards to show understanding: 11, asking teacher after lesson: 6, would like to ask by email: 2

Other information

PF will put hand up if happy to contribute – otherwise ask for written feedback. OS may shut down if noise reaches 'shouting' level and may take time to calm down. AO would like to stand at side of room in science labs, or be at front of class. NG likes colour coding and prefers to do mind maps if plenty of time/at home, if not – bullet points. NE needs short movement break after 30 mins and moves in chair, learns best in middle at side. AH needs RAG cards

HOW THIS CLASS LEARNS – SUMMARY SHEET

Class: Date: Teacher:

What do they enjoy in school?
What do they enjoy out of school?
Presentation preferences
Groupings
Answering questions
Asking for help
Other information

HOW I DESIGN LESSONS - QUESTIONNAIRE FOR TEACHERS

Why

Since student variability is inevitable, it can feel overwhelming to try and make adjustments for everyone.

This last tick sheet is a simple way to look at what you are already doing that is helping your students, and maybe help you come up with some new ideas to help build certainty in the classroom.

How

→ **For each question either tick 'yes' or 'not yet'.**

→ **The 'yes' answers are what you are already doing** to help your students who learn differently.

→ **The 'not yet' answers are a guide** to what you could try next.

Next steps

→ Fill in a Lesson design sheet and think about how to increase certainty using the UDL approach.

HOW I DESIGN LESSONS

MULTIPLE MEANS OF ENGAGEMENT (HOW WE MOTIVATE)	YES	NOT YET
DO STUDENTS HAVE CHOICES ABOUT WHAT AND HOW THEY LEARN? *level of challenge – type of reward – tools for gathering information – colour design or graphics for layouts – order of tasks*		
CAN STUDENTS SET THEIR OWN LEARNING AND BEHAVIOUR GOALS? *long term – lesson by lesson – reflection/self-monitoring sheets*		
DO ACTIVITIES AND SOURCES OF INFORMATION RELATE TO STUDENTS' PERSONAL EXPERIENCE WHENEVER POSSIBLE? (SEE 'HOW THIS CLASS LEARNS') *real-life examples – cultural diversity – opportunities for personal response*		
IS THE PURPOSE OF THE LESSON EXPLICIT AND PERMANENTLY DISPLAYED? *flipchart paper stuck on wall – visuals to support text*		
ARE THERE CLEAR CLASS ROUTINES? *consistent start and finish – charts – countdown timers – schedules*		
ARE THERE CLEAR SIGNPOSTS FOR NEW KEY LEARNING POINTS OR EVENTS? *'brains to maximum' – 'key learning note' – 'this is the science bit' – other signal*		
IS THERE A VARIETY OF SENSORY INFORMATION? *individual/group work noise levels – breaks – time-outs – slow/fast pace*		
IS THERE A VARIETY OF SOCIAL DEMANDS? *individual work – pairs – friendship groups – new groups – public presentation*		

MULTIPLE MEANS OF REPRESENTATION (HOW WE PRESENT INFORMATION)	YES	NOT YET
IS THERE CLEAR VISUAL SUPPORT FOR SPEECH-BASED PRESENTATIONS? *bullet point notes – diagrams – charts – written transcripts – symbols – photos – equipment*		
IS THERE VARIETY AND FLEXIBILITY IN DISPLAYS/ PRESENTATIONS? *size of text – contrast colours for text – breaks in video/audio – well-spaced layouts – different fonts – borders – icons for key learning points*		
MULTIPLE MEANS OF ACTION AND EXPRESSION (HOW WE COMMUNICATE)	YES	NOT YET
ARE THERE CHOICES BEYOND PEN AND PAPER? *laptop – tablet – objects – equipment – interactive whiteboard – voting software*		
ARE THERE CHOICES FOR MULTI-MEDIA FEEDBACK? *text – speech – illustration – design – film – music – dance/ movement – visual art – sculpture – video – storyboards – comic strips – animation – PowerPoint*		
ARE THERE TOOLS TO SUPPORT STUDENT FEEDBACK? *spell-checkers – grammar checkers – word prediction software – text to speech software – dictation – recording – calculators – pre-formatted graph paper – blank mind maps – essay structure formats – sentence starters – concept mapping sheets*		
ARE STUDENTS SUPPORTED TO REGULATE THEIR EMOTIONS IN CLASS? *five-point scales – red, amber, green cards in planners – thumbs up/down – other pre-agreed signals – breaks*		

MARYAM AND THE NOTE

Maryam was 15 and has just started Year 11. She liked school and she liked learning but one Thursday she stopped coming to school.
Maryam found social communication difficult to interpret and experienced high anxiety in Years 7 and 8. She now had a mentor, who met with her every week and helped her with her social understanding. Her form tutor sent round a feedback request to all her teachers and set up a meeting for Maryam, her form tutor and her mentor.

The feedback from all but one of her lessons was positive – although Maryam found it difficult to know how much to contribute, she was doing well in most of her subjects. Except in Geography, on Thursdays.
Mr H, her Geography teacher, reported that since the start of term Maryam had become increasingly rude and unresponsive, refusing to take part in group discussions, and the week before he had had to talk to her in front of the class about her attitude to learning.

His lessons were varied, based on whole-class discussions, video and a mixture of creative individual and group work – all of which Maryam enjoyed.
Further discussion revealed that at the start of the year, Mr H had explained that he liked to revisit previous topics throughout the year, with 'spot tests' quizzes and prizes so that there were lots of opportunities for repeated learning.

Maryam liked to do well; it was extremely important to her that her teachers thought well of her, and during the meeting it became clear that the fear of not getting a high mark in an unplanned assessment (uncertainty around structure) had started an anxiety spiral, which ended in her non-attendance at school on Thursday (Maryam trying to control the situation) and avoiding her mentor.
Mr H agreed that he would give the class one week's warning (increasing certainty around structure) before he gave a topic quiz. Maryam agreed that she would try to email her mentor as soon as she realised she was 'beginning a new worry'.

These agreements were drawn up into a written document which Maryam, Mr H and Maryam's mentor signed. Maryam kept a copy of this agreement in her planner.
She described the process like this: 'If I start to feel stressed about the tests, I know I can look at the note. I probably won't have to even look at it soon.'

LESSON DESIGN

One of the most fundamental things from a UDL perspective is that we have a clear learning objective. The *'at the end of the lessons my students will be able to...'* sentence. It may seem obvious, but if we are absolutely certain of our destination (and can communicate this to our students) it is very much easier to see different possible routes we might take to get there.

You will of course have your own planning formats, but we share this here as an example of how you can build in a mixture of **flexibility** as well as **certainty** at this stage of the teaching process.

Inclusion on demand or by design?

Have a look at these two different approaches to a drama module. Both are carefully planned with specific students in mind. What effect do you think each of the different approaches would have on the student experience?

INCLUSION ON DEMAND	INCLUSION BY DESIGN
Alex (the teacher) takes a register. She will then also specifically greet those students who have been identified with SEMH, autism and ADHD, to make sure they are attending at the start of the lesson.	Alex sets some warm-up exercises that focus on students reflecting on commonalities and help to strengthen and create a trusting classroom community. This helps students to work well together and to self-reflect on their strengths.
Alex provides students with an extract from *King Lear*. For those students with dyslexia, Alex finds a version of the play produced for primary-aged students with simplified language and includes more images.	To teach about a genre (tragedy), Alex provides students with a written extract from *King Lear*, shows a section of the film version and gets students to do their own research about the play online. Alex also helps them to relate what they are looking at in class to some TV shows (*Empire* and *Bloodline*) that some of them have watched.

cont.

INCLUSION ON DEMAND	INCLUSION BY DESIGN
The whole class watches a ten-minute clip from a theatrical production of the play. Alex has provided a list of terms and their meanings for the autistic students, those with dyslexia and those with ADHD who may find them confusing or who she feels will have forgotten what the terms mean. The students individually take notes on the video; Alex has provided writing frames (templates) to support those students with dyslexia, ADHD and autism.	Students work in groups to examine a ten-minute clip from a theatrical production of the play and each group has the same set of instructions: • Look at a list of words and stage directions Alex has provided and discuss what they mean. • Watch the video. • Take it in turns to analyse three roles, for example discuss why an actor has chosen to deliver a line in a certain way. Alex pauses them as they work to ask them to reflect on their discussions and write notes on their reflections. They present their notes to the rest of the class and students give them feedback.
Students write their own opening scene for a tragedy. Alex prints out a simplified template for her students with ADHD and dyslexia. Students perform the script in front of Alex and the rest of the class.	In small groups, students practise performing the opening scene from *King Lear*. Then they individually write their own piece using an online script planner, they rehearse it together, work in groups to give constructive criticism, then perform it in front of the class. The students discuss the outcomes of the performance, present their views of this to the rest of the class for discussion and they also write their reflections.

Throughout the process, Alex ensures a quiet learning environment. She ensures that the two students with ADHD and her autistic student are given movement breaks by offering them a break and/or asking them to help with classroom tasks and/or take notes to another classroom down the hall and up some stairs.	Alex encourages students to assess their work and engage in peer assessment. Throughout the lesson, she chats briefly with students one on one and asks simple questions to help them reflect on what they are doing. At times, Alex gives suggestions and examples to help them move forward. They are encouraged to draw on personal experiences to help shape their work. Group by group students are encouraged to record their performance, watch it and reflect on it. Alex also encourages them to record their voice as they speak and listen back to it and analyse the impact of voice alone.
Alex uses their performance and their script for assessment. Alex ensures that those students who have been identified as meriting extra time in examinations are given more time to complete the written work while the remainder of the class are asked to read the play quietly. Alex provides written feedback for all students.	Various assessment formats are available for Alex to assess the students, for example peer assessment, self-assessment, teacher oral feedback, practical observation assessments and written assignments.

Following on from this idea of widely available options, the next pages contain a suggested lesson planning format, and two completed examples.

PLANNING FORMATS FOR BUILDING CERTAINTY

TOPIC:	CLASS:	DURATION:	DATE:

This links to the previous lesson because...

Main lesson objective (visible throughout lesson):

By the end, they should know/be able to...

Students will demonstrate knowledge through:

- ☐ Discussion
- ☐ Reading
- ☐ Writing
- ☐ ICT
- ☐ Demonstration
- ☐ Other
- ☐ Independent work
- ☐ Collaborative work

Information will be presented as:

- ☐ Video
- ☐ Graphics
- ☐ Objects
- ☐ Audio
- ☐ Text
- ☐ Lecture
- ☐ Other

I will particularly engage them today by...

I will provide extra certainty by...

LEARNING EPISODE (MAIN POINTS)	NOTES (ADAPTATIONS FOR SENSORY, SOCIAL OR STRUCTURAL CERTAINTY)
Homework:	Link to next lesson:
Notes:	

LESSON DESIGN EXAMPLES

TOPIC:	CLASS:	DURATION:	DATE:
Romeo and Juliet — the Friar	Year 11	80 mins	16 Feb

This links to the previous lesson because...	Main lesson objective (visible throughout lesson):
We are revising minor characters.	To understand the role of the Friar and identify key quotes to support evidence.

By the end, they should know/be able to...

Understand the role of the Friar, have detailed revision notes and evidence to support written work next lesson.

Students will demonstrate knowledge through:	Information will be presented as:
☑ Discussion ☐ Other ☑ Reading ☑ Independent work ☑ Writing ☐ ICT ☑ Collaborative work ☐ Demonstration	☑ Video ☐ Text ☐ Graphics ☐ Lecture ☐ Objects ☑ Other ☐ Audio

I will particularly engage them today by...	I will provide extra certainty by...
Showing video clips of three different productions. Supporting them to make shared resources for revision (and to reduce anxiety).	Explaining lesson objectives and how it relates to exams and revision. Providing support to all: buff paper, writing framework, quote banks (email to laptop users). Ensuring plenty of space to work. Schedule written up on poster, lesson divided into chunks, sensory break (stretches).

LEARNING EPISODE (MAIN POINTS)	NOTES (ADAPTATIONS FOR SENSORY, SOCIAL OR STRUCTURAL CERTAINTY)
Work in pairs — brainstorm existing knowledge of the Friar.	Use established working pairs.
Watch three clips of the Friar from different productions — stop between each to share ideas and make notes.	Give out timeline of Friar's part in the plot. Offer structured note sheets to all — be clear that these are for revision only and will not be marked.
Pairs share ideas with the class — students add them to notes.	Students choose to speak or not, can pass written feedback to partner or teacher to read out.
Quote banks given out. Students match quotes to features discussed independently.	Quote banks have space next to each quote for notes if student prefers this structure.
Homework: Finish notes/quotes matching, learn three quotes.	Link to next lesson: Written work on Friar, using today's notes.

NOTES: Make sure there are extra resources for those who might want to rewrite work at home, make sure there are enough highlighters, revision cards, etc. Put links to videos on website for student access at home.

TOPIC:	CLASS:	DURATION:	DATE:
Governance of Ocean Piracy (Eduqas Geography A-level Global Governance Unit 2.2.6)	Year 13	50 mins	19 Feb

This links to the previous lesson because...

Continuation of the Ocean Governance Unit – previously covered laws and agreements and maritime superpowers. Oil choke points done for last week's homework – strong links to piracy hotspots discussed last week.

Main lesson objective (visible throughout lesson):

What is and where are ocean piracy hotspots?

What risks are associated with piracy hotspots? What governance approaches have there been?

How successful is the governance of ocean piracy?

By the end, they should know/be able to...

Locate at least two ocean piracy hotspots on a map and by name.

Understand there are a range of geopolitical <u>risks</u> (security issues) associated with piracy.

For one (or more) piracy hotspots, outline approaches that have been taken to trying to <u>govern (manage)</u> ocean piracy.

<u>Evaluate</u> how <u>successful</u> governance of piracy has been in one (or more) piracy hotspots – need evidence of both success and lack of success.

Students will demonstrate knowledge through:

☑ Discussion ☐ Other

☑ Reading ☑ Independent work

☑ Writing

☑ ICT ☑ Collaborative work

☐ Demonstration

Information will be presented as:

☑ Video ☑ Text

☑ Graphics ☑ Lecture

☐ Objects ☐ Other

☐ Audio

I will particularly engage them today by...	I will provide extra certainty by...
Showing three minutes of 'Captain Phillips' (2013 film about Somali Pirates) and two minutes of BBC documentary.	Hard copy of lesson plan with full notes provided. Also available on VLE (virtual learning environment) and can be accessed at any time before, during or after the lesson.
	In addition: Provide a summary sheet of one-sided A4 with images of key ideas: Location: Somalian Coast, Captain Phillips (Tom Hanks). Risks: shown in lightning bolts. Governance: image of US navy ship. Water cannons & United Nations Convention on the Law of the Sea. Evaluation: Speech bubbles of basic evaluation – positive views in plain speech bubbles and grey-infilled speech bubbles for negative evaluations of governance.
LEARNING EPISODE (MAIN POINTS)	**NOTES (ADAPTATIONS FOR SENSORY, SOCIAL OR STRUCTURAL CERTAINTY)**
DEFINITION of piracy hotspot – discuss and then highlight in prewritten notes (handed to all students). LOCATION of Straits of Malacca, Hormuz + Panama and Suez Canal on a map (independent).	Definition already in the notes – so no need to write out. Text book p.55 open with map. Can use Google maps/ArcGIS to locate places and contextualise them by being able to zoom in and zoom out. (M really enjoys using Google maps.)
RISKS: Discussion around risks associated with piracy hotspots should allow students to draw on their oil choke points homework – for example, energy security, world trade risks. Working in small groups of two or three (collaborative).	Encourage everyone to have their completed homework out of their files and on the desk right at the start of every lesson.
GOVERNANCE APPROACHES: Read provided notes and highlight (independent).	Offer choice of length of reading – students mark in pencil how far they have managed to read.

cont.

LEARNING EPISODE (MAIN POINTS)	NOTES (ADAPTATIONS FOR SENSORY, SOCIAL OR STRUCTURAL CERTAINTY)
EVALUATION OF GOVERNANCE: Interpretation of tables of data + reading notes + reflection on videos seen (independent and collaborative).	Summary sheet for basics. Colour-coded speech bubbles to support identification of differing viewpoints.
Homework: Eduqas A-level questions: 1. Data response question based on a data table of piracy incidents: Use Table 1 to compare piracy trends in different shipping regions. Include relevant data from the table in your answer. (5 marks) 2. With reference to one or more piracy hotspots, suggest how successful attempts to reduce piracy have been. (5 marks)	Link to next lesson: Growth of smuggling and people trafficking (across oceans) and international efforts to manage these flows (our case study Sub-Saharan Africa migrations crossing the Med).

Notes: Double check sound levels on video before students enter the room. Leave windows open until start of class. Offer movement break at halfway point.

Other resources

We think UDL is a game changer for inclusive teaching. If you're interested, go to the **CAST website** and look at the UDL guidelines – they are colourful and easy to navigate.

BUILDING STRUCTURAL CERTAINTY

Art's good. There's a set plan. Wednesday you start a page and you finish it for homework. I know exactly what's going to happen, it's quiet, you do your own thing and ask for help if you need it. (Alex, Year 10)

Earlier in the chapter we looked at the principles of the **Universal Design for Learning**, making support available to each and every student, should they need it. By doing this we have an opportunity to raise everyone's game.

We can look at providing more structure, more certainty and greater agency in dealing with uncertainty by paying attention to these three areas:

▶ **Representation** – visual support, variety and flexibility of presentation.

▶ **Action and expression** – options for student feedback and emotional regulation.

▶ **Engagement** – choices, goal-setting, personal experience, explicit purpose, routines, signposts and a variety of sensory and social demands.

In addition, we keep in mind the balance between offering consistent, certain structure and making sure that our students feel a strong sense of agency as they go about their tasks. A lesson may end up looking a bit like this:

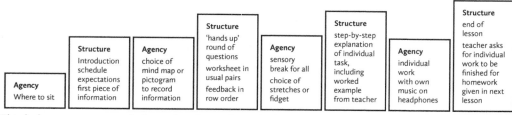

This helps everyone stay balanced and certain, reducing anxiety and allowing access to learning.

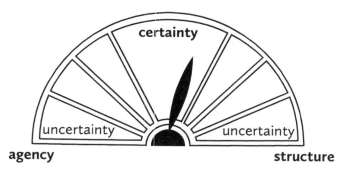

The following pages follow the UDL framework and contain some simple ideas to build certainty through classroom structure. Many of them will be familiar to you and are common to good teaching practice, but we include them here as examples of the certainty-building that our students rely on in order to engage.

Structure through representation

Why

> Reading anything is like reading a dictionary. I can only see one word at a time, the rest are out of focus and after five words I'm somehow expected to know what's happening. (Molly, Year 12)

We can build certainty in the way we present information. Too much, too fast, too inconsistent and students who struggle with uncertainty may get anxious, shut down or search for their own certainty (possibly causing distractions for others in the room). It's rare these days to see students having to copy information from a screen or whiteboard, but it happens, and our students have strong feelings about it. Even transferring a few lines from screen to paper can cause great uncertainty and stress at times.

Jessa, one of our students, wrote us a list to describe what happens when she is expected to copy things down from the board; for example, that week's homework, written up at the end of the lesson.

1   Panic I won't get it done in time.

2   Read the first bit and try to remember it.

3   Write it down.

4   Worry that I've remembered it wrong and go back and check.

5   Panic I won't get it done in time.

6   Look around to see if everyone else has finished.

7   Finish writing the first bit.

8   Read the second bit.

9   Notice that some people are leaving the room and panic more.

10   Write it down in a rush before I forget.

11   Miss bits out.

12   Realise I probably won't be able to read it but carry on like this until the end.

13   Get home and realise I can't read it.

14 Panic about not doing the homework and stress about how I can find out.

15 Maybe ask someone, maybe not.

16 Maybe do the homework, maybe not.

17 Maybe get in trouble, maybe not.

The same can apply to spoken instructions, particularly when we don't have a student's full attention, either because they are deeply involved in a task, or dealing with one end of a transition. It's so easy to find ourselves giving last-minute instructions or reminders as our students pack up at the end of a lesson, and for anyone who struggles with executive function, this can be extremely challenging.

How

The following are suggested guidelines which we try to stick to when thinking about how to present teaching materials. The information is a combination of guidelines from the British Dyslexia Association[2] and ideas that come from observation and listening to our students.

FORMAT	GUIDELINES	AVOID
Slides	• 6 x 6 rule (maximum six bullet points, six words per line) • One clearly defined subject per slide • One clear, relevant, engaging image/icon per slide • Flow charts, pictograms, graphics, grids, charts whenever possible • Sans-serif font only (e.g. Tahoma, Arial, Verdana, Comic Sans, Century Gothic, Trebuchet, Calibri, Open Sans)	• Highlighting • Underlining • Italics • Justifying • Text special effects

cont.

---

2 www.bdadyslexia.org.uk

FORMAT	GUIDELINES	AVOID
Slides	• Large font size, 22–26 point • Cream or pastel coloured background to slides • Consistent font style and size (headings and text) • Use bold for emphasis • Align text to the left or centre • Gradually reveal bullet points by using the 'appear' function • Make slide transitions consistent and simple • Check understanding before moving on	• Complex visual effects • Moving, flashing or dissolving images
Whiteboard	• Clean board *thoroughly* at start of every session • Use dark blue ink for text • Double spaces between key points • Draw boxes to highlight key information • Use bullet points more than free writing • Use flow charts, pictograms, graphics, grids, charts whenever possible	• Overcrowded text • Full paragraphs • Cursive text • Inconsistent-sized writing • 'Wonky' lines • Pens that don't work properly • Words entirely in uppercase

Handouts	• Single image/icon to signpost subject • Group related content together • Leave space between key points • Use flow charts, pictograms, graphics, grids, charts whenever possible • Sans-serif font only (Tahoma, Arial, Verdana, Comic Sans, Century Gothic, Trebuchet, Calibri, Open Sans) • Font size 12–14 point • Cream/pastel paper where possible • Bold for emphasis • Headings at least 20 per cent larger than text	• Underlining and italics • Words entirely in uppercase • Abbreviations • Double negatives • Crowded text • Unclear photocopies
Worksheets	• Clear heading • Clear purpose • Unambiguous instruction at top • Worked example • Tasks broken into sections, in boxes • Specific word bank available to all • Sans-serif font only (Tahoma, Arial, Verdana, Comic Sans, Century Gothic, Trebuchet, Calibri, Open Sans) • Font size 12–14 point • Cream/pastel paper where possible • Space for 'overflow' of writing for those with large handwriting	• Not leaving enough space for students to write in

cont.

FORMAT	GUIDELINES	AVOID
Feedback	• Consistent format (grids/ repeated categories) • Written/spoken/recorded, in-document auditory feedback	• Asking for verbal feedback without some kind of prior warning - 'I'm going to ask some of you questions about X, have a think for a few seconds.' • Asking for verbal feedback as a way to check attention levels (for example, if the student seems distracted)
Displays	• Current • Relevant • Signposted with clear headings • More flow charts, pictograms, graphics, grids, charts than free text • Securely fastened • Legible from across the room • Useful (e.g. subject word banks, key formula)	• Busy displays at the front, near whiteboard or screen • 'Flappy', ripped or faded paper • Irrelevant or out-of-date information

It can be really helpful to draw up a list of how we present information, take feedback and engage students and compare it with the lists of other staff in our school, team or department; consistent font or PowerPoint styles across subjects can really help students who struggle with uncertainty. This helps them manage the transition between classes, subjects and teachers and can lead to a reduced warm-up time and more certain behaviour.

Structure through action and expression

> I really like answering questions in lessons. Sometimes people get annoyed when I try and answer too many. I just don't think it's right when teachers pick on someone who they don't think has been listening. I think it's best when we write our answers down and hold them up – then everyone gets their answer seen. (Sean, Year 8)

Students who struggle with uncertainty often report difficulties with active participation in classroom activities. They are uncertain about how they will be perceived by teachers and peers, find it hard to work out the flexible rules for feedback and may lose access to key information as they try to regulate their uncertain feelings.

By now, the framework of 'choice within a structure' should be familiar to you. Giving all students (not just those with a recognised learning difference) choices for how they record and feed back information can increase their sense of agency considerably, reducing uncertainty, anxiety and distracting behaviours in the classroom.

The last few years have seen some exciting developments in '**edu-tech**' for feedback:

Electronic polling – students often respond with high levels of engagement as they use a simple app on a handheld device to contribute to debates, true or false activities and multiple-choice formats. It encourages contributions from students who are usually reluctant to 'risk' an answer, or too uncertain to speak in front of a group, yet may be motivated by having a tech option.

Whole-class use of tablets – these have revolutionised some classrooms, with sophisticated options for two-way information exchanges. Again, many students who struggle with uncertainty find this approach more easily accessible.

Cloud-based learning – many teachers are setting tasks and taking feedback in an online 'classroom'. This creates the opportunity for flexible options such as auditory feedback, where students and teachers can leave each other voice notes attached to specific points in homework or coursework.

Individual use of IT – this differs from school to school and usually depends on an assessment of typing speed versus writing speed. Many of our students take exams apart from the majority of other students, sometimes in an IT suite, sometimes with a laptop, which makes other adjustments such as extra time, rest breaks or prompts more practical. Some students use a laptop in their classes, and early lessons in touch typing for all our students, but particularly those with dyslexia, can be game changing.

However, we recognise that the majority of schools we work in do not yet have access to all this. The following ideas focus on the more readily available options and are recorded here to remind us of the strategies we use that build certainty.

ACTION OR EXPRESSION	EXAMPLES
Answering questions in class	• Individual whiteboards and pens available (helps students who call out feel their answer is 'seen' each time, even though they may not always be called on to speak). • Wipe clean white page in diary/planner – whiteboard pens available. • Small cards or sticky notes, passed to front and grouped on board at front according to answer. • Students write or draw on main whiteboard. • Pre-arranged systems for asking questions: 'I'm going to ask this row the first question, then this one number two, then the back row', or for highly anxious students, 'If I don't ask you first, I'm not going to ask you to answer in this round of questions.' • Student has option to walk while thinking through answers.
'Voting' for true or false, multiple choice or debate answers	• Gesture: thumbs up/down; stand up/sit down; raise no arms, one arm/two arms (for choice of three options). • Pages in planners: show red/amber/green page. • Movement (where space allows): move to chalk circles on ground, one side of a rope, one side of a room to express choices.

Asking for help	• Pre-agreed sign arranged: coloured card or object on desk. • Small group, extra help or 'overlearning' session offered as regular part of lesson structure, at set point in every lesson (e.g. halfway through a double period) – students opt in or continue with individual work.
Written feedback	• Choice of diagrams, pictograms, mind maps, use of colour, illustrations, comic strips, posters, animations, video, voice recordings to replace or support writing for homework. • Scaffolding: sentence starters, pre-formatted graph paper, essay structures, blank mind maps, 'fill in the blanks' sentences, blank flow charts, etc. • Spell checkers/grammar checkers on laptop.
Taking exams	• Laptop. • Voice recognition software. • Adult scribe. • Use of different colour pens for questions that the student finds difficult to understand. • Use of highlighter to emphasise key parts of questions.
Emotional regulation	• Use of colour-coded scale on desk to communicate rising levels of anxiety. • Whole-class movement breaks built in to every lesson. • Written agreements for specific self-regulation strategies: extra movement breaks, fidget breaks (in or outside the classroom), drink breaks, change of seat, etc. when needed.

Structure through engagement

The first two sections of this element of the chapter looked at how we present information and take feedback can reduce uncertainty. This section looks at how increasing our students' sense of agency through higher levels of engagement can increase certainty and improve outcomes for learning, behaviour and wellbeing.

In Chapter 2, you will find questionnaires to help you find out what motivates your students, what they like to do outside lessons. We may already have this information about many of the young people we teach, but it can be a useful way to get to know some of our more uncertain students, who may not engage so easily.

This information can be useful when designing examples to demonstrate any teaching point, for example using skateboards to explain elements of physics, talking about dog breeds as an example of genetics or making up stories about the students in your class to illustrate maths problems all help students engage more easily.

We summarise some of the options below using the UDL framework:

TYPES OF ENGAGEMENT	EXAMPLES
Choice of what and how to learn	• Choice of order of tasks within a lesson or assignment. • Options to choose different levels of challenge. • Option to 'skip' one question (of the student's choice) in a test or homework. • Choice of reward: points, credits, biscuits, stickers, five-minute game at end of lesson or other privileges according to interests. • Use of colours, graphics, different layouts in classwork according to personal style.
Student goal-setting	• Students set and reflect on own behaviour goals on a daily/weekly/termly basis (e.g. 'writing down my comment instead of calling it out' or 'asking if I need a break'). • Students set own specific learning goals within a broader target (e.g. 'changing colour pen to show I'm finding it hard' or 'always trying two questions before asking for help').

Personal experience	• Encourage sharing of student experience, written or verbal (e.g. they may have visited a country mentioned in a Geography case study or English literature text, practise a certain religion, have a family member who experienced a historical or world event first hand). • Use real-life examples to explain concepts whenever possible. • Check examples (photographs, videos, stories) drawn from a representative cultural mix.
Clear purpose to each task	• Explain lesson 'purpose' at start of every task and make visible on each slide/worksheet. • Use flipchart paper poster stuck next to whiteboard if necessary, so the purpose/schedule is visible at all times.
Clear routines (examples)	• Familiar beginning to each session – greeting and lesson schedule. • Familiar end to each session – summary and homework details/next lesson. • Movement break exactly halfway through lesson. • Familiar repeated phrases for setting up experiments or equipment/getting into pairs/packing up/before key information. • Review and test at end of each module. • Progress through curriculum timeline displayed at end of every module.

cont.

TYPES OF ENGAGEMENT	EXAMPLES
Other signposts?	• Visual 'traffic light' timers to display exact times for short tasks, whole lesson or time till a movement break. • Visual timetable written or drawn on flipchart poster as schedule is presented – can nominate student to cross off as each section ends. • Visual map of all subject units as timeline or mind map; refer to as each unit ends to show progress through curriculum. • Clear signals for key points: same student writes it on board each time, everyone stands up to listen and repeat to their neighbour, 'this is the science bit', 'brains turned up to 11', etc.
Variety of sensory learning	• Combination of listening, looking, speaking, listening to music out loud/on headphones and silence. • Build movement into lessons where possible. Students come up to the board/move to small groups/pairs and vote by moving to one side of room/standing up/ sitting down. • Experiment with options for seating: on floor, sitting at desk or standing. • Use classroom yoga between tasks. • Vary pace: quick fire versus deeper thought and learning.
Variety of social learning	• Individual. • Pairs. • Small groups. • Whole-class learning. • Encourage students to contribute to decisions on groupings for collaborative work and where possible allow for flexibility and 'trial arrangements' until productive student combinations are found. • Experiment with side-by-side (as opposed to face-to-face) learning for students with social uncertainty.

These are strategies that we see often in schools; much of it will have been familiar and some may seem difficult to implement with limited time, space or resources. However, we have seen great change come from simple structural adjustments and often the time that's spent setting up a new routine or presentation format is more than paid back in better engagement from a whole class.

IF YOU ONLY HAVE FIVE MINUTES

Tips for building structural certainty in the classroom:

- **Balance familiar structure with student choice:**
  - Introduction and link to last lesson
  - New information in a familiar structure
  - Students manipulate/evaluate new information – give options for methods
  - Build in movement breaks
  - Student feedback – give options for methods
  - Summary/questions/homework – give options for methods
  - Preview of next lesson.
- **Be consistent with presentation:** use the same PowerPoint theme, fonts and layouts across your lessons and subject department.
- **Allow for freedom of student expression:** offer options to write, draw pictograms, use mind maps, grids or bullet lists for recording of information, giving feedback and homework.

- **Give structured, visual, certain feedback:** use grids (example below). Print or stick them in books. Use the three-to-one rule – three positives: one improvement.

What went well	50% correct (30% last time) Much clearer numbering Neater graphs
One thing you could do to improve	Show ALL your working out.
Notes	I know you find this a challenge but your marks have improved every week since the start of term.

- **Use self-regulation systems** to help students let you know how they are doing. Use red, amber and green pages in planners and encourage students to display their levels of certainty as you work through the lesson.

REFERENCES

Bowe, F. G. (2000). *Universal Design in Education: Teaching Non-Traditional Students.* Westport, CT: Bergin & Garvey.

Bowers, J. S. (2016). The practical and principled problems with educational neuroscience. *Psychological Review, 123,* 600–612.

Bradley, R., Doolittle, J. & Bartolotta, R. (2008). Building on the data and adding to the discussion: The experiences and outcomes of students with emotional disturbance. *Journal of Behavioral Education, 17*(1), 4–23.

Carleton, R. N. (2012). The intolerance of uncertainty construct in the context of anxiety disorders: Theoretical and practical perspectives. *Expert Review of Neurotherapeutics, 12*(8), 937–947.

CAST (2011). Universal Design for Learning guidelines version 2.0. Retrieved from https://udlguidelines.cast.org.

CAST (2014). CAST through the years: One mission, many innovations. Retrieved from https://www.cast.org/impact/timeline-innovation.

Cook, S. C., Rao, K. & Collins, L. (2017). Self-monitoring interventions for students with EBD: Applying UDL to a research-based practice. *Beyond Behavior, 26*(1), 19–27.

Coyne, M. D., Kame'enui, E. J. & Carnine, D. W. (2011). *Effective Teaching Strategies That Accommodate Diverse Learners* (fourth edition). Boston, MA: Pearson.

den Houting, J. (2019). Neurodiversity: An insider's perspective. *Autism, 23*(2), 271–273.

Dymond, S. K., Renzaglia, A., Rosenstein, A., Chun, E. J., Banks, R. A., Niswander, V. & Gilson, C. L. (2006). Using a participatory action research approach to create a universally designed inclusive high school science course: A case study. *Research and Practice for Persons with Severe Disabilities, 31*(4), 293–308.

Edyburn, D. (2010). Would you recognize universal design for learning if you saw it? Ten propositions for new directions for the second decade of UDL. *Learning Disability Quarterly, 33*(1), 33–41.

Edyburn, D. & Gardner, J. E. (2009). *Readings in Special Education Technology: Universal Design for Learning*. Arlington, VA: Council for Exceptional Children.

Fiske, S. T. (2002). Five Core Social Motives, Plus or Minus Five. In S. J. Spencer, S. Fein, M. P. Zanna & J. Olson (eds) *Motivated Social Perception: The Ontario Symposium*, Vol. 9 (pp.223–236). Mahwah, NJ: Erlbaum.

Gable, R. A., Hendrickson, J. M., Tonelson, S. W. & Van Acker, R. (2002). Integrating academic and non-academic instruction for students with emotional/behavioral disorders. *Education and Treatment of Children, 25*(4), 459–475.

Hitchcock, C. & Stahl, S. (2003). Assistive technology, universal design, universal design for learning: Improved learning opportunities. *Journal of Special Education Technology, 18*(4), 45–52.

Jolivette, K., Wehby, J. H., Canale, J. & Massey, N. G. (2001). Effects of choice making opportunities on the behaviors of students with emotional and behavioral disorders. *Behavioral Disorders, 26*, 131–145.

Landau, M. J., Kay, A. C. & Whitson, J. A. (2015). Compensatory control and the appeal of a structured world. *Psychological Bulletin, 141*(3), 694.

Lieber, J., Horn, E., Palmer, S. & Fleming, K. (2008). Access to the general education curriculum for preschoolers with disabilities: Children's school success. *Exceptionality, 16*(1), 18–32.

Lieberman, L., Lytle, R. & Clarcq, J. A. (2008). Getting it right from the start: Employing the universal design for learning approach to your curriculum. *Journal of Physical Education, Recreation & Dance, 79*(2), 32–39.

Lowrey, K. A., Hollingshead, A., Howery, K. & Bishop, J. B. (2017). More than one way: Stories of UDL and inclusive classrooms. *Research and Practice for Persons with Severe Disabilities, 42*(4), 225–242.

Mangiatordi, A. & Serenelli, F. (2013). Universal design for learning: A meta-analytic review of 80 abstracts from peer reviewed journals. *REM, 5*(1), 109–118.

McIntosh, K., Chard, D. J., Boland, J. B. & Horner, R. H. (2006). Demonstration of combined efforts in school-wide academic and behavioral systems and incidence of reading and behavior challenges in early elementary grades. *Journal of Positive Behavior Interventions, 8*(3), 146–154.

Meyer, A., Rose, D. H. & Gordon, D. (2014). *Universal Design for Learning: Theory & Practice*. Wakefield, MA: CAST Professional Publishing.

Orkwis, R. (2003). *Universally Designed Instruction* (Report No. EDO-EC-03-02). Washington, DC: Special Education Programs.

Ostroff, E. (2001). Universal Design: An Evolving Paradigm. In W. F. E. Preiser & K. H. Smith (eds) *Universal Design Handbook*. New York: McGraw Hill.

Patalay, P. & Fitzsimons, E. (2016). Correlates of mental illness and wellbeing in children: Are they the same? Results from the UK millennium cohort study. *Journal of the American Academy of Child & Adolescent Psychiatry, 55*(9), 771–783.

Pennebaker, J. W. & Stone, L. D. (2004). Translating Traumatic Experiences into Language: Implications for Child Abuse and Long-Term Health. In L. J. Koenig, L. S. Doll, A. O'Leary & W. Pequegnat (eds) *From Child Sexual Abuse to Adult Sexual Risk: Trauma, Revictimization, and Intervention* (pp.201–216). Washington, DC: American Psychological Association.

Pittman, T. S. & Zeigler, K. R. (2007). Basic Human Needs. In A. Kruglanski & E. T. Higgins (eds) *Social Psychology: Handbook of Basic Principles* (second edition) (pp.473–489). New York, NY: Guilford Press.

Presson, P. K. & Benassi, V. A. (1996). Illusion of control: A meta-analytic review. *Journal of Social Behavior and Personality, 11*(3), 493.

Rose, D. & Meyer, A. (2002). *Teaching Every Student in the Digital Age: Universal Design for Learning.* Alexandria, VA: ASCD.

Rose, D. H. & Strangman, N. (2007). Universal design for learning: Meeting the challenge of individual learning differences through a neurocognitive perspective. *Universal Access in the Information Society, 5*(4), 381–391.

Scanlon, D. & Baker, D. (2012). An accommodations model for the secondary inclusive classroom. *Learning Disability Quarterly, 35*(4), 212–224.

Skinner, E. A. (1996). A guide to constructs of control. *Journal of Personality and Social Psychology, 71*(3), 549.

Spencer, S. A. (2011). Universal Design for Learning: Assistance for teachers in today's inclusive classrooms. *Interdisciplinary Journal of Teaching and Learning, 1*(1), 10–22.

Thomas, M. S., Ansari, D. & Knowland, V. C. (2019). Annual research review: Educational neuroscience: progress and prospects. *Journal of Child Psychology and Psychiatry, 60*(4), 477–492.

United Nations (2006). United Nations Convention on the Rights of Persons with Disabilities. Retrieved from www.un.org/disabilities/documents/convention/convention_accessible_pdf.pdf.

Whitson, J. A. & Galinsky, A. D. (2008). Lacking control increases illusory pattern perception. *Science, 322*(5898), 115–117.

4

SENSORY

ACTIVITIES TO SUPPORT SENSORY CERTAINTY

This chapter is about the sensory uncertainties that our students might experience – how they cause anxiety and how we can help. The Sensory S is the central of our 3S's because it plays such a fundamental role in how we understand the world and therefore the amount of certainty we experience as we move through it. The way in which we process and manage both **external** (sounds, sights, smells, tastes, textures) and **internal** sensory information (balance, movement, body awareness, digestion, pain and emotions) can have a significant impact on our ability to learn and function as a *social* being, which in turn affects our needs for *structure* and predictability.

Introduction

Theory

▸ Uncertainty and sensory

▸ The what and why of sensory support

▸ Interoception – the eighth sense

▸ Linking theory and practice

▸ How we can help

Practice

▸ Sensory uncertainty in the classroom

▸ The ~~five~~ eight senses

　• Interpreting sensory-based behaviour

▸ The search for sensory certainty

　• What does it look like, what could it mean?

　• Using the 3S framework to understand behaviour

　• Sensory observation

　• Sensory survey

▸ Building sensory certainty – four steps to self-regulation

　• 1. Recognise sensory signals

　　– Chair-based pressure activities

　　– Walking in the present

　　– Sensory moments

　　– Tracing the breath

　　– Yoga practices for the classroom

　　– The body scan

　• 2. Link sensory signals and emotions

　　– Interoceptive body mapping

　　– What's in my head?

- 3. Notice thoughts
  - Thinking out loud
  - Using journals
- 4. Trying new responses
  - What to do with worry
  - Using scales

Other ideas to increase interoceptive awareness

If you only have five minutes

Further reading

References

INTRODUCTION

The sensory-rich nature of the everyday school environment can threaten the learning and full educational participation of young people with differences in sensory processing if their differences are not recognised and accommodated. All school-based activities, such as completing class work, playing, socialising or eating in the lunch hall, require students to process and integrate sensory information, in environments that can be perceived by all students as new or unpredictable (Villasenor, Smith & Jewell, 2018). The lunch hall is a good example of an unpredictable sensory environment, with its different smells, sounds and sights, and the uncertainty associated with sensory processing in these dynamic environments can result in what might be considered atypical, irregular or even 'challenging' behaviour. For example:

> I might not expect to perceive a certain smell in the world, in this case the lunch hall – it might be a new recipe(!); this would lead me to question my model of the world (the lunch hall). I would, in the face of this uncertainty, then try to look for some certainty – I might have an exaggerated need for control. So, I shout loudly, as I predict that this would feel/sound a certain way, and as my prediction is fulfilled it brings some certainty, and therefore control, back to the situation.

What this example illustrates is that the behaviour the student is displaying is not the problem, it is their **solution** to a problem. That problem is uncertainty, and their behaviour is a bid for certainty. In this example, and many others that you might think of, the certainty-seeking behaviours might not always be the most effective way to manage difficulties in that context. In this case, they could have social repercussions that the student might not want.

The aim of our work is to reduce sensory uncertainty, where possible, by adapting the environment, and then support students to use more effective strategies to manage unaccommodating sensory environments, thus increasing their capacity to cope with them. This is because the main function of school is to prepare us for life outside school, and the world can sometimes be a chaotic, noisy place.

THEORY

UNCERTAINTY AND SENSORY

As we saw when we looked at predictive processing (PP) in Chapter 1, sensory information is fundamental in determining our worlds and our certainty within them. Not only does it provide the raw materials that we use to build our models of the world, it is also the yard stick that helps us to measure how good a fit our models are. It is sensory information that signals to us that our predictive models might not be as good as they could be.

Prediction error comes from the perception of sensory changes in the body (interoceptive sources) and/or the surrounding world (exteroceptive sources) that were unexpected. When it comes to sensory, we can experience both internal and external prediction errors. Internal prediction error refers to unexpected information about the condition of the body (signalling, for example, heart rate, respiration, metabolic and immunological functioning; Barrett & Simmons, 2015; Craig, 2015; Seth, 2013). External prediction error refers to unexpected information in the environment (signalled by sights, sounds, etc.). It is fundamentally important that we perceive sensory information as **precisely** as necessary so that we can (1) build good models of the world and (2) recognise when those models do not fit and if they should be updated.

As discussed in Chapter 1, precision in the PP story is an approximation of certainty. If something has high precision it is allocated a high level of certainty. If something has low precision it is the opposite. When weighing up our prior models and current sensory information, carrying out our compromise calculation, we might turn the strength dial up or down on one or the other depending on the amount of precision we give to it. This will influence how we experience the world and how we build models of it. Imprecise sensory information limits how good our models are and makes us more prone to experience uncertainty. For example, we experience more uncertainty about what we are seeing when it is dark than when it is light. Equally, physical differences in our sensory hardware, such as a visual or hearing impairment, can impact how we build our models and how good a fit they are for the world.

Crucially, even without a physical difference in our sensory hardware, information does not reach us 'loud and clear'. It is always adulterated/modified by our prior models and the learning glasses we are wearing. We might not process some sensory information as precisely as we could do if our model of the world tells us it's not very important, such as visual input when it is dark. Or we might miss important new sensory information when we are somewhere that is very familiar to us (or if we are with someone we are very familiar with). It means we can genuinely not 'see' that our partner has changed their hairstyle. In this situation, we have turned the strength dial on our prior model up as this is a highly predictable situation and turned down the strength dial on current sensory input as we would expect any errors to likely be just random noise.

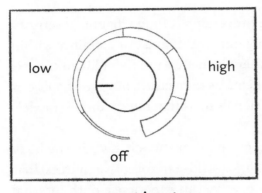

current input

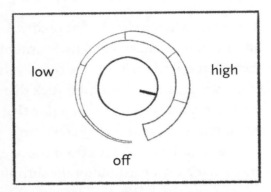

priors

This might explain what happens in cases of attentional blindness, a phenomenon made famous in Simons and Chabris's (1999) 'gorilla' experiment (give it a try, though keep in mind that reading this might have given you a different prior model to someone who has not and could impact the effect!).[1]

So, we can see how, according to the PP story, differences in the way we process sensory information and the precision we then give it causes discrepancies between *our* world and *the* world. This then leads to uncertainty (prediction errors). It is due to this central role that sensory plays in everything we see, understand, feel, think and do that it is the central S in our 3S model of uncertainty.

The examples of practical support for sensory uncertainty in the second half of this chapter, as with all the support described in this book, are not aimed at young people with any specific diagnosis and would benefit all students. Current estimates of the prevalence of children **without** identified diagnoses experiencing challenges in processing and integrating sensory information ranges from 15.8 to 16.5 per cent (Ben-Sasson, Carter & Briggs-Gowan, 2009; Fernandez-Andres *et al.*, 2015) and from 40 to 88 per cent in children **with** specific diagnoses (Cheung & Siu, 2009; Fernandez-Andres *et al.*, 2015). These sensory difficulties can be a result of differences in an individual sense (see the senses listed in the next section) or, more often, due to difficulties with multisensory processing. It is also important to keep in mind that all of us experience differences in the way our senses operate (and therefore the precision of the information we receive) not only as we grow and develop but also throughout the day depending on other factors. For example, differences in sensory certainty can happen more frequently, and temporarily, such as when we are tired, stressed or excited. So all of us, and all our students, benefit from greater sensory certainty.

---

1   www.youtube.com/watch?v=vJG698U2Mvo

THE WHAT AND WHY OF SENSORY SUPPORT

Below we provide a brief description of sensory intervention programmes you might come across and the reasons behind their development. Not all of these reasons explicitly highlight the aim, which is to reduce uncertainty, but it is hoped that we all now know that this is (of course) what any effective type of support is ultimately aimed at doing!

Sensory interventions

The main types of sensory support in schools are currently these: sensory integration (Ayers, 1972), sensory processing (Miller & Lane, 2000), sensory modulation (McIntosh *et al.*, 1999) and sensory perception (May-Benson & Schaaf, 2015).

The confusing thing with these terms is that they are often used interchangeably, despite representing very different constructs, both across and within research and practice. Whichever process or practice we are thinking about, we need to consider all eight senses:

▸ Vision (sight)

▸ Olfactory (smell)

▸ Gustatory (taste)

▸ Auditory (hearing)

▸ Tactile (touch)

▸ Interoception (sensory information relating to internal body senses)

▸ Vestibular (balance, orientation, space and acceleration)

▸ Proprioception (sense of position/movement of body parts).

The two overarching terms we need to be aware of are sensory integration and sensory processing (Brown, Tse & Fortune, 2019). From a practice perspective, sensory integration is often used to refer to a specific class of interventions, the most notable being sensory integration therapy (SIT; Ayres, 1972). SIT is provided by occupational therapists, often clinic based, and traditionally involves the use of specific equipment (swings, therapy balls, trampolines) to increase a young person's ability to integrate sensory information (Case-Smith, Weaver & Fristad, 2015). The approach seeks to use enhanced sensory experiences to improve neurophysiological processing of sensation to promote change in sensory responsiveness, thereby supporting better learning and behaviour (Reynolds *et al.*, 2017). It aims to make a deep change at the neurological level. However, as not all of us are qualified occupational therapists, we will be focusing on sensory-based interventions.

Sensory-based interventions (SBIs)

These take place in the young person's natural environment and typically aim to have a shorter-term impact on supporting self-regulation, attention or organisation (Watling & Hauer, 2015). They aim to make a change at a behavioural level as opposed to necessarily a neurophysiological one. Within education, SBIs focus on how sensory input within the school environment affects student participation (Foster & Cox, 2013). Typically, SBIs might be systematically programmed into a young person's day (such as scheduled sensory/movement breaks), so a sensory diet would be an example of an SBI. Equally, they may be put in place in response to an immediate self-regulation need, particularly to lower a high arousal state, such as stress or hyperactivity.

SBIs in school settings typically involve the application of Dunn's (1997) conceptual framework of sensory processing. While the majority of work around this has been looking at young children, recent studies have shown the model can successfully be applied to adolescent and adult populations (Metz *et al.*, 2019). Dunn's model is based on two central constructs: neurological threshold and behavioural response (Dunn, 2007).

Neurological thresholds measure how people respond differently to sensory information on the basis of how sensitive they are to it, that is, the limit that sensory input (e.g. sound) needs to meet (or exceed) for it to be detected and attended to (this in turn is impacted by the precision they apply to it as a result of their prior models of the world). These limits are unique not only to each individual but also to each of their senses, so each sense can have a different threshold. They also vary across the lifespan and contexts. For example, a young person may have a low threshold for auditory input and a high threshold for proprioceptive input and as such may find it particularly difficult to manage in a noisy environment (because their auditory system registers very small amounts of sensory stimuli) and struggle to maintain their posture when sitting (because their proprioceptive system requires a lot of input to register it).

Low threshold is often referred to as being hyper-sensitive (high precision) and high threshold as being hypo-sensitive (low precision). These thresholds are important for us to understand, as it follows that 'typical' levels of sensory input might then generate what will seem to be an atypical response – over-reaction for someone with a low threshold to input in that sense (hyper-sensitive) and under-reaction for someone with a high threshold (hypo-sensitive). As discussed below, these thresholds can lead to two types of behaviour, **sensory-seeking** behaviour or **sensory avoidant** behaviour.

Behavioural responses define how we manage sensory stimuli. Behavioural responses also run along a continuum ranging from people actively engaging with their external environment or passively allowing their environment to act on them. The responses are often referred to as sensory-seeking and sensory avoidant behaviours. Based on these two axes, sensory behaviours have been divided into four patterns: sensory under- (hypo-) reactivity, sensory over- (hyper-) reactivity, sensory seeking, and sensory avoidance (Ben-Sasson *et al.*, 2009; Dunn, 2001).

THE RELATIONSHIP BETWEEN NEUROLOGICAL THRESHOLDS AND BEHAVIOURAL RESPONSES (DUNN, 1997)

Neurological Threshold Continuum	Behavioural Response Continuum	
	Responds in ACCORDANCE with threshold	Responds to COUNTERACT threshold
High (habituation)	Poor registration	Sensation seeking
Low (sensitisation)	Sensitivity to stimuli	Sensation avoiding

These are useful distinctions to make in practice when designing support. Dunn (1997) describes these patterns as follows:

> young children with high 'sensory' thresholds would respond to very few stimuli, while young children with low thresholds would respond to many stimuli. On the other end of the continuum, young children can respond to counteract their thresholds, these children might either try to exert excessive energy seeking stimuli to try to meet high thresholds or exert energy to avoid triggering low thresholds. (p.27)

Another way to think of our senses and their thresholds is like a cup.

Sensory cups

We can think about our sensory systems as being like cups and sensory input as liquid being poured into them. If we are hyper-responsive to a certain sense it is like having a small cup, where a small amount of input will cause us to overflow. If we are hypo-responsive we have a large cup. We need a lot of sensory input to fill it up. Full cups are our home state (homeostasis). Anything other than a full cup causes uncertainty and creates the drive to get back to our home state (fill up or empty our cups).

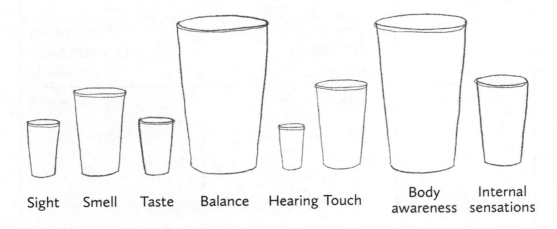

| Sight | Smell | Taste | Balance | Hearing | Touch | Body awareness | Internal sensations |

We also need to recognise that our cups change both in the longer term as well as day to day. The most frequent change to our cups that we are likely to experience is when we are **stressed**. This can lead us to a hypervigilant state and cause our visual and auditory cups to shrink (turning the precision on these right up – see below).

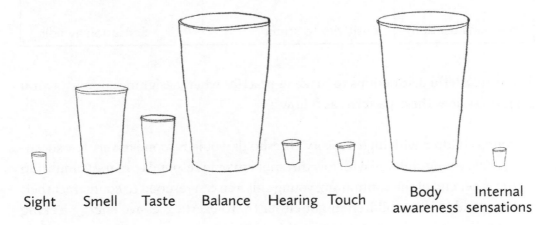

| Sight | Smell | Taste | Balance | Hearing | Touch | Body awareness | Internal sensations |

As a result, as the cups shrink, we are more likely to experience overwhelming feelings, uncertainty, and the distress this brings.

Sensory sensitivities and responses

A sensory over-responsive (hyper-responsive) young person may present with negative or seemingly aggressive behaviour in response to what appears to be non-threatening sensory information (i.e. anxiety when hearing the school bell, not liking to be touched or a dislike of certain food textures/tastes). The sensory under-responsive (hypo-responsive) young person seems not to detect sensory information (i.e. does not respond to their name when called, may not 'know their own strength' or craves the strong flavoured foods they need to register taste).

A young person who is sensory seeking needs what can seem to be unusually excessive amounts of sensory stimuli (i.e. incessant running/jumping around or humming), with the obvious consequence within an education setting of interrupted attention (Miller *et al.*, 2007). The sensory avoidant young person will try to avoid sensory input, for example placing their hands over their ears or withdrawing from/avoiding certain environments. While this might not be the most overtly difficult problem for a setting to manage, it can have a significant impact on an individual and also affects attention, as the student is focused on trying to avoid possible sensory overload. More generally, seeking and tolerating novel sensory environments supports learning and development throughout childhood, and not doing so can have a negative impact on learning (Thelan & Smith, 1998). **It is important to note that these (seemingly unusual) responses to sensory stimuli are never conscious acts of defiance, but a response to uncertainty**.

Even the excitement caused by something positive can be overwhelming and create a state of uncertainty – 'something's changed inside my body that is costing me energy and I need to get back to being my most energy efficient'. The excitement has moved us out of our 'home' state (homeostasis) and created a biological drive to get back to it. We are pushed to find some certainty.

For example, we may be confused by a young person refusing to get out of the car to go to a place they may really, really like, say a concert by their favourite band. This may be because the anxiety caused by their uncertainty over how they are feeling (a mixture of excitement and fear of the unknown) compels them towards the certainty of staying put, rather than getting out of the car (Donnellan, Hill & Leary, 2013).

Sensory modulation (precision) and stress

It would be a significant oversimplification to presume that behaviours we see accurately capture the complexity of sensory processing, but behaviour is a way of creating certainty to manage sensory input that an individual cannot modulate. The emotional uncertainty caused by the excitement of arriving at a concert by my favourite band may be experienced at such a high level that it is almost intolerable and yet I may have no way of reducing the uncertainty being communicated by my internal state.

SBIs, therefore, often specifically aim to target and support sensory modulation (akin in the PP story to the **precision** we apply to sensory information). Sensory modulation is often used to describe both a neurophysiological process and an intervention approach addressing observable behaviour (Wallis, Sutton & Bassett, 2018). We will focus on the intervention approach. Broadly speaking, this looks to address the registration (sensing) and integration (interpreting) of multisensory information (information from more than one sense).

As an example of sensory modulation, when we eat we need to register and integrate information from all our senses to see, smell, touch and taste the food, register and integrate the proprioceptive information we get as we chew, the vestibular information as our head moves while chewing and the process of the food moving down our throats. We must do all this while taking in the background noise and speech of any companions, regulating our movements and knowing when we are full.

Sensory modulation describes the process by which we interpret sensation according to previous experience (prior models) and how it links with emotional and cognitive states to evoke regulating and behavioural responses. It allows us to self-regulate effectively in response to sensory demands (including prediction errors) from the environment, both external and internal. An external demand might be to manage in a loud environment and an internal demand might be the need to address our sensation of hunger! It is the precision setting that we apply to current sensory input in light of how certain we view the situation to be (the specific type of certainty glasses we are wearing, as discussed in Chapter 1) that will impact our sensory modulation.

Individuals who have difficulties with sensory modulation have been found to have low vagal tone (which indicates activity in functioning of the vagus nerve) (Schaaf *et al.*, 2010). A low vagal tone in children and adolescents has been associated with heightened emotional reactivity, poor attentional and inhibitory control and clinically significant anxiety (McLaughlin *et al.*, 2015). Vagal tone is seen as a useful biomarker for the parasympathetic nervous system (PNS). The PNS (rest and digest) helps us to calm, and keeps the sympathetic nervous system (SNS) fight or flight in check. Together, the PNS and SNS form part of the autonomic nervous system (ANS). The ANS plays a central regulatory function of maintaining homeostasis activity. Homeostasis can be considered the state we always want to be in, our physiological home(*ostasis*). When we are stressed we have moved out of homeostasis, away from certainty, and our sympathetic nervous system (fight or flight) will kick in try to regulate us back home. Having a low vagal tone might indicate that we are not as efficient as we could be in finding our way back home, that the parasympathetic nervous system is not effectively holding the sympathetic nervous system back. There are times when we would like to suppress vagal tone (lower it) as this would give the sympathetic system free reign to kick in and therefore might help us fight or run away from a threat, something that, if a bear was about to eat us, would be more adaptive than 'resting and digesting'.

However, a consistently low vagal tone might mean we are always bubbling away, primed to react to a threat, never quite in our full rest and digest state. It would be the state we would be in if we were frequently experiencing uncertainty.

This relationship between sensory modulation (precision) and greater vulnerability to stress (a manifestation of uncertainty) can end up creating a vicious circle. Inaccurate estimates of the precision of sensory input (such as paying too much attention to what might just be random pieces of information or slight, inconsequential variations) causes uncertainty as these random pieces of information or slight variations were not predicted by our models (as they are random or slight variations!). However, as we have turned up the precision of sensory input, we might use this slight variation or random piece of information to build a new model of the world. As these are built on random pieces of information or slight variations, they will not be very useful, they will over-fit the data. It is a bit like seeing one Sphynx cat and updating your model of cats as being hairless. This poor model leads to more prediction errors, which causes more stress. This leads us to view the world as highly volatile and unpredictable (we put on our unexpected uncertainty glasses) and we end up having the default setting for our current sensory input dial being 'all the way up'.

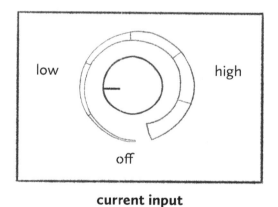

current input

So, it becomes vitally important to be able to understand how volatile our environment is and therefore how to modulate our senses. Ultimately, one of the key sensory players which helps us understand the volatility of our world is **interoception**.

INTEROCEPTION – THE EIGHTH SENSE

They are called feelings because we feel them.

Interoception is defined as the detection of the internal physiological condition of the body or the sensing of internal bodily changes (Craig, 2002; Garfinkel *et al.*, 2015; Wiens, 2005) and is the key steering point for sensory modulation. It gives us some baseline indications as to where to set our precision levels as it ultimately tells us if we are stressed (experiencing a prediction error). Interoception is our sense of the internal physiological condition of our body – the process by which the nervous system senses, interprets and integrates signals originating from within us, providing a moment-by-moment mapping of the body's internal landscape across conscious and unconscious levels. Interoception plays a fundamental role in managing anxiety in both helping us to react to threat but also to calm down again.

The basic process of interoception is how sensory signals relating to internal body experiences such as pain, temperature, itch, sensual touch, muscular and visceral (from our major organs) sensations, heart rate, hunger, thirst, fullness, nausea, need for the toilet, tickle and emotional states such as anger, calmness, distraction or fear reach our conscious awareness (Craig, 2003, 2015).

Interoception allows us to answer the question 'How do I feel?'

The feelings we receive from inside our bodies define our emotional world. Interoception determines how information about invisible internal physiological states is communicated to the brain in order to support physical and emotional wellbeing. This includes making effective responses to stress (uncertainty) using emotional awareness and regulation (Craig, 2003; Critchley & Garfinkel, 2017). Interoception can be seen as a precursor and even a blueprint for all our emotional responses (Damasio, 1999). So, when students have difficulties with emotional regulation, the underlying difficulty will be one of uncertainty around interoception.

Exteroceptive information (the processing of sensory signals coming from *outside* the body, such as sights, sounds, smells and touch) is always going to be highly unpredictable and volatile. The world is a noisy place and much of this noise is ambiguous, filled with uncertainty: was that bang the sound of a car backfiring, a firework or a gun shot? Interoception is a system that can anchor us when navigating the volatile waters of exteroceptive input. For example:

> When we are riding a bike, we need to keep track of a lot of information, the sights, sounds, smells, balance and body awareness as we speed along. This information is constantly changing. The crucial information we need to be aware of, however, in order to stay alive, is internal: how much effort are we putting in, how much our heart rate and breathing need to be increased. This information allows us to stay alive in the face of all the rapidly changing exteroceptive information.

However, if we have difficulties modulating information (misestimating precision), this might mean we are surrounded by uncertainty both inside and out. Good interoceptive awareness – the ability to identify, access, understand and respond appropriately to the patterns of internal signals – would be a distinct advantage to manage life's uncertainties (Craig, 2015). It can equally be assumed that poor interoceptive awareness can lead to difficulties managing life's uncertainties. When we support students to become more aware of internal signals, we may not necessarily support them to improve their interoceptive awareness. A clear example of this is when we are supporting students to regulate their emotions. We may not help them to tie their emotions to how their body feels.

Interoceptive awareness is a construct that is made up of two other abilities: interoceptive sensibility and interoceptive accuracy.

Interoceptive accuracy is how reliably and accurately you can actually detect internal signals, such as heartbeats. This is measured objectively through performance on behavioural tests, most commonly heartbeat detection tests such as judging when you experience a heartbeat and a tone ('a beep') at the same time. **Interoceptive sensibility** is how good at interoceptive processing you think you are. This is a subjective measure of perceived awareness that can be looked at through questionnaires that include questions (answered on a five-point scale ranging from Never to Always) on aspects such as 'Most of the time I can feel how fast I am breathing' and 'Most of the time I can feel if I need to go to the toilet'. In addressing interoception, students may show an increase in their sensibility, their perceived ability: 'I know how I am feeling.' It is important that we recognise this is not necessarily a marker of increased interoceptive awareness. It is the combination of accuracy and sensibility that can tell us someone's awareness.

Interoceptive awareness is a **metacognitive** (*thinking about thinking*) insight into your own interoceptive skills (i.e. a student saying they know when they feel angry and being right about it). Poor awareness would be a mismatch, thinking you are accurate when you are in fact not or thinking that you are not accurate when in fact you are. The association between poor awareness and anxiety, in light of predictive processing, is not a surprise. It represents a prediction error – I thought I needed a wee but I am then unable to go for one. It also highlights the importance of developing students' understanding about emotions and not just giving them knowledge.

A risk of the work we might do to support students with emotional understanding is that, without tying the emotions to the interoceptive information, they will only have a superficial knowledge. They might think they understand their emotions (increased interoceptive sensibility), but because they do not have a deeper understanding of how they feel in their body they are not very accurate. This will then leave them even more anxious. They will experience more prediction errors (my prior model says I know how I am feeling but the current sensory input is not what I was expecting) and even greater uncertainty.

LINKING THEORY AND PRACTICE

Sensory information provides the foundation for our understanding of the world and sensory differences have a significant impact on the precision of our models, as well as the precision of the sensory data we receive. Sensory information also plays the key role in the learning process as it alerts us to possible error in our models so we can decide whether we update our models or not. Frequent misestimation of the precision of sensory information can lead to many more prediction errors, a great deal of uncertainty and ultimately a world full of surprises.

According to Dunn (1997), from a practical perspective, effective modulation (allocation of precision) requires a balance between habituation (prior model) and sensitisation (current sensory input). **Sensitisation** occurs when sensory input is considered highly significant, something to be given a great deal of attention. When this happens, we are giving greater precision to current sensory input, and it has caused a prediction error.

If we take the example of young children trying on new shoes, sensitisation occurs if the sensory input is seen to be significant or threatening:

> 'My model did not predict this sensation; I may need to remove these shoes to get me back to certainty.'

Habituation refers to when sensory stimuli are recognised as being familiar and a response is not needed. This would correspond to more precision being given to our prior model – the sensory input was either predicted by it and therefore no further action is required in addressing it, or it was not paid attention to.

> 'My previous experience of shoes meant I predicted this feeling; I can keep them on.'

Getting the balance right

> If I am driving down the road back home, I am less likely to pay attention to current sensory information, as my prior model has served me well in the past, so the precision dial for my model is turned right up. Yet if I am driving around unfamiliar roads I may well drive more slowly, paying more attention, as my prior models will not be as good a basis for predicting what is happening, so my dial for current sensory input will be turned up higher than my prior model.

This driving example shows how we need to get the balance right and adjust our dials to best suit the situation – though it can also explain why so many road accidents happen close to a driver's home. (They were not paying as much attention to unexpected sensory information – like the car coming out of the drive.)

It has been suggested that groups of individuals with sensory processing differences, when faced with a prediction error, might rely less on their prior models, as they are considered to be less precise and therefore more uncertain. As a result, the volume of their current sensory input is turned up, resulting in increased sensory sensitivity and a tendency to perceive the world more accurately or 'as it really is' moment by moment, unfiltered and full of prediction errors that demand our attention (Pellicano & Burr, 2012, p.504).

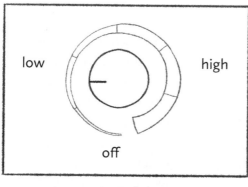

current input

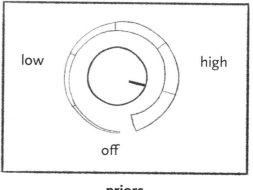

priors

This can lead to feelings of being overwhelmed. If we perceived the world 'as it really is' it would be exhausting, we would be constantly aware of all of the sensory input we were receiving, the feeling of our T-shirt on our body, our breathing, heart rate, the sounds of distant cars, the hum of the computer fan, the socks on our feet. We would have to pay attention to all of this information, none of it would be explained away by our prior model (we'd have no inattentional blindness), and we would perceive it all to be providing us with a clear signal to update our model of the world.

Some researchers have argued that the feeling of sensory overload, being overwhelmed, comes about not due to having imprecise prior models but as a result of overweighting of irrelevant prediction errors (Van de Cruys et al., 2014), that is, being unable to decide which information that might challenge our model is important. So we do still rely on our prior models but we just give current sensory information too much weight. We misestimate precision.

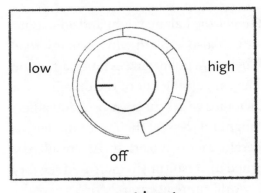

current input

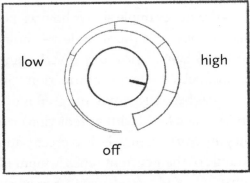

priors

As an example:

> You're at work when you hear a delivery lorry outside and men shouting, along with the crashing of a trolley. You may register it but quickly dismiss it as 'unusual but not significant' and habituate to it without experiencing much uncertainty or needing to update your model of the world. A colleague who gives too much weight to this sensory information might experience uncertainty and a considerable anxiety spike at this sound and need to investigate its source, double checking for threat/danger (look out of the window). They then may have to wait for the physiological effects of the anxiety to drain from their body and engage in some self-regulation activities: have a cup of tea, walk around, talk to someone about the noisy delivery. You carry on with your work, but your colleague may find it hard to focus for the rest of the morning. They may have moved into a hypervigilant state and, if we were being particularly invasive, you might check out their vagal tone and see that it was low!

Either way, having less reliance on prior models or overly precise perception of current sensory input, the end result is the same – too much precision is being given to sensory signals, which are pushing us into ineffective learning, where we are heading down path 2, updating our models when it is not required, and making them less precise. Without a precise prior model to guide interpretation, sensory information that should seem irrelevant may be enhanced. Over the long term, an uncertainty loop can then develop that leads to the precision being 'turned up to 11' as a default setting. This increased precision of sensory input leads to the development of less accurate prior models, and as they will be based on exceptionally precise information they will over-fit the world. Therefore, unless the sensory information received the next time is exactly in line with what was perceived before and due to heightened sensitivity – and this is highly unlikely to be the case – then we will once again be faced with ongoing prediction errors, with surprise and uncertainty about the current situation. Eventually this will impact on the precision of our hyper-priors about our priors, our confidence in our models.

A simplified example might be:

> We could build our model of 'a horse' based on the precise details of a specific horse, brown with a white spot on its nose just above the left nostril. With this as our model, in order to recognise something as 'a horse' it must be brown with a white spot on its nose just above the left nostril, that is, look *exactly* like the last horse we saw. If the next horse we see does not look like that then we have an error and we update and build again; this time our model of a horse is grey with a black tail, and so it goes on.

Unsurprisingly a tendency to perceive sensory information more precisely results in what have been described as overly fearful cognitive models of the environment, which is seen as highly volatile, always unpredictable (Houghton, Stein & Cortese, 2019). This then becomes our prior model – the world is unpredictable and scary. When we find ourselves in a highly volatile environment, we turn up our learning rate; we know that our prior model is unlikely to provide a precise model of the world, so we pay more attention to current sensory input. We put on our unexpected uncertainty glasses.

Seeing the world full of unexpected uncertainty will lead us to a state of hyper-vigilance where we are not only more likely to notice sensory information that we misperceive as threats but also less likely to successfully disengage from it (Green & Ben-Sasson, 2010). 'My learning rate is high – I am paying attention to everything and am unable to ignore it as it might be something important that will help me to build a better model of this highly volatile environment.'

This can in turn lead to a general mindset of 'anything uncertain is bad'. Within this, sensory information that has been associated with uncertainty (and stress) will receive even greater attention because it signals a threat – it caused a stress response last time which confirms to us it is something that causes stress! This can then lead to anxious catastrophising in the face of any uncertainty, so that an unthreatening piece of sensory information (e.g. a mild smell of smoke from some burnt toast) can be perceived catastrophically – 'The house is on fire!' – or abnormally intense – 'That smell is too strong!' Thoughts, emotions and behaviours that are traditionally associated with anxiety then become activated: 'I feel as if I am going to die; I need to escape from this situation.' Our body then goes into fight or flight as we have perceived a threat. This information then confirms to us that we are in a threatening situation – 'I am freaking out. I would only be freaking out if it was a threatening situation, therefore it must have actually been a threatening situation' – and we go into crisis, a panic attack.

I couldn't really articulate how busy classrooms made me feel or at certain stressful moments so it just led to me having a panic attack and having to leave the classroom a lot and some of the staff would question me about if I was faking them (some even made assumptions that I was) because I couldn't find the words to tell them exactly why I had to leave right at that moment. (Anja Melissa)

Our students who are finding it difficult to regulate their emotions can easily become trapped in the uncertainty loop:

1   They are unable to accurately recognise what their body is telling them when they experience an emotion (an interoceptive change, moving out of our 'home' state).

2   This causes uncertainty.

3   They then experience a stress response.

4   This confirms that the emotion was something to be stressed about.

This loop repeats and the young person ends up in crisis.

In this situation, there is no objective physical danger, and to help them to break this loop we need to support them to identify the origin of their uncertainty, the change in interoceptive information, what the emotion was that caused it and therefore give them better strategies to regulate (e.g. 'It's okay, I recognise these signals as just a panic attack – it will go away in a few minutes and I'm not going to die').

Desperately seeking certainty

Over time, the increased experience of uncertainty as a result of differences in sensory processing (misestimation of precision) means that a highly negative association is then attached to the uncertainty itself, meaning that all subsequent uncertainty, even positive novel experiences that will help build better models in the long run, is automatically perceived negatively. This might then result in us starting to withdraw from all novel situations, retreating into certainty to cope with the trauma related to uncertainty.

We are then desperately seeking certainty – behaviours/actions/environments that will not result in prediction errors, fidgeting, self-stimulatory behaviours and even self-injurious behaviours, so as to create sensory certainty. **All of these behaviours involve actions that are generated to fulfil predictions and therefore create certainty.** This might lead to high levels of avoidance: a new subject at school, trying to make some new friends, going to that party or even refusing to go to school so as to avoid all the uncertainty associated with it. This is why support for sensory uncertainty is so important. We can help by helping students to:

▸   develop strategies to help modulate sensory input and arousal to help students address anxiety caused by sensory uncertainty

- ▸ reduce their bias towards interpreting situations as threatening
- ▸ filter out irrelevant sensory input ('noise')
- ▸ better attend to relevant sensory input ('signals'), including cues of safety (Cisler & Koster, 2010)
- ▸ better understand emotions
- ▸ regulate their emotions
- ▸ **provide more certainty**.

We can support students to address the uncertainty loop they might be in, by first helping them identify **where** they are experiencing a feeling in their body (and later explore ideas why). Having access to this information can help ground us (provide knowledge and therefore certainty) when we are feeling overwhelmed by feelings of anxiety or low mood.

The focus in practice terms regarding sensory modulation is on behavioural sensory modulation: developing and supporting the conscious management of physiological feelings resulting from sensory input from various objects, activities and environments (Champagne, 2011), helping our students turn their precision dials to the optimal setting and wear the best glasses. Ultimately, the aim is for young people independently to recognise when and how to use sensory strategies. As with all support we put in place to address uncertainty, we want them to be able to understand: (1) which pair of certainty glasses to wear (these will influence their likely learning rate) and (2) what setting to turn their precision dials to.

Initially, an adult may need to prompt an individual to use these, and in situations of acute stress those with knowledge of an individual's sensory preferences may need to provide the right sensory environment to de-escalate their anxiety, by providing certainty or removing the uncertainty (Sutton *et al.*, 2013).

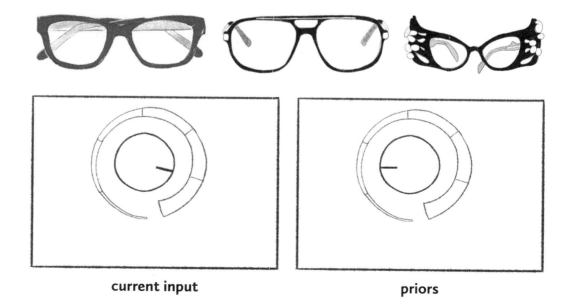

current input   priors

HOW WE CAN HELP

A combination of strategies can be used to help students recognise and regulate the type and intensity of auditory, gustatory, visual, olfactory and tactile systems, as well as vestibular input and proprioception, and better understand interoceptive information. The general aim of modulating sensory input is to achieve our home **'calm and alert'** state (Abernethy, 2010; Brown, 2002; Lane, Lynn & Reynolds, 2010; Pfeiffer, 2012). Modifying the type or amount of stimulation to specific sensory systems through SBIs can support individuals to learn the best settings for their precision dials. They can learn to better attend to important sensory stimuli (such as the teacher describing how to complete a task), filter irrelevant stimuli (such as the noise of traffic outside), and directly affect physiological arousal (such as staying calm) (Abernethy, 2010; Brown, 2002; Champagne, 2011; Champagne, Koomar & Olson, 2010; Lane, Lynn & Reynolds, 2010; Pfeiffer, 2012).

Sensory modulation interventions are also fundamental in supporting adolescents to regulate their emotions. For example, proprioceptive, deep tactile and vestibular input (e.g. yoga, massage and trampolining) can have a calming, organising effect on the central nervous system, and can lower arousal levels for adolescents with sensory over-responsiveness by giving a single, certain, point of focus. In contrast, visual, auditory and oral sensory input (e.g. use of colour, playing music and eating hard crunchy snacks) can have an alerting effect on individuals with sensory under-responsiveness, making them turn up their learning rate, which can support the discrimination of sensory input and emotional states. Most important, however, are interventions addressing interoception.

For adolescents with difficulties understanding their emotions, teaching them how to identify internal states and the emotions associated with them will support them to be able to regulate their emotions and to better communicate their feelings with parents, teachers and peers, and improve social functioning. We do this by developing our understanding of interoception, ensuring that in any emotional literacy work we do, emotions are tied to the way our bodies feel. This will also help us to recognise that it is the feelings that can help us identify our emotion, not simply the context we find ourselves in, so certain places don't simply become 'bad places'.

INTERNAL UNCERTAINTY + EXTERNAL CERTAINTY = SELF CONTROL LEARNING SELF BELIEF

Emotional literacy support is designed to reshape the young person's response to their environment and to make internal (interoceptive) responses more knowable, accessible and tolerable. This allows for more 'expected' emotional responses and gives us – carers, parents, teachers and mentors – information that we can use to offer more targeted support. If we can help a student to recognise and understand their emotions and express this effectively, so they can learn to show us, for example, that they are actually confused or afraid (although their certainty-seeking behaviour might be misinterpreted as defiance), we can then offer more suitable strategies. Emotional literacy interventions (ELIs) aim to gently nudge students towards greater interoceptive awareness and emotional regulation by incrementally moving them towards a greater understanding and awareness in a safe and familiar environment (school!).

We increase external certainty to minimise the impact of the internal uncertainty our students are managing. All ELIs follow a general principle of helping students to first of all recognise their feelings, then to understand the causes and consequences of them, and then what to label them, how to express them and finally how to regulate their feelings.

Recognise, *then* regulate

We begin by supporting students to tie emotions to the physical sensations that they are associated with, for example by learning that sweat on our palms and a sick feeling in our stomach might indicate anxiety. We then need to help them to correctly label those feelings, rather than seeing them as 'something different/wrong' and therefore uncertain, as we bring more certainty to those sensations. The ability to identify and describe sensation is fundamental for interoceptive awareness as it provides a pathway for linking the body, experiences of sensation and environmental triggers. 'I know that tense muscles often mean I'm feeling angry, and I'm learning that being ignored often creates that emotion in me. Knowing that means I can develop better coping strategies when it happens.' This will help them to recognise and *understand* what they are feeling.

Labelling and writing down emotional experiences can help reduce their intensity, with important therapeutic implications (e.g. Kircanski, Lieberman & Craske, 2012; Lieberman *et al.*, 2007; Pennebaker, 1997). Interventions should be designed to also ensure that they effectively teach emotional language and concepts (e.g. Hagelskamp *et al.*, 2013) as this can better lead to shifts in emotional meaning-making, facilitating communication and greater shared understanding.

Once we can recognise and understand our emotions we can then identify and work on strategies to help us regulate them. Emotion regulation, and, therefore, interoceptive awareness, is particularly important for developing socio-emotional competence. Interoceptive accuracy is related both to empathy (Fukusima, Terasawa & Umeda, 2011) and emotion processing (Barrett, 2004; Wiens, 2005).

Furthermore, it has been proposed that developing an understanding of others requires accurate representation of our own interoceptive states (Fotopoulou & Tsakiris, 2017; Ondobaka, Kilner & Friston, 2017). This, again, reiterates the fundamental role that sensory and in particular interoception plays in bringing certainty to our world. Addressing sensory uncertainty can also help us with addressing social uncertainty, which we will consider in the next chapter.

PRACTICE

SENSORY UNCERTAINTY IN THE CLASSROOM

> I don't know what would happen if I couldn't move. In lessons I start tapping, whistling, beatboxing, then I just trail off, but I'll kind of be in my own dimension, like nothing around me is really happening, I'm just thinking about stuff to myself and then minutes go past and I'll suddenly snap back. (Luke, Year 10)

> I don't always talk because I'm bored or because it's fun, it's because I genuinely can't concentrate. It's soothing, it helps me process — like when other people draw. (Molly, Year 12)

The first part of this chapter shows that as we learn more about how the senses and the brain work together, it seems clear that unless we are able to recognise and process the information that we are receiving *all the time*, the world can be an uncertain, confusing, even terrifying place.

Without sensory certainty it's difficult to learn, socialise and achieve. So, we support students by trying to reduce any sensory uncertainty that might be coming from the learning environment and then helping them to manage any remaining uncertainty by developing self-regulation strategies. The following is a useful diagram that illustrates how sensory information and processes are the foundations needed for effective academic learning to take place. It highlights the fact that teaching students to develop sensory knowledge is not something we might do instead of teaching academic knowledge but how by failing to teach students to develop sensory understanding can reduce the impact of our academic teaching.

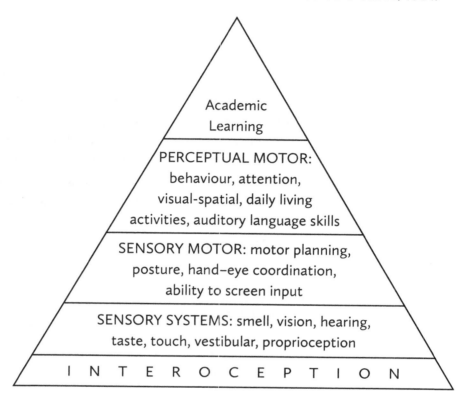

Our sensory systems start to develop before we are born and continue as our primary sources of information throughout our lives. Educators generally start to support development at the top end of the pyramid, around the sensory motor section. We work on hand–eye coordination, toileting, listening and attention in the nursery/kindergarten years, assuming that all the lower systems are working as well as they can be. However, we know that for many of the students we work with not all these systems 'run' in the same way and this can have a huge impact on the amount of uncertainty they experience.

THE ~~FIVE~~ EIGHT SENSES

Most people agree on the basic five senses as proposed by Aristotle in around 300BC:

Touch, Vision, Hearing, Smell, Taste
(tactile, visual, auditory, olfactory, gustatory senses)

Two more senses are considered important in the worlds of education and therapy:

Balance, Body Position
(vestibular and proprioceptive senses)

These last two senses are about our whole bodies and tell us about balance and where our bodies are in space. A good way to understand them is to think about ourselves on a trampoline in a completely dark space. Even though we can't see, we still know which way up we are (vestibular sense) and our proprioceptive sense tells us whether our arms are up or down. In a classroom, we use these senses to know when our bottom is fully on our chair, our legs are straight or bent or if our finger is on our nose. If the information we are receiving is too low for us to register (mid-way through a double lesson) we may need to move in order to seek it.

And finally, the eighth sense:

Interoception

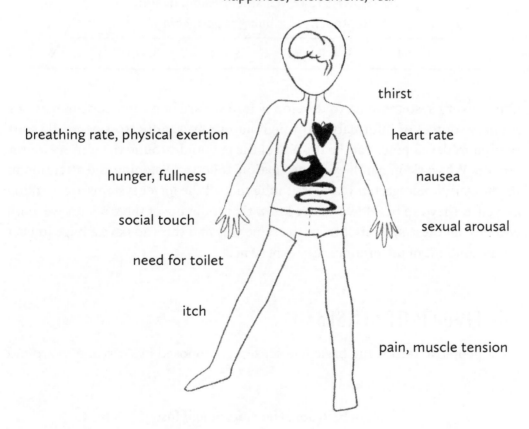

anger, embarrassment,
happiness, excitement, fear

thirst

breathing rate, physical exertion

heart rate

hunger, fullness

nausea

social touch

sexual arousal

need for toilet

itch

pain, muscle tension

This is our ability to recognise our internal states. These signals are felt in different parts of the body and might indicate that we are feeling things like pain, hunger, embarrassment or that we need the toilet.

We need to be able to make sense of these signals, so that we can respond in a way that returns us to the ideal 'calm alert' state. For example, if we are feeling pain, we might need to get medical help, or take a painkiller. If we are hungry, thirsty or need the toilet, we might need to fix that fairly urgently, and if we are feeling embarrassed, we might need to ask for clarification, apologise or sometimes just leave.

These difficulties can cause significant problems, in the classroom and in life. Knowing that 'something's wrong' but being uncertain about what it is, or what to do about it, can cause intense anxiety, social isolation and potentially serious health issues. For example, a student may experience all pain as a 'stomach ache' (over-fit the information) and risk missing serious disease somewhere else. For some individuals who struggle with processing interoceptive information, it can cause incontinence or difficulties with sexual relationships.

The school environment can add to any sensory struggle, coming across as a highly volatile environment, and significantly impact how we learn. Large, bright, noisy rooms full of unwritten social rules can make life intolerable and cause our students to develop unhelpful responses. For example, many students we see have worked out that they find it easier to listen without looking (focusing on one sense at a time). This causes confusion because the 'rule' is that when a teacher is speaking, students are expected to look, listen and give non-verbal feedback, all at the same time. If a student avoids eye contact, and an adult doesn't know why, they can seem defiant or uninterested and create an unnecessarily negative impression.

MALIKA AND THE MATHS LESSON

Malika waits in the corridor outside the maths room. She feels 'wrong' but doesn't realise that her pencil case is digging into her through her backpack (interoceptive uncertainty). She likes her backpack straps tight as it helps her feel calm (proprioceptive certainty), but this is making the pain more extreme. She also has period pains but is unaware of this (interoceptive uncertainty). These unrecognised states mean that right now everything else is  a blur of sound and movement as students move from one class to the next. She's vaguely aware of someone making a screeching noise but can't tell if it's near or far away and whether it's a happy noise or means that something bad is happening (auditory uncertainty).

The bell went off a couple of minutes ago. It doesn't bother her too much these days, although it did when she first came to this school. It's always the same sound for the same length of time and she knows it means that at some point in the very near future the door of the classroom will open, and students will come out (auditory certainty).

As her class jostles into the room, she is aware of other students moving against her, sometimes just a bump, sometimes for longer periods of sustained pressure. She has no idea whether she needs to respond – smile? apologise? – at any of these moments; she watches other students, but she finds it hard to work out (social touch uncertainty).

She goes to her regular desk for this class and starts to get her books out as usual (structural certainty). There is a tree surgeon working somewhere nearby, but she can't identify the sound as one she knows and is unsure if it's something bad (auditory uncertainty). She is looking at the board while she assesses this risk, but she can't process what the teacher is saying. Ms A is going through the list of tasks and allocating them to groups. Once Malika is ready, however, she is able to work out what to do because her teacher leaves the instructions on the screen while everyone begins work (visual certainty).

The pain and a need for the toilet grows but Malika is unaware of this; she only feels more 'wrong'. She has a general sense of heat and sees that her hands are wet with sweat. She knows that she needs to do the expected thing and complete the tasks. She is in a group with two other students; they are pleased to have her in their group as she is good at maths. They both seem to be talking and pointing at the sheet at the same time, every now and then looking at her and asking her questions, but because of the 'wrong' feeling she can't process what they are asking (multisensory uncertainty) and she starts to panic.

Malika's habitual response to stress is to shut down. She stops talking or responding in any way and 'zones out'. The other students notice, and it confirms their view that she's 'weird'. They continue the tasks without her. Her teacher later considers sanctioning her for not doing the work and refusing to explain why. She just keeps saying 'I don't know'.

Interpreting sensory-based behaviour

While it's impossible to experience someone else's internal states, there are some outward signs that might indicate sensory-based uncertainty. Two key types are: 'repetitive motor behaviours' and 'insistence on sameness behaviours'.

Repetitive motor behaviours: these are exactly what you might expect them to be. These are behaviours that give us certainty as we carry out actions that purposefully look to fulfil internal predictions. For example, if we are experiencing uncertainty (from any or all of the 3S's), we know that rocking on our chair will bring us certainty. These behaviours are typically seen as **adaptive** responses. They are behaviours we have developed to help us regulate – great! We also do not need anyone else to be involved for us to be able to use this strategy (other than them recognising the function of the behaviour and not simply telling us to 'stop fidgeting!'). What we as educators need to understand, though, is that these behaviours are possibly signalling to us that a student is managing some uncertainty, so our job is to ask 'Where's the uncertainty?' and work on helping them to reduce it.

Insistence on sameness behaviours: these are also exactly what you might expect them to be – behaviours that are motivated by keeping things the same. They might look a little like obsessive behaviours and reflect an exaggerated attempt to control an aspect of the environment, imposing our own routines and rituals on the world to try to bring certainty. For example, when anxious we might need to have all the doors closed or all our things lined up perfectly on our desk. These are generally seen as **maladaptive** behaviours. They do not effectively reduce uncertainty and can increase our anxiety. We are driven to these behaviours by some sort of uncertainty around one or all of the 3S's and we need to do this to get certainty. However, now we have a secondary source of uncertainty – someone might leave a door open or nudge something on our desk. As educators, when we see these behaviours we should not only ask ourselves where the uncertainty is but also how we can teach this student a better way of managing it.

More generally, all behaviours that we might see our students display when they are struggling are useful for us as educators because they are a signal that someone is trying to manage their uncertainty, and may hold the key to where, in terms of the 3S's, we need to build more certainty.

Before we look at some resources to help us understand these behaviours (and how they can help us work out where we need to build more certainty), let's quickly recap two key concepts.

The size of our cups

All of us have different levels of sensitivity within our eight senses. Some of us are easily distracted by a buzzing strip light, others won't notice at all; some of us love hot chillies, others can't stand the tang of black pepper; some of us love the firm embrace of a sleeping bag and others can only sleep with their feet outside the duvet; some of us know when we are anxious and take deep breaths and some of us don't and may get angry instead. It's how we've set our precision dials.

We have different **neurological thresholds** – the point at which sensory information is registered. For many students we work with, these thresholds can be significantly different. We might describe them as:

▸ hyper-sensitive: someone who has a high sensitivity to a certain type of sensory information – a low threshold – and may be easily overwhelmed by sensory information

▸ hypo-sensitive: someone who is less sensitive to a certain type of sensory information – a high threshold – and may seem unaware of certain sensory information.

It is important to remember that just because a student may be hyper-sensitive (have a small cup) in one of their senses does not mean that they are hyper-sensitive across them all. The size of their cups will also change as they grow and develop and may also change throughout the day, particularly if they are stressed. So, someone whose auditory cup may shrink as the day goes on (and experience noise sensitivity) may at the same time have a growing cup for proprioception and need lots of movement in the last lesson to stay focused.

And the other key concept? This is about what happens next and is our route to understanding what's going on for some of our students.

Behavioural responses

In the example of Malika in the maths lesson we saw how easy it is to misinterpret behaviour. Her classmates labelled her as 'weird' and her teacher as 'defiant'. Yet from a sensory point of view she was simply doing what she had to do to avoid being completely overstimulated (by pain, needing the toilet and people talking). Typically, we respond in two different ways:

▸ Sensory avoidant: someone who reacts to uncertainty due to hyper-sensitivity by avoiding sensory input; for example, pulling a sweatshirt over their hands (touch), refusing to attend whole-school assemblies (sound, light, movement) or only eating bland food (smell and taste).

▸ Sensory seeking: someone who reacts to uncertainty due to hypo-sensitivity by searching for sensory input; for example, constantly moving in their chair (proprioception), humming (auditory) or chewing pens (proprioception and possibly taste?).

The practice section contains checklists, observation schedules and activities that you can use to explore these ideas and tailor your support to students who may be struggling to manage their sensory uncertainty throughout the day.

THE SEARCH FOR SENSORY CERTAINTY
What does it look like, what could it mean?

The chart below focuses on the Sensory part of the 3S framework and works like this. Each row contains:

▸ a commonly observed behaviour which indicates a search for certainty

▸ the potential underlying sensory uncertainty causing this behaviour

▸ some ideas that might help to build more sensory certainty through greater self-knowledge and a sense of agency.

You can use the blank 3S chart at the end to create your own record of behaviours that you observe, in terms of Sensory, Social and Structure. These are included in each of the 3S chapters.

The example below just considers explanations based on sensory uncertainty. In practice, we need to consider a possible underlying cause of uncertainty from each of the 3S's, so we must consider how the behaviour could be motivated by sensory uncertainty, how it could be motivated by social uncertainty and how it could be motivated by structural uncertainty.

These ideas are from and for the classroom. They are based on unexpected reactions to uncertainty that we observe in schools, and some that are taken from our interviews with students. Each behaviour is linked to a possible sensory uncertainty, with a brief note on what you could try to provide the student with more certainty.

Many of these behaviours also occur in the **the search for structural certainty** and **the search for social certainty** sections of the book, with a different analysis. Here we look at sensory certainty and uncertainty only.

Sometimes we need to refer on. In extreme cases, where the search for sensory certainty causes behaviours that put physical or mental health at risk, we might refer a student for support from occupational therapists, psychology or psychiatry for intensive, individual therapeutic support.

If you think your student may be experiencing sensory uncertainty, you can ask them to complete the **Sensory survey** while you complete a **Sensory observation questionnaire** (both in this chapter).

WHAT IT MIGHT LOOK LIKE	WHERE'S THE SENSORY UNCERTAINTY?	IDEAS FOR CERTAINTY
Excessive movement: finds it hard to stay put/sit on a chair/finish a meal without moving.	Proprioceptive/ vestibular uncertainty: needs to move to feel calm/alert. *'I feel out of balance, uncertain; I need to move to feel "right".'*	**Work with class/ teachers/extended family to explain sensory thresholds and increase tolerance for those that need more movement.** **Build in movement breaks/chair-based sensory activities/ stand and stretch/ go for a run between home and school tasks/ ask to give out books/ take in papers, etc.**

Always sitting with legs up/crossed/folded.	Proprioceptive uncertainty: needs pressure to feel calm/alert. *'I feel uncertain if I sit with my legs down. I need pressure and the information this brings to feel "right".'*	**Allow unconventional seating positions in class.** **Experiment with allowing students to stand at the back or side of room. Offer 'standing desks' or folding frames which students can carry around with them to raise books and so on to standing height. Try using yoga blocks or books for students' feet if they don't touch the floor securely.**
Fidgeting with equipment.	Tactile, visual, proprioceptive uncertainty: strong impulse for certainty through objects. *'I feel uncertain. Touching familiar objects gives me predictive certainty – I can correctly predict what they will feel like.'*	**Chair-based sensory activities. Teach useful (and non-distracting) 'mini' stretches.**
Humming/singing.	Auditory uncertainty: *'I feel out of balance, uncertain when it's quiet. I need sound to feel "right".'* OR *'The sounds I'm hearing are unpredictable; they make me feel uncertain. Making my own predictable sounds makes me feel more certain.'*	**Use repeated, familiar language to signal key points in lesson. Play low-level background music for silent study. Allow students to listen to music on headphones.** **OR** **Try to identify any sound issues and remove (e.g. equipment fans off during silent work where possible) or explain source and reason for problem sounds.**

cont.

WHAT IT MIGHT LOOK LIKE	WHERE'S THE SENSORY UNCERTAINTY?	IDEAS FOR CERTAINTY
Tapping or flapping with fingers/items.	Auditory/ proprioceptive/visual uncertainty: seeking certain sensory input. *'Doing this repetitive predictable activity makes me feel more certain.'*	**Allow behaviour if undisruptive to other students and arrange seating for minimal disruption. Suggest student adapts activity, e.g. brings sponge mat to use on table to reduce (but not remove) sound.** **Work with class/ teachers/extended family to explain sensory thresholds and increase tolerance for those that need more movement.**
Finds room changes hard to manage.	Multisensory uncertainty: may need time to process new sounds, smells, visuals, etc. *'The room changed. It feels as if everything about this lesson is now different and unpredictable.'*	**For planned changes, arrange for student to visit new room when quiet. Discuss seating before the lesson.** **For unplanned changes, allow time (and expect unexpected behaviours) while student adjusts.**

Unresponsive in class.	Shutdown due to multisensory uncertainty, from too much information. *'The sensory demands of this lesson are too much. I can't tolerate it and contribute.'* OR Undersensitive but not sensory seeking: disengaged due to multisensory uncertainty (not enough information to stimulate a response).	**Ask – use the Sensory survey in this chapter. Consider seating position in class, offer noise cancelling headphones, build in extra structural certainty wherever possible.** **Increase physical activity in lesson – move seats for small group activities, use students at front of class as physical examples (maths/ science) or characters (languages/literature). Further increase variety of teaching styles (see Chapter 2).**
Insists on wearing non-regulation items.	Tactile uncertainty: may be oversensitive. Items function as 'object of certainty' connecting student to home/ parent. Exaggerated need for control as a response to uncertainty.	**Explore all possible options with student and school management: removal of labels/wearing leggings under uniform skirt/larger sizes/ different shops for non-branded items (add school logo, etc.).** **Trial discreet wearing of non-regulation item.**
Unwilling to participate in practical tasks.	Multisensory uncertainty: unsure of ability to process senses appropriately in new activity.	**Encourage participation only after clear modelling by teacher or another student.**

cont.

WHAT IT MIGHT LOOK LIKE	WHERE'S THE SENSORY UNCERTAINTY?	IDEAS FOR CERTAINTY
Clumsy, drops equipment, frequently trips/falls.	Vestibular/ proprioceptive uncertainty; needs more or less information about body in space.	Allow extra time for practical activities and give very clear instructions. Consider whole class mindfulness/tapping/ warm-up activities at start.
Food around mouth/on clothes causing social difficulties in school.	Tactile uncertainty: can't 'feel' the food debris.	Teach regular self-monitoring in mirror after food/at start of afternoon.
Hygiene issues: unusually messy or dirty hair/clothes causing social difficulties in school.	Tactile, proprioceptive or vestibular uncertainty leads to uncomfortable/ painful experiences and avoidance of hair brushing and washing.	Consider a meeting with young person, school and parent and design steps to independent self-care. Explain social consequences (see Chapter 5). Consult occupational therapist if problem persists.
Refuses touch in drama or sport activities.	Interoceptive or tactile uncertainty: may have low tolerance for 'social touch' or specific textures.	Consider adaptations to activity. If touch is necessary, communicate the reason to student and listen to uncertainties. Collaborate for practical solutions, e.g. pulling clothing over hands, firm touch only.

Regularly eats in class.	Sensory uncertainty: may be seeking sensory certainty through familiar foods. May not experience feeling of 'fullness' due to interoceptive uncertainty.	**(With family) encourage student to eat hard, crunchy foods outside lessons. Suggest jaw massage in lessons.** **Monitor food intake with family if diet thought to be an issue.**
Rarely eats or drinks in school.	Multisensory uncertainty: shutdown due to high levels of sensory input in noisy eating areas. May not experience feelings of thirst or hunger due to interoceptive uncertainty. May experience exaggerated need for control in this area.	**Suggest quieter space with small group for eating at lunch. Work with family to ensure that the student is eating well at home.** **Consider referral to eating disorders team if not, due to high incidence of eating disorders in students with low tolerance to uncertainty.**
Seems to drink water excessively.	Interoceptive uncertainty: may not experience feelings of 'thirst quench'.	**Be certain across classes about rules for drinking/ fetching water.** **Research 'healthy' amount of water per day with student. Make it visual and support them to measure out daily limits, draw a water bottle with times of day and amounts.**

cont.

WHAT IT MIGHT LOOK LIKE	WHERE'S THE SENSORY UNCERTAINTY?	IDEAS FOR CERTAINTY
'Explosive' emotions observed.	Interoceptive uncertainty: may go from 0–5 due to lack of emotional self-awareness. *'I can't feel the mood coming – then suddenly it all explodes.'*	**Use scales and activities in this chapter to help student recognise early signs of any difficult emotions and teach self-regulating strategies.**
Excessive fear of vomiting affecting daily life.	Interoceptive uncertainty: may find it hard to recognise difference between anxiety, hunger and the need to vomit. *'I can't tell the difference between the signals – it's not safe for me to go anywhere in case I miss the signal to vomit and then vomit in public.'*	**Use activities in this chapter to develop greater understanding of signals from body and their link to thoughts and emotions.** **Look specifically at 'body' signals in examples and talk about your own. Refer for individual cognitive behaviour therapy if possible.**
Does not use toilet in school.	Multisensory uncertainty: may find toilet space overwhelming or lack interoceptive awareness to realise need.	**Explore options: help student find quietest times/toilets in school. Consider early release from lesson if possible.**

Using the 3S structure to understand behaviour

The next page contains our 3S analysis sheet completed to look at the Sensory aspects only of Jordan's behaviour at lunchtime only. This sheet repeats at the same point in the Social and Structural chapters, with a different analysis.

On the following page, there is a blank version for you to use to help you interpret your student's behaviour using a sensory, social and structural approach.

3S ANALYSIS

Name of student: Jordan   Year group: 10   Date: 10 Jan

Adult(s) completing checklist: Ms B, Mr H

WHAT'S THE BEHAVIOUR?	WHERE'S THE SENSORY, SOCIAL AND STRUCTURAL UNCERTAINTY?	IDEAS FOR CERTAINTY?
Avoids lunch — spends time in bathroom or classroom. Talks about feeling ill.	Sensory: overwhelmed by noise and unpredictable movement in canteen. Social: Structure:	Teach breath/mindful practice for lunchtimes. Explain links between what we think and what we feel in our body. Try wearing headphone ear buds to reduce noise. Share ideas for managing busy environments. Develop interoceptive awareness.
	Sensory: Social: Structure:	
	Sensory: Social: Structure:	
	Sensory: Social: Structure:	

3S ANALYSIS

Name of student: Year group: Date:

Adult(s) completing checklist:

WHAT'S THE BEHAVIOUR?	WHERE'S THE SENSORY, SOCIAL AND STRUCTURAL UNCERTAINTY?	IDEAS FOR CERTAINTY?
	Sensory: Social: Structure:	
	Sensory: Social: Structure:	
	Sensory: Social: Structure:	
	Sensory: Social: Structure:	

SENSORY OBSERVATION

An observation framework for understanding sensory differences.

Why

Some people experience unusual patterns of sensory processing (vision, touch, hearing, taste, smell, proprioception, vestibular and interoception). Many of the unexpected behaviours in our classrooms are an expression of anxiety and have a sensory basis. This structure helps find out what these might be.

How

→ **Think of a student** who is struggling with expected behaviour.

→ **Make a list** of the behaviours that are unexpected.

→ **Look at the examples** of sensory-based behaviours in the next section. See physical – think SENSORY. Does the behaviour seem to 'fit' any of these categories? Might the student be using the behaviour to return to a 'calm alert' state?

→ **Write your answers in the corresponding space** on the chart provided. For example, always jumps when the door bangs/taps pencil when working in silence/may seem angry or get into disagreements at the start of PE lesson.

→ **Look for patterns.** Can you see any generalisations in the chart? Might they have oversensitive hearing/undersensitive proprioception? This can help everyone understand the behaviour more accurately and plan regulation interventions more effectively.

→ **Remember that sensory sensitivities change** over time and may become more extreme in times of anxiety.

→ **Communicate your findings.** Let other people know what might be going on for that student.

→ **Plan together.** When we are trying to build sensory certainty we often collaborate with colleagues in the drama or sport departments, who have more access to body-friendly spaces and activities. Students sometimes find it easier to engage in these types of activities outside more desk-based lessons.

→ **Make notes on ideas you come up with** to support sensory differences in class.

Sensory observation

Below are some examples of behaviours that might indicate sensory uncertainty. Consider all eight senses as you think about your student.

EXAMPLES OF OVERSENSITIVE OR SENSORY-AVOIDING BEHAVIOUR:	EXAMPLES OF UNDERSENSITIVE OR SENSORY-SEEKING BEHAVIOUR:
Easily startled by unpredictable noises or flashes of light	Moves constantly in chair/around the room and may invent excuses to move – needing the toilet/fetching equipment
Easily upset by smells	Doesn't respond first time when name is called
Easily distracted by tiny details (e.g. particles in the air/on the floor)	Messy eater – may be unaware of food on mouth/in hair/on clothes
Easily distracted by small sounds (e.g. a pencil dropping)	Strongly attracted to bright lights and colourful objects
Low pain threshold	Responds dramatically better to 'hands-on' lessons
Appears to dislike brushing hair	Doesn't seem to mind (or craves) 'weird' tastes or textures
Easily irritated by the sounds or movements of other students and often communicates this openly (or seems completely unable to)	High tolerance of pain – may not notice injuries or even broken bones
Overreacts to heat or cold	May not feel hunger or thirst and eat or drink furiously when given the opportunity
Dislikes having feet off the ground for any activity	'Floppy' body
Reluctant to take part in messy art/craft/cooking	Calls out repeatedly
Insistent on same clothes day after day	Clumsy, may drop things, bump into things and fall often
May prefer to look down when speaking	Likes to sit with legs crossed/one knee bent to chest/legs wrapped around each other
Attention affected by certain rooms in school	Compulsive eater
Avoids sport/drama or physical contact	May eat non-food items like grass or paper
Refuses to wear a coat, even in cold weather	Fidgets – finds it hard not to touch things on desk
Prefers short sleeves to long, smooth textures to rough	Chews sleeve/pencil/pen/hair ties/hair
Finds it hard to copy from a screen	Draws on paper/desk/book/hand during most lessons
Makes sounds while working	Likes to lean on people, furniture or walls
Easily irritated by labels in clothing	Loves to go fast (running, riding bike, fairground rides)
Sensitive gag response to certain foods	Loves to engage in rough sports/play
Excessively frightened by thunderstorms	Likes to spin or swing and enjoys climbing/trampolining
Excessively upset by hair in food	Prefers tight clothes
Dislikes having haircut (maybe as a young child)	Enjoys crowded corridors, loud music, festivals, etc.
Dislikes fairground rides/theme parks	Likes to wrap things around wrist/body/arm
Does not show interest in going to concerts/parties/loud events	Makes sounds while working (finds silence hard to tolerate)
Makes sounds while working (to drown out sounds around them)	

SENSORY OBSERVATION

Name of student: Date: Teacher:

SIGNS OF OVERSENSITIVITY OR SENSORY-AVOIDING BEHAVIOURS	SIGNS OF UNDERSENSITIVITY OR SENSORY-SEEKING BEHAVIOURS

Notes:

SENSORY SURVEY

Why

If we don't ask, we can't know how our students experience their sensory environment. This is useful where you have a sense that a group is behaving differently, compared with other lessons in school. The questionnaire is quick and can have some really interesting results, often highlighting issues that have a simple fix.

How

→ **Explain** that you will be asking students to tell you how their senses experience lessons in this room.

→ **Hand out the questionnaire**, talk through examples on a screen and leave them up. Allow plenty of time for completion.

→ **If you have time go through the answers as a group**, encouraging students to explain their answers in more detail. Collect, review and communicate findings to other teachers.

→ **Make accommodations where you can**, or help students develop their tolerance, for example with a rating scale, to help them understand whether the sensory input is annoying/uncomfortable/unbearable.

→ **Help students identify and use their own strategies** – for example, asking to sit away from noisy equipment, near a light source, at the front/to the side.

SENSORY SURVEY (EXAMPLE)

Name of student: Will B   Date: 27 January   Teacher: Mr Z
Lesson/situation: Double Science – Monday afternoons

SENSE	WHAT'S GOOD AND BAD	WHAT I'D LIKE...
What I see	Too many old posters, feels dark and weird in here.	Individual lights on desks. One poster on each board. New each term.
What I hear	It's quiet, which is good, but the projector is noisy if you have to sit near it.	Silent projector, or for it to be turned off when it's not being used.
What I feel	The tables in here are old and bumpy. The lab coats have scratchy labels.	I'd have the lab benches cleaned smooth and I'd be allowed to cut out the label on a lab coat.
What I smell or taste	I HATE the smell in here.	I'd have the windows open between lessons. I'd be allowed to chew gum.
How I move or sit	I don't like the stools in here, I hate having my feet off the ground.	I'd be allowed to stand up at the bench for this lesson.

My dream classroom would have... Bean bags, a teacher at the back for anyone who didn't understand, pets (rabbits?), standing and sitting desks. ☺

SENSORY SURVEY

Name of student: Date: Teacher:

Lesson/situation:

SENSE	WHAT'S GOOD AND BAD	WHAT I'D LIKE...
What I see		
What I hear		
What I feel		
What I smell or taste		
How I can move or sit		
My dream classroom would have...		

BUILDING SENSORY CERTAINTY – FOUR STEPS TO SELF-REGULATION

The following pages contain ideas on how to reduce anxiety by building sensory certainty in each of these four areas with a strong focus on **interoception** – the awareness of our internal states.

Step 1: Recognise sensory signals (sight, sound, taste, touch, smell, proprioception, vestibular, interoception).

Step 2: Link sensory signals and emotions.

Step 3: Notice thoughts.

Step 4: Try new responses.

1. Recognise sensory signals

We are looking to build sensory certainty. If we can help the young people we work with understand the many and various signals they receive, we reduce uncertainty and anxiety. We replace 'What am I feeling?' with a greater understanding of thinking and feeling and as a result see fewer unexpected behaviours, leaving the way clear for easier learning and socialising.

Research suggests that practising mindfulness, in its various forms, can increase certainty:

1 **Improve interoceptive awareness:** I know what my body is telling me.

2 **Increase the clarity of mental processes:** I think more clearly.

3 **Increase meta awareness:** I can think and talk about my feelings.

4 **Create a change in habitual behaviours and thought patterns:** I have a new way to respond to this.

This work can also help students see difficult times as a sensory event, rather than a state of being:

'I find lunch times noisy and confusing.'

instead of:

'I'm no good at socialising.'

There are many school-based programmes and packages available which help young people focus on the present, for example 'mindfulness' activities. We regularly suggest the following activities to young people to help them stay more in the present, helping them to 'lean in' to whatever they are going through and understand their experience more fully. In this way we hope to reduce anxiety and avoidance and support sustained engagement.

Whichever activity you choose, try and do it regularly with your students. You may like to start the day with a breathing activity or the afternoon with a body scan. We almost always incorporate a physical element, as it gives the practice a more accessible structure for students and then repeat, repeat, repeat.

Watch out for...

It is not uncommon for anyone beginning these exercises for the first time to experience initial resistance and a slight increase in anxiety. This may be evident in anxious laughter, an increase in 'messing about' or flat refusal to participate.

The theory goes like this: an increase in body awareness may be associated with negative emotions, as we move from a safe place of low awareness into a new, unfamiliar state of heightened awareness. The body may perceive this as a threat and our fight, flight or freeze system is activated. This triggering confirms our thoughts that the shift in awareness is a bad thing and we try to avoid it.

Calm repetition of these activities, using increasingly familiar language, will eventually help brain and body re-evaluate the threat level and accept the raised awareness as a safe state of being. Do not enforce participation, it often comes with repetition.

CHAIR-BASED PRESSURE ACTIVITIES

These exercises provide movement and resistance (proprioceptive input) to achieve a calm and alert state, **without the student having to leave their chair**. These can be really helpful for students who find it hard to feel calm and alert in lessons and during long tests and exams.

Demonstrate the exercises to the whole class. For these to work safely, students need to be seated on a four-legged stable chair, one in which their feet reach the ground and the table height meets the middle of their trunk.

Thera bands/resistance bands

These are strong, slightly stretchy bands which can be bought online fairly cheaply in a roll, which you cut and tie as needed. Otherwise try using wide, strong elastic.

→   Tie the band tightly round the lower half of the front legs of a classroom chair.

→   The student can either place their legs in front of the band and kick back against it to provide a foot fidget or place their legs behind the band and push into it.

→   Students who find this particularly useful are given a band to take to all lessons and sign a written agreement on how and when it can be used.

Hand pushes

→   Students bring their palms together in front of their chests and press firmly five times, with their elbows bent out to the side. Breathe out slowly as you press, relax shoulders.

Table holds

→   Students grip the table, palms down, shoulder width apart.

→   Breathe slowly in and out, being aware of the shoulders softening with each out-breath.

→   Good for exam times.

WALKING IN THE PRESENT

Useful for students who struggle with unstructured times at school and who may experience social anxiety. Best done where there is room for everyone to walk around (obviously): outside, in a sports hall, drama studio, empty corridor or anywhere with space.

Session one

→ Tell the group that you are going to learn a technique that is scientifically proven to reduce stress and increase clear thinking. You may like to introduce it as part of a 'preparation for exams' session and it might be helpful to share some of the research with them.

→ Explain the practice: 'In a minute we are all going to walk slowly around the room. I want you to focus completely on your feet. Notice which part of your foot hits the ground first and which is the last bit to lift off. Feel the pressure of the ground underneath your feet, the texture of your sock, how your shoe moves as you lift and lower your foot. See what else you become aware of as you walk. If you find yourself thinking about anything else, that's okay. Notice what you're thinking about and then return the focus to your feet.'

→ Explain that for the practice to work, we need to do this silently. Use your knowledge of the group to decide how long this first attempt lasts.

→ Ask students if they can think of anything else they noticed (whether their feet were hot/cold, the way their ankle reacted, how the rest of their body moved from side to side, etc.).

→ Explain how this practice can be very useful if we are feeling anxious, for example travelling somewhere, or when we aren't sure what to do with ourselves in social situations.

Session two onwards

→ Repeat as above until the students are able to carry out a minute's walking in (near) silence.

SENSORY MOMENTS

These develop an 'accepting awareness' of sensory information. Depending on the focus you choose, they can help with all aspects of sensory processing and interoceptive awareness.

As before, if the focus shifts, notice where it's shifted to and gradually return to the chosen sense.

Vision

A slow, silent walk similar to the previous one, but focusing on colours, shapes, light and shadows.

Listening

Sit for a minute at the start, middle or end of a lesson, with eyes open or shut. At the end, encourage students to write down as many sounds as they can hear and make a whole class list at the end. Good for a break in a double lesson.

Smell

Although this is best done somewhere with some obviously strong smells – in a cooking lesson/near the school kitchens/on a school trip – it can be interesting to see what smells some students are aware of in the classroom. You may be surprised.

Taste

Probably easiest for teachers of food technology/cooking or science. Dip lolly sticks into different spice pastes or fruit jams and get your students to feel *where* on their tongue they sense which taste. Use blindfolds and put students into pairs; get one to describe tastes and textures of different unknown foods as their partner writes them down.

What to watch out for

As always, be on the lookout for uncertainty and create as much certainty as possible, by using the same language as you introduce the activity and running it at the same time of day/in the week.

TRACING THE BREATH

Useful for 'grounding' students and increasing certainty before a lesson begins.

Session one

→ Photocopy and distribute the sheets on the following pages.

→ Explain that over the next few weeks you are going to start each session/afternoon/ lesson/group with a breathing activity.

→ This is to help everyone in the room to think more clearly and to reduce stress.

→ Ask the students to stand and place their hands lightly against their ribs.

→ As they breathe, ask them to feel the breath entering and leaving their body. Take a few slow breaths, then sit everyone down.

→ Use a visual aid or project the images onto a screen so that every student can watch you as you trace the shapes **slowly** with your finger.

→ As your finger moves slowly across the shape, inhale and exhale slowly but gently. Try not to do this in an exaggerated way! Encourage the students to imagine that it's the breath moving in and out of their lungs, rather than them pulling it in and pushing it out.

→ Let the students explore the different shapes and see which one they prefer. They can trace the printed hand, or their own. Find out which shapes were more or less popular and encourage students to remember their favourite. They could also design and colour their own.

Session two

→ Project the shapes onto the screen.

→ Ask the students to draw one of the shapes in the back of their planner or diary.

→ Lead the breath exercise as before, modelling an appropriate speed.

Session three onwards

→ Use minimal speech as you begin the activity.

→ Work up to one minute.

→ Watch for students who may be moving their finger too fast and remind the group that it's important to move slowly.

→ Fade modelling as appropriate. Repeat regularly.

TRACING THE BREATH #1

Either follow your actual hand with your finger, trace your hand onto paper or use the drawing below. Trace slowly round the hand shape, breathe in as you move up the fingers and out as you move down.

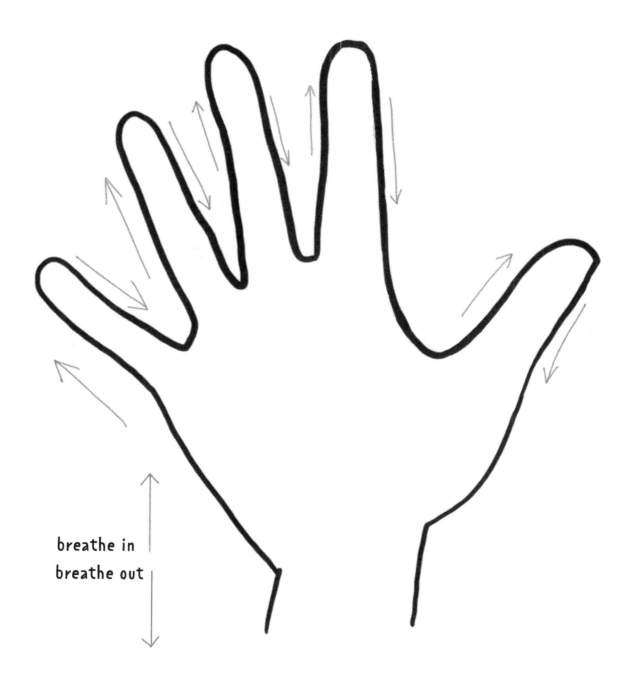

breathe in
breathe out

TRACING THE BREATH #2

Trace slowly round each shape, breathing as shown. Choose one you like, or design your own.

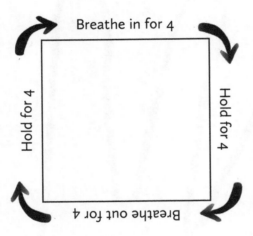

YOGA PRACTICES FOR THE CLASSROOM

The next four activities are from Jyoti Manuel, founder of Special Yoga.[2] They are standing activities, useful for the beginning, the middle or the end of a lesson. Follow the instructions as you lead each activity for the students.

Many of our students experience uncertainty if they do not receive enough sensory information, particularly during long, physically inactive lessons. We can increase feelings of sensory certainty for all students by including some short breath and movement activities in our daily practice.

From experience, students often display signs of uncertainty at the start of a new practice, but with repetition most settle and engage.

Tapping

This activity is particularly good for students who struggle with inattention, impulsivity or hyperactivity. It settles the body quickly and has had a dramatic effect on many of our students. It is also good just before bedtime for students who find it hard to get to sleep.

→ Stand with feet shoulder width apart – arms by your sides.

→ Take a moment to feel the feet on the ground and the contact that your feet make with socks/shoes/earth.

→ Take a couple of deep breaths in and out – slowly and deeply.

→ On the next in-breath, tap the back of the top of the shoulders once, quite firmly.

Ha!

→ As you breathe out, bring the arms down and firmly tap the back of your thighs in a similar way as you say 'Ha!'

→ Repeat ten times, focusing on a slow, regular rhythm to the firm taps.

→ Then stand quietly – eyes closed or look down – and feel the sensations in your body.

---

2   https://specialyoga.org.uk

Breathing with movement – balloon breath

A short activity to calm and regulate.

→ Bring your hands together in front of your solar plexus (below the heart and just above the belly) as if you are holding an average-sized balloon.

→ Breathe in slowly and, as you do, imagine the balloon is filling with air and open the arms out wide.

→ Breathe out and slowly bring your hands back to their starting position.

→ Count the breath – e.g. breathe in for four and out for four. The key here is to get the same length of in-breath as out-breath and slow the breath right down.

→ Continue for three to five minutes.

→ Stand quietly – eyes closed or look down – and feel the sensations in your body.

Stretches

→ Take the arms up over the head, link fingers and turn palms up to the sky stretching the body up as much as possible.

→ Move the arms to the left side as you breathe in, keeping arms up and both feet evenly planted.

→ As you breathe out, move your arms back to the centre.

→ On the next in-breath, move to the right and back to centre on the out-breath.

→ Repeat three to five times on each side – allow the movement to get deeper each time you do it.

→ Finish by returning back to the centre feeling the breath, and any sensations in the body.

Shake it off

Find a piece of rhythmic, energetic music that the majority of your students like. This may take some doing but it's sometimes possible (Taylor Swift, anyone?).

→ Stand again with feet hip width apart and take a moment to feel the feet on the ground/in socks/shoes.

→ Start to shake the body loosely, in time to the music, imagining that you are shaking off all tension and uncomfortable feelings.

→ Begin with hands and arms, then add shoulders and head.

→ Add a bounce through the knees and feet.

→ Keep shaking for two to five minutes.

→ Slow down and stop. Feel the feet again. Notice sensations in the body.

THE BODY SCAN

These types of activities are useful for young people who find it difficult to fix awareness on the breath or body. They involve visualisation, but no movement, and are best done with eyes closed. There are lots of body-scan meditation scripts available online. Session two can be used for a short body-scan activity with groups.

Session one

Explain that you are going to start using a technique called 'body scanning'. We do this because our minds and bodies are connected, and if we relax our body, we can relax our minds. It can be really useful if you get stressed or if you have difficulties going to sleep at night. You can practise it lying down, or in a chair. Use the script below:

→ Ask the students to sit in their chairs with their feet flat and their backs slightly off the back of their chairs, eyes closed and hands loosely placed on the thighs (palms up). They should relax their mouth and let their jaws go soft.

→ Students notice the feeling of their feet on the floor, their hip bones sinking into the chair, hands heavy on their legs.

→ Ask them to focus attention on their neck and shoulders and see if they can feel any stress there. 'See if you can imagine the tension melting like butter and drifting away.'

→ Model and direct long slow breaths for a few seconds.

→ Tell students to open their eyes slowly but stay still.

→ They stand up and gently shake their bodies.

Session two

At this point we start to introduce the scan. There are lots of different techniques available online, and you may like to choose one of these. Below is an example of a short technique we use.

→ Repeat the steps of the process outlined above in session one, to prepare the body, and once everyone is still and breathing slowly, tell students, 'As you breathe in, imagine your breath filling your lungs. As you breathe out, imagine sending it down to your toes. Notice how they feel.' Remain here for a few breaths.

→ Move through the body, asking students to continue breathing slowly, allowing the air to flow in and out, without forcing. We focus on the breath reaching feet, ankles, knees, hips, belly, wrists, elbows, shoulders and neck, as the joints are where we get most proprioceptive information about our bodies in space.

→ You may like to start with one part of the body (legs/arms/head/neck/shoulders) and progress to a whole-body scan.

→ Always finish by opening eyes slowly, standing up and gently shaking the body.

2. Link sensory signals and emotions

These are activities to help students develop a greater awareness of how our senses and our feelings are interlinked. We know that for many of our students there is one question they often struggle to answer:

'How do you feel?'

Low interoceptive awareness means that it can take longer for some people to learn to link internal body changes with the labels we use to describe them. These links can be fragile and may be affected by things like sensory overwhelm, low energy levels or times of uncertainty.

We use these labels as a kind of shorthand, to describe a combination of internal body signals; signals that we may need to do something to help us get back to a calm alert state. For example:

The feeling	The label
Burning face, hot body (especially hands)	Embarrassed
Sweat on back of neck	
Dry, itchy and heavy eyes	Tired
Weak arms and legs	
Sick feeling in stomach	

Difficulties with making these links can cause our students to experience greater levels of anxiety than their peers, as this sensory uncertainty may cause them to interpret any internal change as 'bad'; but this low awareness can have other consequences too.

We know from talking to families that some of our students experienced difficulties as a result of their interoceptive awareness when they were younger, and some continue to do so. We hear stories of students who took considerably longer than their peers to understand when they needed the toilet (either going too frequently due to a hyper-sensitive sense, or not frequently enough due to a hypo-sensitivity) and stories that suggest difficulties with the sensory aspects of 'letting go'.

Processing pain accurately is another vital skill; some of our students have a dramatic medical history as a result of their difficulties interpreting pain signals; these signals may be mislocated (infections in the ear or throat all being described as a 'stomach ache'), missed (not noticing a serious injury) or experienced as completely overwhelming (vaccinations and minor medical interventions being a particular issue).

The following activities continue to work on interoceptive awareness, this time linking body awareness to emotions.

INTEROCEPTIVE BODY MAPPING

This is a creative activity to help students develop interoceptive awareness.

How you run this activity will depend on the levels of awareness in your students. Some older teenagers are able to explain where in their body they feel changes and even describe some of them. With other students, we sometimes need to 'provoke' feelings – we might play a simple game that requires a response within a time pressure (e.g. Pass the Bomb or similar) and 'freeze' it if we observe a student experiencing positive (winning) or negative (stress/losing) emotions. We can then ask them to describe where they feel the feeling in their body.

→ **Give each student a body map worksheet.**

→ **Explain that interpreting our internal feelings can give us clues** to what we need to do to get back in balance. Give the example of feeling really hungry and explain how missing these signals can make people feel 'hangry' (hungry + angry). If we realise we are hungry early on, we can eat and avoid the distress (for us and everyone else).

→ **Describe how you might recognise a feeling in yourself** and represent it with writing/drawings/colour/collage on your sheet. Or use the example below.

→ **Ask each student to describe a recent situation where they experienced unusual feelings** – this could be positive or negative. It can help to start with body changes that might signal the following: thirst, hunger, fullness, heat, cold, physical exhaustion, illness, the need for the toilet, before moving on to emotions.

→ **Use the word bank worksheet** and encourage students to add more descriptors.

→ **Encourage conversation about how different people process experiences in different ways** and ask students to try and identify where in their body *they* might feel these signals. Some beautifully descriptive examples of how @happy_nd_lady experiences different emotions are recorded below.

happy	radiating warmth, I feel my heart beat
anxiety	tight band around diaphragm, curled toes, thought spirals in head
depression	cold hands and feet, hollow chest, heavy head
worry	temples hurt, sweaty hands, butterflies in stomach
excitement	warm fuzzy feeling in my chest, active hands

→ **Use this as an opportunity to let your students participate according to their own style** – encourage them to use writing, drawing or colour to express themselves.

→ **Store the art work carefully** – some students like to have them made into booklets; in fact notebooks are often popular as they bring more certainty than loose sheets.

BODY MAPPING WORD BANK

energised   electric   pounding

              pressure   prickly

fluid   shivery

              shaky   tight

wobbly   sinking

              heavy   buzzy

aching   fizzy

              tingly   cool

light   fluttering   glowing

              radiating   warm

empty   spinning   dull

MY BODY MAP – EXAMPLE

A situation I remember:

When I got my dog – I didn't know we were getting one

What I felt in my body:

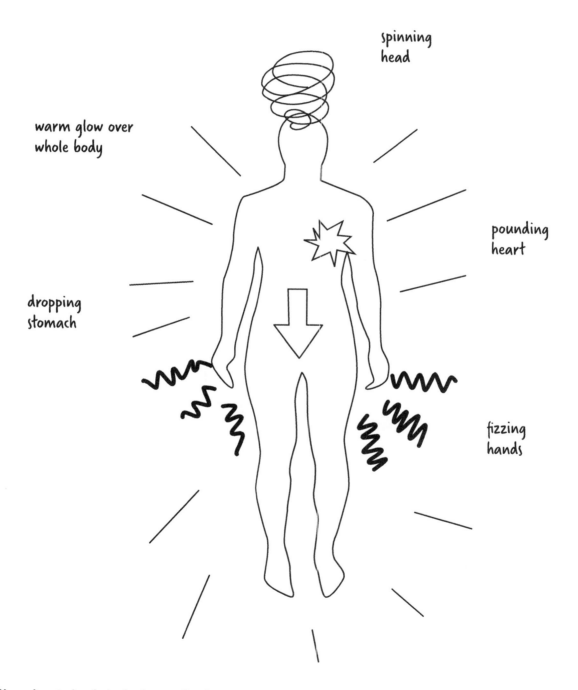

spinning head

warm glow over whole body

pounding heart

dropping stomach

fizzing hands

How I might label these feelings:

excited, surprised, shocked, a bit overwhelmed, really happy

MY BODY MAP

A situation I remember:

What I felt in my body:

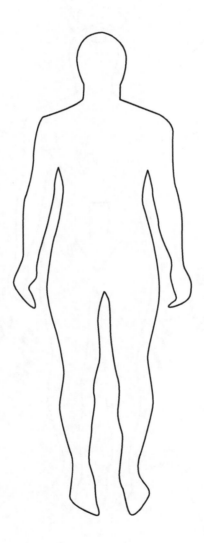

How I might label these feelings:

WHAT'S IN MY HEAD?

A game to develop emotional vocabulary and link these labels to situations and internal feelings. The aim is for everyone to guess the emotion label that they have in their headband.

→ **Choose a level of emotion vocabulary** from the next few pages.

→ **Print two copies of this vocabulary block** onto card and cut up one copy to make small cards. Keep the other for reference during the game.

→ **Put all the emotion cards face down** on the table and ask students to take turns turning them over, each time describing the emotion on the card in greater detail – encourage all students to join in with their definitions or examples. You can record these if you like.

→ **Teach and play a 'Headbanz'-type game** – this is available commercially or easy to make with strips of wide elastic sewn together to make a headband.

→ **Begin with pictures of animals or household objects** stuck in the headband. Students have to ask closed questions of each other and guess what's in their band. 'Does it have four legs?' 'Is there one in this room?' Adults play too.

→ **Once the game is established, start using the emotion cards in the headbands.**

→ **Go around the group taking it in turns to ask one question about the emotion.** Encourage students to ask these types of questions. You might like to write some sample questions on the board:

- Is it a positive emotion? A negative emotion? A neutral emotion?

- What might make you feel like this?

- What might make me feel like this?

- Where might I feel this in my body?

- What facial expression might I make?

→ **Students can make a guess after three rounds of questions.** Keep going until everyone has guessed their emotion.

EMOTION WORD BANK

Level one emotions

Scared	Angry	Disgusted	Surprised
Sad	Happy		

Level two emotions

Rejected	Frustrated	Depressed	Aggressive
Guilty	Lonely	Optimistic	Trusting
Peaceful	Powerful	Proud	Interested
Excited	Amazed	Confused	Panicky
Stressed	Bored	Anxious	Disappointed
Calm	Sleepy	Stressed	Exhausted

Level three emotions

Creative	Curious	Cheeky	Successful
Confident	Brave	Sensitive	Inspired
Isolated	Embarrassed	Withdrawn	Annoyed
Jealous	Furious	Disrespected	Resentful
Nervous	Insignificant	Overwhelmed	Helpless
Out of control	Sleepy	Pressured	Shocked
Irritated	Frustrated	Depressed	Aggressive

3. Notice thoughts

Being aware of the specific thoughts that might be causing us uncertainty can help us avoid feeling overwhelmed and give us useful ideas for how to help ourselves return to a calm alert state, a state of greater certainty.

For example, if we can identify the thoughts that are part of our stress on the way to a train station we might be able to identify the uncertainty we are experiencing (rather than becoming so overwhelmed that we panic and go the wrong way):

> 'I don't know if I'm going to catch the train or not. I might be late home.'

Once we have identified this more specific uncertainty, we can work out what to do to build certainty.

Increase our knowledge

> 'I can use the travel app to find out what time I'll get to the station and find out if the train is on time.'

Increase our tolerance of the uncertainty

This might involve assessing the implications of missing the train:

> 'If I miss the train, I can get the next one. I can call my mum and let her know. It doesn't matter if I'm a bit late home tonight.'

or using some strategies to reduce the stress:

> 'I can do some mindful walking, breathe slowly and listen to music on my headphones.'

Developing an awareness of thoughts is a key part of emotional problem solving. The activities in this section help students learn to identify their thoughts. Thoughts are sometimes easier to access than emotions, although some students may find this difficult too, initially.

We can support all young people (we all experience uncertainty) by being explicit about this 'life hack' and why it's so useful. We can explain the importance of being aware of thoughts and watch out for moments in the classroom, in a small group or at home, when someone may be feeling mildly uncomfortable or annoyed (emptying their bag on the floor by mistake, leaving a book at home or forgetting something) and give options for what they might be thinking. With modelling and repetition, we find that most students are able to start identifying thoughts which may help them develop coping strategies in times of uncertainty.

Negative thoughts:

- ▸ You overhear the student complaining about forgetting a form for a school trip.

- ▸ Ask them what thoughts are going through their head – it might be something like 'It's the last day to bring in the form, I'm worried I'll get in trouble' or 'I'm annoyed with myself – it's the third day I've forgotten it'.

Positive thoughts:

- ▸ Someone wins a sports prize.

- ▸ Ask the students what thoughts might go through someone's head at times like these – 'I did so well!', 'Can't wait to tell my mum/dad/brother/sister', 'I like feeling good at something'.

The answers aren't too important – the point of this is that students realise we all have an internal monologue that goes along with our day-to-day experiences. Writing these comments down or saying them out loud helps make them more concrete and raises awareness, increasing our chances of building our certainty.

THINKING OUT LOUD

→ Explain to students that you are going to do an activity that can help them cope in times of stress. Understanding what we are **thinking** can sometimes make us feel less anxious and can also help with problem solving.

→ Ask students to think about a time when they felt a positive feeling – they don't need to name it, nor does it have to be too significant (see the first worksheet).

→ Use the example below, or another of your own, to explain how the activity works.

→ Get them to write a brief description of the situation in the box.

→ Now ask them to try and remember/imagine some of the thoughts they might have been thinking and write them below the box. They can draw think bubbles around them.

→ Repeat with a moment you experienced a kind of negative feeling – again emphasise that it could be something really ordinary and give an example before getting them to fill out the sheet on this.

→ You will notice that although you haven't asked for them, many of the clouds will have feelings in them. This is good preparation for the next level of awareness – labelling emotions.

A positive memory:

I got really wet in the rain on the way to school. Someone had a spare sweatshirt and just offered it to me. I didn't even ask.

I'm so glad I don't have to sit in wet clothes all day.

I liked not having to ask.

I like them for doing that.

A negative memory:

I was waiting to get on a crowded train and someone with a massive backpack shoved me out of the way and got on. There was no more room and I had to wait for the next one.

I got a shock when they pushed me.

I'm tired and I want to get home.

It's not fair, I've been waiting longer.

THINKING OUT LOUD (POSITIVE)

Think of a positive memory from last week.

A positive memory was when...

My thoughts might have been...

1 Think of a positive memory from the last week, try and remember a moment when you felt really good.

2 Write a short description in the box.

3 Now try and remember the thoughts you might have had in your head and write them in the cloud. You can add more if you like.

THINKING OUT LOUD (NEGATIVE)

A negative memory was when...

My thoughts might have been...

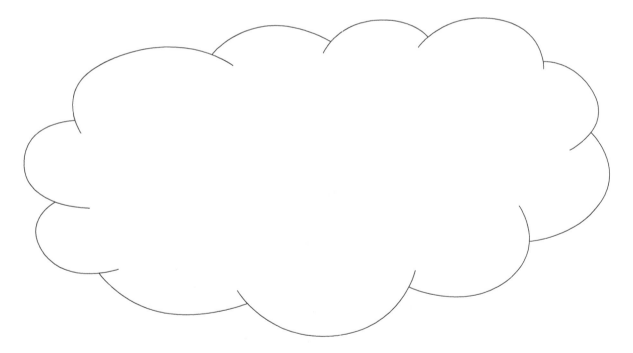

1 Think of a less positive memory from the last week, try and remember a moment when you felt not so good.

2 Write a short description in the box.

3 Now try and remember the thoughts you might have had in your head and put them in the cloud. You can add more if you like.

USING JOURNALS

Why

Regularly 'checking in' on how we are feeling and thinking can help us develop a greater awareness of our thoughts and feelings about ourselves and other people. This can make them more manageable. Books are great for certainty, and some of our more creative students really enjoy the process of recording questions or concerns.

Some of our students use journals to record and 'hold' their worries:

If I'm really stressed about something, I'll write it down in my phone on my way to or from school, then at the end of the day I'll write them down in my book — it's like I'm getting them out of my head before I go to sleep. It kind of helps. (Isha, Year 11)

How

Some students need little encouragement and really enjoy the process. For reluctant students, begin by encouraging them to use a book in school.

→ Model how writing down our stresses can sometimes make them seem more manageable, by using the book to record specific uncertainties that may be behind a worry – you can use the 'What to do with worry' worksheet from the next section for this. It can also be a way for students to record specific concerns for a class or group discussion.

→ Use it for students to record information during group work. They can list things like the sentence starters they can use when asking for help, or their own tips for more confident body language.

→ Set short tasks to be done outside school – for example, watch how people in your family get a turn to speak, see how many people on the train wear headphones to help them deal with the commute (we all have to deal with sensory overload sometimes) or draw three pictures that represent different teenage styles of dress. Ask the students to use the book to record them.

→ Help students put their own style into what they record by showing them different options for journal writing on Pinterest (or similar) to inspire them.

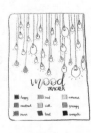 

4. Try new responses

The final part of the self-awareness process is to encourage students to use their increased self-awareness to plan more certain and helpful responses to difficult moments. To learn how to act more than react.

This section is included here because when we raise awareness, we need to teach students to use this knowledge to develop their own self-regulation strategies and promote a more certain engagement with their peers, teachers and families.

It can be difficult for teachers and students to understand the reasons behind some of the more unexpected behaviours we see in school; it is easy to assume that what might be a reaction to uncertainty is a more planned and deliberate action. The interviews we carry out with young people give us some interesting insights into this:

> I need to do my own thing in PE because it doesn't feel like an actual lesson, it's so free. I either just sit on a bench, or if I'm made to do something like play badminton, I wouldn't want to play with someone — I'd want to smack the little thing around. If I'm made to do running, I always want to have a little skip to it, because running's so boring. So, I'd run, walk and skip around, see who's near me and chat to them. (Antoni, Year 11)

Antoni has excellent gross motor skills – he's part of a track cycling team – but he finds it difficult to engage in PE in school. This may originally have been a response to uncertainty in all three areas, Sensory (seeking 'more' than running), Social (seeking social certainty from his friends) and Structure (needing more structure in the 'free' lesson), but has become an established pattern over the years.

For our students to manage the requirements of the school day, and life beyond, we need to help them increase their awareness of uncertainty so they can develop some strategies for living a more certain life.

The following pages contain two simple activities to help students come up with options for actions as well as understanding their reactions.

WHAT TO DO WITH WORRY

Why

A structure for helping students take ownership of their uncertainty. If we can increase their awareness of some of the uncertainties that may underlie their anxiety, they can begin to use this knowledge to help themselves in times of upset or high anxiety.

We often find that by simply identifying and categorising the underlying uncertainties, our students feel more in control of their anxiety. Once these are written down, what to do next often flows more easily.

It's best if students get the opportunity to practise using this framework in a calm moment, but it can be used in an emergency. It can also be practised in a group setting.

How

→ Give your student a copy of the '**What to do with worry**' worksheet.

→ **Work through an example** (one is provided, but you may like to use your own).

→ **Ask the student to choose a situation they are finding difficult to manage**; this might be a lesson, a conversation, a friendship or something else, and write it down.

→ **Work through each section**.

→ Sort worries into types: **expected**, **unexpected** and **temporary** (remember the glasses from Chapter 1?).

→ **Encourage discussion and sharing of experiences**, if working in a group. Find the worries we can do something about and acknowledge the worries we can't immediately remove. Life is uncertain and it can make all of us have uncomfortable feelings.

→ **Record any strategies for certainty in the appropriate boxes.** You may need to offer options for ideas in the early stages, but with repetition students can learn to develop their own.

There will be some uncertainties that we can't fix – in the example the student can't know what she and her new teacher will think of each other – and that's okay. By focusing on what we **can** make more certain we hope to increase agency and reduce anxiety that way.

And finally, we can remind students that sometimes...

@sootmegs

WHAT TO DO WITH WORRY (EXAMPLE)

The situation: My maths teacher is leaving. We are getting a new one.
The feeling: I'm stressed.

What do I not know?

If I will like the new teacher.

If the new teacher will like me.

If the teacher will know where we've got to in the syllabus.

If the teacher knows what I'm like at maths.

If the teacher will run the Tuesday catch-up session.

What kind of worry is it? (expected, unexpected, temporary)

I think it's expected.

What could I find out?

If the Tuesday session will run.

If the teacher has records of our maths tests this year.

What the teacher's name is.

What could I do?

Ask my maths teacher about the Tuesday session, the syllabus and the test results before he goes.

Talk to my form teacher and see if I can meet the new teacher before the lesson next term.

What could I think?

It's okay if I feel stressed when things change, most people do.

It might take time for me to get used to a new teacher but that's okay.

If the old teacher liked me, then maybe the new teacher will too.

WHAT TO DO WITH WORRY

The situation:

The feeling:

What do I not know?
What kind of worry is it? (expected, unexpected, temporary)
What could I find out?
What could I do?
What could I think?

USING SCALES

Why

We use scales to grade reactions and build certainty, particularly for times when our students experience loss of control. Many young people we work with seem to experience uncertainty when working out how intensely they are experiencing an emotion (and how big a problem is) and it can help them to get a more certain measure down on paper.

By creating scales, we can help increase awareness of different **degrees** of awareness. If we add new response options, we can create some really useful action plans which may well avoid the loss of control that causes such distress.

How

→ Work with students, either one to one or in a group, to help them work out the different ways they might respond to a tricky situation.

→ Encourage them to think about the interoceptive information, thoughts and emotions they might experience.

→ Support them to grade their reactions from 1–5. Colouring in the scale squares from cool to hot colours (1 = cool, 5 = hot) makes for a stronger image.

Prompting students to scale their emotions can really help diffuse a situation when someone feels that it's the 'end of the world'. By setting the emotion down on paper and talking about where it is on a larger scale, we can reduce feelings of anxiety surprisingly quickly.

THE STRESS SCALE (EXAMPLE)

Name of student: AS   Date: 10 April   Teacher: KD

Situation: Classroom in non-lesson time

LEVEL	THOUGHTS ☼	BODY ⛑	EMOTIONS ♡	ACTION ▷
1	I'm about to lose control I have to get out of here	Hot, shaking, sweating, can't hear properly	Frightened, completely overwhelmed	Go to The Hub. Do some mindful walking on the way Find Miss H and tell her I'm feeling stressed or sit quietly and breathe
2	I think I'm going to lose it I bet everyone's staring at me	Very hot, sweating	Rejected Overwhelmed	Do a mindful walk to the water fountain and fill up my bottle
3	I think my face is going red Can they see I'm sweating?	Sinking feeling in my stomach Hot, heart is beating fast	Anxious	Drink some water from my water bottle Trace an infinity curve on the desk Do some work
4	I'm not sure what to do	Shallow breaths, churning stomach	A bit stressed	Ask someone a question about work/ the day
5	I'm doing okay	Body still, breathing slow	Calm	Smile at someone

THE ANXIETY WORKBOOK FOR SUPPORTING TEENS WHO LEARN DIFFERENTLY

THE STRESS SCALE

Name of student:　　　　　Date:　　　Teacher:

Situation:

LEVEL	THOUGHTS ☼	BODY ☺	EMOTIONS ♡	ACTION ▷
1				
2				
3				
4				
5				

OTHER IDEAS TO INCREASE INTEROCEPTIVE AWARENESS

▶ **Build a mood chart** on the classroom wall, talk about it in form time, literature lessons or PSHE.

▶ Make a grid with axes from high to low energy and good to not-so-good feelings. Get students to write down the feelings they experience or observe on sticky notes and stick them on to show type and intensity: are they mostly **happy** (low energy, good feelings), **excited** (high energy, good feelings), **sad** (low energy, not-so-good feelings) or **angry** (high energy, not-so-good feelings)? Get students to decide on the intensity. Which emotion goes in the middle?

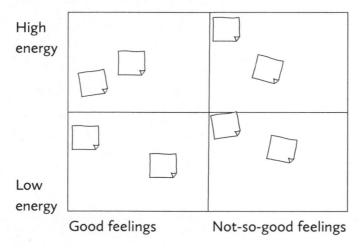

High
energy

Low
energy

Good feelings   Not-so-good feelings

▶ Refer to it when discussing characters in stories/literature and use it as a prompt for emotion vocabulary, building word banks with sticky notes.

▶ **Investigate 'mood' apps** and encourage students to rate their mood on a regular basis.

▶ **Use an emotions wheel** as a vocabulary bank (lots of versions available online).

▶ **Talk about your own emotions** and model out loud your coping strategies for day-to-day situations, such as making a mistake, being disappointed, preparing for a challenge.

▶ **Encourage 'individual' team sports** – structured physical activities like running, swimming and cycling, especially in groups, can be highly beneficial for raising interoceptive awareness. Experience suggests that sports which are more individual (like running or cycling) and less communication based (like football or basketball) are more suitable for uncertain teens. This may be because they find it hard to predict what will happen next. Sports where the space is marked and contained (a running track, a swimming lane, a cycling course) are really popular with some of our students. This doesn't mean that solitary sport is the only option – many of our students take part regularly in these types of team sports and are often highly successful.

- ▸ **Develop a whole-school yoga programme.** There are many available. Special Yoga offers online training.

- ▸ **Get creative.** Activities such as cartoon drawing, illustration, animation, journal writing, photo-editing, film-making, sewing, knitting, crochet and even pom-pom making can also act (for some!) as a form of meditation/mindfulness. Setting up this type of club after school or during lunch for students who struggle to find 3S certainty can make a big difference to a stressful day and their creativity may amaze you.

IF YOU ONLY HAVE FIVE MINUTES

Tips for dealing with sensory uncertainty in the classroom:

- ▸ **Understand that some people struggle with their filters** and may be acutely aware of sounds, smells, vibrations or lights that we screen out. Their sensory cups may be full before we begin.

- ▸ **Remember that sensory-seeking behaviour can cause low-level disruption** – movement and sound particularly. Some cups are empty and the need to fill them is irrepressible.

- ▸ **Understand that some feelings take time to leave the body.** High levels of emotion (either positive or negative) may take longer to process and we can help by allowing for this, especially around transitions.

- ▸ **Allow for regular movement** for whole groups. Use warm-ups, movement breaks, stretches and shake-outs whenever you feel a group seems over- or under-stimulated. Particular 'stress points' include first day back, last day of term/half term, exam or test season, double lessons, a change of venue and long stretches of 'passive' learning.

- ▸ **Remember that low interoceptive awareness can cause confusion for everyone** – not knowing how you feel can also mean that you don't know what you think. Students who struggle with independent study may experience this.

- ▸ **Identify thoughts and link them to feelings** – model your thoughts as you experience a lesson or group. 'When you said that it made me think...', 'When he came in like that I wondered if...', 'When that happened, I felt...' and so on.

- ▸ **Remind students that some level of uncertainty is to be expected**, even the unexpected or temporary variety – reinforce this message when you observe it at exam time, when a class had a change of teacher, or venue, or timetable. We need to learn to sit with uncomfortable feelings sometimes. It's okay not to be okay.

▶ **Make it visual** – use charts, scales, emojis, colour cards in planners, charts in journals, word banks, drawings or emotions wheels to support students to express levels of confidence or anxiety.

FURTHER READING

Bogdashina, O. (2016). *Sensory Perceptual Issues in Autism and Asperger Syndrome: Different Sensory Experiences – Different Perceptual Worlds.* London: Jessica Kingsley Publishers.

Buron, K. D. & Curtis, M. (2003). *The Incredible 5-Point Scale: Assisting Students with Autism Spectrum Disorders in Understanding Social Interactions and Controlling their Emotional Responses.* Shawnee Mission, KS: AAPC Publishing.

Khalsa, S. S., Adolphs, R., Cameron, O. G., Critchley, H. D. *et al.* (2018). Interoception and mental health: A roadmap. *Biological Psychiatry: Cognitive Neuroscience and Neuroimaging, 3*(6), 501–513.

Mahler, K. J. (2016). *Interoception: The Eighth Sensory System: Practical Solutions for Improving Self-Regulation, Self-Awareness and Social Understanding of Individuals with Autism Spectrum and Related Disorders.* Shawnee Mission, KS: AAPC Publishing.

Mahler, K. (2019). *The Interoception Curriculum: A Step-by-Step Guide to Developing Mindful Self-Regulation.* Shawnee Mission, KS: AAPC Publishing.

REFERENCES

Abernethy, H. (2010). The assessment and treatment of sensory defensiveness in adult mental health: A literature review. *British Journal of Occupational Therapy, 73*(5), 210–218.

Ayres, A. J. (1972). *Sensory Integration and Learning Disorders.* Los Angeles, CA: Western Psychological Services.

Barrett, L. F. (2004). Feelings or words? Understanding the content in self-report ratings of experienced emotion. *Journal of Personality and Social Psychology, 87*(2), 266.

Barrett, L. F. & Simmons, W. K. (2015). Interoceptive predictions in the brain. *Nature Reviews Neuroscience, 16*(7), 419–429.

Ben-Sasson, A., Carter, A. S. & Briggs-Gowan, M. J. (2009). Sensory over-responsivity in elementary school: Prevalence and social-emotional correlates. *Journal of Abnormal Child Psychology, 37*(5), 705–716.

Ben-Sasson, A., Hen, L., Fluss, R., Cermak, S. A., Engel-Yeger, B. & Gal, E. (2009). A meta-analysis of sensory modulation symptoms in individuals with autism spectrum disorders. *Journal of Autism and Developmental Disorders, 39*(1), 1–11.

Brown, A., Tse, T. & Fortune, T. (2019). Defining sensory modulation: A review of the concept and a contemporary definition for application by occupational therapists. *Scandinavian Journal of Occupational Therapy, 26*(7), 515–523.

Brown, C. (2002). What is the best environment for me? A sensory processing perspective. *Occupational Therapy in Mental Health, 17*(3–4), 115–125.

Case-Smith, J., Weaver, L. L. & Fristad, M. A. (2015). A systematic review of sensory processing interventions for children with autism spectrum disorders. *Autism, 19*(2), 133–148.

Champagne, T. (2011). Attachment, trauma, and occupational therapy practice. *OT Practice, 16*(5), CE1–8.

Champagne, T., Koomer, J. & Olson, L. (2010). Sensory processing evaluation and intervention in mental health. *OT Practice, 15*(5), CE1–8.

Cheung, P. P. & Siu, A. M. (2009). A comparison of patterns of sensory processing in children with and without developmental disabilities. *Research in Developmental Disabilities, 30*(6), 1468–1480.

Cisler, J. M. & Koster, E. H. (2010). Mechanisms of attentional biases towards threat in anxiety disorders: An integrative review. *Clinical Psychology Review, 30*(2), 203–216.

Craig, A. D. (2002). How do you feel? Interoception: The sense of the physiological condition of the body. *Nature Reviews Neuroscience, 3*(8), 655–666.

Craig, A. D. (2003). Interoception: The sense of the physiological condition of the body. *Current Opinion in Neurobiology, 13*(4), 500–505.

Craig, A. D. (2015). *How Do You Feel? An Interoceptive Moment with Your Neurobiological Self.* Princeton, NJ: Princeton University Press.

Critchley, H. D. & Garfinkel, S. N. (2017). Interoception and emotion. *Current Opinion in Psychology, 17*, 7–14.

Damasio, A. (1999). *The Feeling of What Happens: Body and Emotion in the Making of Consciousness.* New York, NY: Harcourt.

Donnellan, A. M., Hill, D. A. & Leary, M. R. (2013). Rethinking autism: Implications of sensory and movement differences for understanding and support. *Frontiers in Integrative Neuroscience, 6*, 124.

Dunn, W. (1997). The impact of sensory processing abilities on the daily lives of young children and their families: A conceptual model. *Infants & Young Children, 9*(4), 23–35.

Dunn, W. (2001). The sensations of everyday life: Empirical, theoretical, and pragmatic considerations. *American Journal of Occupational Therapy, 55*(6), 608–620.

Dunn, W. (2007). Supporting children to participate successfully in everyday life by using sensory processing knowledge. *Infants & Young Children, 20*(2), 84–101.

Fernandez-Andres, M. I., Pasto-Cerezuela, G., Sanz-Cervera, P. & Tarraga-Minguez, R. (2015). A comparative study of sensory processing in children with and without autism spectrum disorder in the home and classroom environments. *Research in Developmental Disabilities, 38*, 202–212.

Foster, L. & Cox, J. (2013). Best Practices in Supporting Students with Autism. In G. Frolek Clark & B. E. Chandler (eds) *Best Practices for Occupational Therapy in Schools* (pp.273–284). Bethesda, MD: AOTA Press.

Fotopoulou, A. & Tsakiris, M. (2017). Mentalizing homeostasis: The social origins of interoceptive inference. *Neuropsychoanalysis, 19*(1), 3–28.

Fukushima, H., Terasawa, Y. & Umeda, S. (2011). Association between interoception and empathy: Evidence from heartbeat-evoked brain potential. *International Journal of Psychophysiology, 79*(2), 259–265.

Garfinkel, S. N., Seth, A. K., Barrett, A. B., Suzuki, K. & Critchley, H. D. (2015). Knowing your own heart: Distinguishing interoceptive accuracy from interoceptive awareness. *Biological Psychology, 104*, 65–74.

Green, S. A. & Ben-Sasson, A. (2010). Anxiety disorders and sensory over-responsivity in children with autism spectrum disorders: Is there a causal relationship? *Journal of Autism and Developmental Disorders, 40*(12), 1495–1504.

Hagelskamp, C., Brackett, M. A., Rivers, S. E. & Salovey, P. (2013). Improving classroom quality with the ruler approach to social and emotional learning: Proximal and distal outcomes. *American Journal of Community Psychology, 51*(3–4), 530–543.

Houghton, D. C., Stein, D. J. & Cortese, B. M. (2019). Exteroceptive sensory abnormalities in childhood and adolescent anxiety and obsessive-compulsive disorder: A critical review. *Journal of the American Academy of Child & Adolescent Psychiatry, 59*(1), 78–87.

Kircanski, K., Lieberman, M. D. & Craske, M. G. (2012). Feelings into words: Contributions of language to exposure therapy. *Psychological Science, 23*(10), 1086–1091.

Lane, S. J., Lynn, J. Z. & Reynolds, S. (2010). Sensory modulation: A neuroscience and behavioral overview. *OT Practice, 15*(10), CE1–7.

Lieberman, M. D., Eisenberger, N. I., Crockett, M. J., Tom, S. M., Pfeifer, J. H. & Way, B. M. (2007). Putting feelings into words. *Psychological Science, 18*(5), 421–428.

May-Benson, T. A. & Schaaf, R. (2015). Ayres Sensory Integration® Intervention. In I. Söderback (ed.) *International Handbook of Occupational Therapy Interventions* (pp.633–646). Cham, Switzerland: Springer.

McIntosh, D. N., Miller, L. J., Shyu, V. & Hagerman, R. J. (1999). Sensory-modulation disruption, electrodermal responses, and functional behaviors. *Developmental Medicine and Child Neurology, 41*(9), 608–615.

McLaughlin, K. A., Rith-Najarian, L., Dirks, M. A. & Sheridan, M. A. (2015). Low vagal tone magnifies the association between psychosocial stress exposure and internalizing psychopathology in adolescents. *Journal of Clinical Child & Adolescent Psychology, 44*(2), 314–328.

Metz, A. E., Boling, D., DeVore, A., Holladay, H., Liao, J. F. & Vlutch, K. V. (2019). Dunn's Model of Sensory Processing: An investigation of the axes of the Four-Quadrant Model in healthy adults. *Brain Sciences, 9*(2), 35.

Miller, L., Anzalone, M. E., Lane, S. J., Cermak, S. A. & Osten, E. T. (2007). Concept evolution in sensory integration: A proposed nosology for diagnosis. *American Journal of Occupational Therapy, 61*(2), 135–140.

Miller, L. & Lane, S. J. (2000). Toward a consensus in terminology in sensory integration theory and practice: Part 1: Taxonomy of neurophysiological processes. *Sensory Integration Special Interest Section Quarterly, 23*(1), 1–4.

Ondobaka, S., Kilner, J. & Friston, K. (2017). The role of interoceptive inference in theory of mind. *Brain and Cognition, 112*, 64–68.

Pellicano, E. & Burr, D. (2012). When the world becomes 'too real': A Bayesian explanation of autistic perception. *Trends in Cognitive Sciences, 16*(10), 504–510.

Pennebaker, J. W. (1997). Writing about emotional experiences as a therapeutic process. *Psychological Science, 8*(3), 162–166.

Pfeiffer, B. (2012). Sensory hypersensitivity and anxiety: The chicken or the egg? *Sensory Integration Special Interest Section Quarterly, 35*(2), 1–4.

Reynolds, S., Glennon, T. J., Ausderau, K., Bendixen, R. M. et al. (2017). Using a multifaceted approach to working with children who have differences in sensory processing and integration. *American Journal of Occupational Therapy, 71*(2), 7102360010p1–7102360010p10.

Schaaf, R. C., Benevides, T. W., Blanche, E., Brett-Green, B. A. et al. (2010). Parasympathetic functions in children with sensory processing disorder. *Frontiers in Integrative Neuroscience, 4*, 4. doi: 10.3389/fnint.2010.00004.

Seth, A. K. (2013). Interoceptive inference, emotion, and the embodied self. *Trends in Cognitive Sciences, 17*(11), 565–573.

Simons, D. J. & Chabris, C. F. (1999). Gorillas in our midst: Sustained inattentional blindness for dynamic events. *Perception-London, 28*(9), 1059–1074.

Sutton, D., Wilson, M., Van Kessel, K. & Vanderpyl, J. (2013). Optimizing arousal to manage aggression: A pilot study of sensory modulation. *International Journal of Mental Health Nursing, 22*(6), 500–511.

Taylor, K. M. & Trott, M. A. (1991). Pyramid of Learning. In M.S. Williams & S. Shellenberger (1994) *How Does Your Engine Run?* (p.4). Albuquerque, NM: Therapy Works.

Van de Cruys, S., Evers, K., Van der Hallen, R., Van Eylen, L. et al. (2014). Precise minds in uncertain worlds: Predictive coding in autism. *Psychological Review, 121*(4), 649.

Villasenor, R. F., Smith, S. L. & Jewell, V. D. (2018). A systematic review of sound-based intervention programs to improve participation in education for children with sensory processing and integration challenges. *Journal of Occupational Therapy, Schools, & Early Intervention, 11*(2), 172–191.

Wallis, K., Sutton, D. & Bassett, S. (2018). Sensory modulation for people with anxiety in a community mental health setting. *Occupational Therapy in Mental Health, 34*(2), 122–137.

Watling, R. & Hauer, S. (2015). Effectiveness of Ayres Sensory Integration® and sensory-based interventions for people with autism spectrum disorder: A systematic review. *American Journal of Occupational Therapy, 69*(5), 6905180030p1–6905180030p12.

Wiens, S. (2005). Interoception in emotional experience. *Current Opinion in Neurology, 18*(4), 442–447.

5

SOCIAL

ACTIVITIES TO SUPPORT SOCIAL CERTAINTY

This chapter is all about social certainty and how, by supporting young people to understand more about themselves, others and the social world, we can help them to develop trusting and accepting friendships and relationships.

The activities include questionnaires and checklists to help you look at social uncertainty and some ideas for activities that might help young people become more socially certain.

Introduction

Theory

▶ Social uncertainty

▶ Behaving as we *should*

▶ Theory of ~~mind~~ body

Practice

▶ The search for social certainty

- What does it look like, what could it mean?

- Using the 3S framework to understand behaviour

  – The social environment

  – The assessment checklists

▶ Building social certainty

- Understanding me

  – Personality pairs

  – I am...

  – Me and not me (yet)

  – Would you rather...?

- Understanding other people

  – Mannequin challenge

  – Finding my tribe

  – Social inference

  – Social filters

  – The thinking machine

- Being socially predictable

  – Conversation Jenga

  – The bad news sandwich

  – Passive, aggressive or assertive?

INTRODUCTION

When I was little, I'd talk to anyone; at secondary there was a total change. I've never really enjoyed people my own age, I was always an outsider and we all stopped doing stuff together. (Maria, Year 13)

The social environment becomes more uncertain and unpredictable as students start secondary school. Events start to be independently arranged as parents are less actively involved, social media use rises and this, as well as daily real-life social interaction, becomes more subtle and difficult to learn and, therefore, teach. You can explain the rules for sharing toys and playing games outside – these are both broad and pretty stable – but it's much harder to give a teenager such a certain guide to 'joining in conversations' or 'making new friends'.

At the same time, peer relationships move centre stage in the lives of young people, as their social attention shifts increasingly outwards, from familiar care-givers to their peer group and the wider world. Acceptance (or rejection) by the individuals or groups around them – the certainty of belonging – becomes the main focus and colours everything else, including learning, as they try to manage the ever-increasing uncertainty around the social demands of adult life.

We know that many of our students struggle with the uncertain 'grey area' of social expectations. Predictions are hard to make and rules are hard to define; 'social skills' manuals can give step-by-step instructions for social behaviours which can be really useful when looking at concepts, but can rarely be applied to all situations, as they have limited precision.

Looking 'not weird' (acting as they *should*) in front of different groups of teenagers may require very different types of behaviours, different models, and it might be hard to build these effectively. Social uncertainty affects all other areas of school life, including academic achievement, as young people use up precious energy in working out what is going on around them:

'Does this student/teacher like me? I can't tell.'

'Did what I just say go well or badly?'

'What does that look mean? Did I do something wrong?'

'I really want to leave. Will it look weird if I do?'

'He's explained it twice, but I can't tell if he was cross last time.'

'Do I risk asking again?'

Over the years, we've seen students try to manage this uncertainty in a variety of ways; some create certainty by removing themselves, to varying degrees, from social situations; they don't use social media, make minimal social contact with their peers and rarely ask questions in lessons or tell us if they haven't understood something, with obvious consequences. In more extreme cases, young people may not speak at all in school or may experience such high social uncertainty that they withdraw completely and are unable to attend school.

Others create their own certainty in more active ways and it is we, the educators, who are left puzzled and uncertain:

'She's quite able, but seems to make no effort at all. Why?'

'He sits sulking at the back with his arms folded. Does he not care?'

'If he stopped messing about, he could do quite well. I don't get it.'

'She needs to stop talking so much. Why is she always distracting all the others?'

'Why is he always so argumentative?'

'It is almost as if they are trying to get the other kids to dislike them.'

For us, the answer is relatively simple:

Uncertainty leads to anxiety and results in a search for certainty and an exaggerated need for control.

MATTHEW AND THE RULES

Matthew finds people hard to understand. His experiences in the last years of primary school made him more aware of all kinds of hidden rules that he's expected to follow, rules that most kids seem to understand. He thought his new school would be different, because everyone would be older (and maybe more like the adults he seems to find easier), but the rules just got more complicated. It now seems that always telling the truth is not the correct rule; you should lie if you're talking about how much work or revision you do or if you don't like someone's new trainers (but then with close friends it seems almost expected that you are rude to them); people expect you to look at them when they are talking, but not when you are talking (but you have to look a bit); and when you pass someone you know in the corridor you need to raise your eyebrows and nod your head (but there's no guarantee they will respond consistently).

The 'rules' now just make him feel anxious, which he often experiences as anger – he'll never get it right every time, so he looks to create his own certainty. If anyone asks him a question, he snaps at them; he openly criticises other students' contributions in class, and if a teacher gives him any negative feedback (with a stern look, a comment or a low mark) he argues in a way that he knows will cause trouble but, more crucially, it will cause certainty and that is all he is looking for. Making people behave more predictably, even if that has negative consequences for him, is preferable to living with the uncertainty of subtle rules. His life is more predictable, and this behaviour and its certainty-creating consequences (they won't like me, but I am in control of making them not like me) bring him much more certainty than trying to understand the less certain rules about what is 'right' to do with which people, in what situations and when.

We all experience social uncertainty, even those of us who find socialising fairly predictable have to manage social uncertainty. Why? Because we come across adults and students who go about their 'search for certainty' in a way that makes us feel uncomfortable. Why do we feel this way? Because if other people are not behaving as we would expect, it makes it harder for us to predict how we should behave. We all struggle to cope with unpredicted behaviour (prediction errors), it makes us feel uncertain too and we also then search for certainty. For example:

WHEN WE OBSERVE THIS BEHAVIOUR IN THE CLASSROOM...	WE TRY TO BRING CERTAINTY TO IT BY INTERPRETING IT LIKE THIS...
• Compulsively talking to friends	= not listening, not following rules
• Answering back to teachers	= rude and disrespectful
• Sitting apart from the rest of the group	= prefers to be on their own
• Sabotaging friendships	= not a nice person

Our uncertainty as to why this behaviour is happening might cause us to feel sensations of irritation, annoyance or even anger; whereas, if our students 'do the expected thing', we feel calm and secure.

The 'Search for social certainty' section later in this chapter provides lots more examples of some behaviours that might provoke these kinds of reactions; all within the framework of recognising uncertainty and providing certainty. It reiterates the fundamental question we need to ask when a student is struggling, **'Where's the uncertainty?'**

Have a look at the story of Lucas and the science lesson, overleaf, which may explain in more detail. Or consider this badge, which sums it up quite neatly, too.

@doodlepeoplexo

As we will see on the coming pages, the social uncertainties people experience often have an interoceptive basis and so it's important to begin by working on these. See Chapter 4 for more on this.

LUCAS AND THE SCIENCE LESSON

Lucas sits in a science lab. It's a double lesson at the end of the day, and although he doesn't mind the subject, he is over-whelmed by the need to move (**sensory – vestibular; proprioceptive – uncertainty**). He daydreams about playing football with his friend after school and then gets lost in remembering that time they went to Power League and ended up playing  against another group of boys, winning 6–0 (**social certainty**). He suddenly realises that Ms O is looking at him. So are the two rows in front of him. He can't work out from Ms O's face whether she is feeling cross or not (**social uncertainty**). Her eyebrows look higher than normal, but her face and body are still and her eyes are looking straight at him. Atiq mutters the question she just asked, and Lucas answers it (correctly). He likes Atiq, they get on in lessons, but he ignores him the rest of the time (**social uncertainty**). Ms O seems annoyed, but he isn't sure – he answered the question, didn't he? (More **social uncertainty**.) He stares hard at her trying to work it out but says nothing.

Now *he* feels annoyed. If he could, he'd go for a toilet break, but he knows she'll say he has to wait. He quite likes Ms O because her rules are firm, and she uses diagrams to explain things (**structural certainty**), but he's not sure if she likes him or not (**social uncertainty**). He's stuck here for another 50 minutes and he's starting to panic because he's missed a bit and isn't sure where they are in the lesson (**structural uncertainty**).

He starts to bang his foot on the bar beneath the lab bench, the rhythm makes him feel slightly better (**sensory certainty**), but Atiq tells him to 'Stop it, you freak' and moves down the bench, away from him. He feels even less sure that Atiq likes him (**social uncertainty**), which causes him to experience an anxiety spike and he shouts at Atiq to 'Shut up'. Ms O comes over, all in a rush. Her face looks funny.

At this point he feels like pushing them all aside and running out of the school – he has a bad feeling and knows something's about to happen, but he can't tell exactly what and the sensation is unbearable (**social uncertainty**). Before the teacher starts to speak, he takes control: 'He started it! He had a go at me and I was just sitting here! Why are you always on at me? I do the work, I hand it in, I...I...I' (**search for certainty**).

Lucas is sent to the behaviour team. Again. He's glad he's out of that class. He knows what comes next (**3S certainty**), and although it's not great, it's more certain than where he was a few minutes ago. Ms O is mystified – he's got the potential to be a good student but she can't explain his behaviour and worries that it's either her teaching style or that he just doesn't like her (**social uncertainty**).

Janice is in the behaviour room today; they know each other well, and though he can tell she's not pleased, she works through what went on for each of the students that day using the 3S analysis (see later in this chapter). By the end of the session he has three strategies for what to do next time (**social, sensory and structural certainty**). She takes all the behaviour room students for a fast walk round the football pitch (**sensory certainty**). He feels calmer for a while.

THEORY

SOCIAL UNCERTAINTY

Sometimes I can walk into a room and sense a really strong emotion in someone – but I find it really hard to work out why they might be feeling like that, and what I need to do. So I do nothing. (Jaya, Year 11)

'Every good regulator of a system must be a model of that system' (Conant & Ross Ashby, 1970). As we discussed in Chapter 1, the brain can be viewed as a predictive model-making machine. Through the ongoing process of inferring, predicting, error-monitoring and updating, the brain develops models of the world. It tries to develop the best fitting models that make it easier to regulate us, with the ultimate aim of keeping us alive. The fundamental model it uses in order to do this is a model of us, our body. It is our model of ourselves that serves as the foundation on which all other models are built. As our body does not exist in a vacuum, we need to build a model of our body-in-the-environment. We need to use our baseline model of our body to build models of our physical environment: trees, skyscrapers, grass, roads, rivers, houses, rain, shops, snow and everything else. We also do not exist in isolation in this physical environment; there are people in those skyscrapers, houses, shops and on those roads. Our environment is social, so our model of our body-in-the-environment needs to effectively model other people. The trouble is, much like everything that the brain is trying to predict, social information is hidden.

Unlike the hidden cause of why we might always feel cold when it is snowing, the hidden cause of social information is not so easily and quickly learned from experience. There are fewer statistical regularities to build good fitting models from. Snow is always cold. People are not **always** anything. It takes a lot longer to try to build a model of what the causes of social information might be.

Let's bring back our imaginary student, Jordan, from Chapter 1. Let's say they have no model of why people shout and imagine them trying to infer this hidden cause, build a model of it. In their interactions with other students, they can pick up some data, current sensory input. The problem is that everyone is different, each operating with their own model of the world. For example, Sarah might usually shout when she is angry, but Gary doesn't, Gary tends to shout when he is excited, except for that time when he was angry with Jess. Then there was the time Sarah was angry in class but did not shout and the other time when everybody in the common room was shouting because England scored a goal. The problem Jordan has in building their model is which of these pieces of sensory data is a 'signal' and which is just 'noise'. Do they build their model of what causes people to shout based on Sarah or Gary and in which situation?

Building a model based on either will lead to a prediction error if they apply it to the other; a model based on Sarah is less likely to predict Gary's behaviour. Not only are the causes of other people's behaviours uncertain (e.g. their thoughts, desires, intentions and beliefs are not directly observable), dynamic (they change depending on the environment they are in) and constantly evolving (as they develop their own models), they are also likely to be very different. This can leave Jordan feeling that they may need to build a specific model for both Gary and Sarah in every situation they may ever find themselves in. The brain energy and capacity needed to do this would be overwhelming and leave Jordan exhausted and they would be likely to end up withdrawing from Gary and Sarah's world. Equally, they may build a model based on just one situation, one instance of one individual shouting. However, this would frequently be wrong, produce uncertainty and need updating again, and then again and again. This would leave Jordan seeing the social world as highly unpredictable; they would end up wearing their unexpected uncertainty glasses and bouncing from model to model. Again, the energy cost of this constant updating could lead to Jordan completely withdrawing from this highly volatile (social) world.

The social world is never going to be entirely predictable. It is also not entirely volatile. While there are some irregularities, there are also some signals (statistical regularities) Jordan can use to build 'good enough' models. Our job is to help Jordan to take off their unexpected uncertainty glasses by introducing them to some of those signals in others and in themselves.

The human saga is just not reliable enough for me to predict. (Willey, 2014, p.90)

As the Gary and Sarah scenario illustrates, social learning will involve making a lot of mistakes, a lot of errors. Unless we can build 'good enough' models and apply the correct amount of certainty (precision) to the predictions they generate, we can quickly find ourselves in a world that appears incredibly complex, volatile and highly unpredictable. As a result, we will put on our unexpected uncertainty glasses and increase our learning rate, running down path 1 and likely building models based on a single event that overgeneralises (Claire laughed once when we told a joke, so *Claire always laughs at our jokes*). These will inevitably lead to more poor predictions and we fall into the uncertainty loop.

Let's look at an example of how quickly our social world becomes complex as the prediction space (the size of the space needed to take into account all possible predictions/models) grows, providing more space for prediction errors.

Let's imagine we have never met another person before. We, therefore, have just one social model, a model of ourselves; this is essentially then our model for *people*. When we then meet a new person, Dani (let's say at the park), we have just one model to call on, *people*, to predict Dani's behaviour. The prediction space is small, however, and just having one model to explain 'all people' will likely cause us to experience a prediction error, as Dani is not us, so unlikely to behave exactly like us. So, we use the current sensory input from Dani to build a new model, *people like Dani*. This also provides us with a second new model *people not like me*. Our prediction space for people has now grown; the next time we meet a new person we have three models to call on. That's three opportunities to make a better prediction as to how they will behave, but also more room to get it wrong.

We then meet another person at the park, Menita. The most accurate one of our three models to use, as Menita is not us or Dani, would be *people not like me*; this should result in the least uncertainty. However, due to the increased size of our prediction space, we also have two other models of *people like Dani* and *people like me* also to call on. If we turn up the precision on either of these too high we will find ourselves experiencing errors and we will start to reach for our unexpected uncertainty glasses whenever we encounter other people.

Let's imagine we manage to use the best fitting model, *people not like me*, and do not experience too many errors, but enough to adjust our learning rate to build another new model *people like Menita*. This, as with *people like Dani*, brings additional models almost by default: *people not like me, people not like Dani, people not like Menita, people not like Dani and me*. We might also start to build broader models too, as a result of meeting more than one other person: *people I know, people at the park*. There would be many more models we might start to build too, around physical features that Dani and Menita may have (*people with dark hair, people with no hair, people wearing glasses, people wearing hats*). To keep things simple (!), in this example we will just stick with the broad models of *people, people like Dani* and so on.

Despite keeping it artificially simple after meeting just two people in the park our prediction space has grown to include (at least) nine models: *people like me, people like Dani, people like Menita, people not like me, people not like Dani, people not like Menita, people not like Dani and me, people I know, people at the park*. So, while this gives us nine possible ways to reduce errors when predicting the behaviour of the next person we meet, Amy, it also gives us much more space to incorrectly predict her behaviours. What further increases the complexity, and, therefore, size of the prediction space, are the two variables (that make up our compromise calculation) that we need to adjust every time we meet with uncertainty, the precision we apply to our model (to keep it simple we will say our dial has three settings: low, medium or high) and the precision we apply to the current sensory input (low, medium, high) that is generating the error. Keeping things simple still means we have (at least) three ways to apply each of the nine models. When we meet Amy, we have to select from (at least) 27 possible ways to apply the best fitting model at the best precision to predict her behaviour as accurately as possible. This gives us 26 ways to fail to apply the best fitting one.

This simple example demonstrates how social uncertainty increases with the number of plausible predictions we can generate about another person. The more people in our social world, the more models we may then bring to our prediction space.

BEHAVING AS WE *SHOULD*

Now imagine Jordan again, this time walking into the lunch hall, a busy, uncertain space both in terms of sensory and structure anyway and looking out at around 200 other people. For each person across multiple lunch hall 'situations' (looking at, talking to, sitting next to, walking past, joking with), Jordan will need to use a model and set their precision dials to the correct setting. Their prediction space will be enormous, and there are thousands of opportunities for errors and uncertainty. Even if they have a pretty stable model of someone, Zak, another student in their class, any interaction is still going to cause uncertainties because they will never have a perfect model of Zak in this specific situation. Jordan can never be sure of Zak's intentions and motivational state 'in that moment'. This makes it hard to know precisely what Zak might do, and crucially it then makes it hard for Jordan to know what they should do to minimise uncertainty in their interaction. If Jordan cannot predict Zak's actions, they will not know how they should behave. *Should* in this instance is 'how Zak is expecting me to behave' (Theriault, Young & Barrett, 2020). If Jordan behaves in a way that violates Zak's expectations (not in line with Zak's idea of how they *should* behave) then he may well behave in an even more unpredictable way. This in turn makes Jordan's world much less certain as it makes it harder for Jordan to work out how they *should* behave and therefore less likely to do so. So begins an uncertainty tango (see below).

As a result of a need to behave in line with others' expectations, uncertainty about everything we *should* do in the social world, be it the clothes we *should* wear, the haircut we *should* have, the jokes we *should* make or the emotions we *should* choose to express, will be magnified when considering the diversity of the social attributes of people we might interact with throughout the day. We *should* behave differently with Zak from how we *should* behave with Mr Doherty. How do we behave as we *should* when there are at least as many different types of *should* as there are people in the world?

With the high stakes consequences of a social misstep, not acting as we *should* (such as making an 'inappropriate' comment) further intensifies the impact of the uncertainty we might feel. An error can be perceived as devastating and long lasting, and for some people this can lead to catastrophising about every stage of a social encounter (before, during and afterwards). The uncertainty about how other people might behave (and therefore how we should behave) before a social encounter, such as going to a party, leads to catastrophising about possible occurrences: 'Everyone will think I am weird.' The uncertainty around how to interpret social behaviour during the encounter can lead to catastrophising about the particularly ambiguous sensory input other humans provide: 'They do all think I am weird.' The uncertainty here is compounded by the fact that humans can deceive; the outward information we provide might not accurately represent what we are actually thinking ('Was that a real laugh or a fake laugh?', 'Are they really listening to me and therefore thinking about what I am saying or not really listening and thinking of something else?', 'If so, what might that be?'). This in turn leads to catastrophising about the consequences after the encounter: 'They are going to post mean things about me on social media.' Even the worry that we do not know how we *should* behave can lead us to worry that we are already sending signals that we *should* not be. For example, we might be wondering if the other person can see we are nervous (and so uncertain)? Can they recognise we are blushing? If so, will they now start to behave even more differently from what we might expect? And so begins the uncertainty tango...

The uncertainty tango

In the earlier example of us meeting Dani and Menita, one of the further complications that we did not introduce was that both Dani and Menita would also have been trying to predict what we might do. Unlike inanimate objects (like rain, chairs or trees) that are not trying to predict our behaviour, people are.

In order to make other people predictable, therefore, we *should* behave in a way that they are predicting. If we behave how they are expecting us to behave then we will be less likely to encounter a prediction error ourselves. The earlier example of Jordan and Zak introduced the idea of an uncertainty tango, the back and forth of uncertainty between two people. Below we will illustrate this idea further with Jordan and the ruler.

If Jordan needs to borrow a ruler and then looks at another student, Rosie (who has a ruler), and asks 'Can I borrow your ruler?', they are behaving as they *should*. Rosie's model would have predicted that someone who wanted to borrow a ruler would carry out those actions. As Rosie is also driven to minimise uncertainty she will act as she *should*, she will likely behave as Jordan's model predicts and hand them the ruler. Jordan and Rosie are in sync, they are creating a flow of certainty between one another by each behaving as they *should*. If, however, Jordan had an inaccurate model of how they *should* behave to get the ruler and they simply looked at Rosie and waved their hand, thinking this is how they *should* behave, it would be unlikely that Rosie would pass them the ruler. Rosie not passing the ruler means she would not be behaving as Jordan felt she *should*. Jordan would have an error as a result of their initial error (not behaving as the other student felt they *should* in order to borrow the ruler). The prediction error that we get in social situations is therefore known as a reciprocal error – reciprocal as there is a relationship between the other person's model about us (how we *should* behave) and the prediction error we get from them, and it likely signals to us that we have violated their model and not behaved as we *should* (Theriault, Young & Barrett, 2020).

An important point to note here is that a reciprocal error (essentially any error in a social situation) also provides us with a learning opportunity. While it does not exactly tell us how another person expects we *should* behave (and therefore helps us build a better model of the other person), **it does tell us how they do not expect us to behave**. If we are struggling to understand others, we might look to undertake behaviours that are more and more unpredictable. This allows us to receive more reciprocal errors and we can attempt, through a process of elimination, to work out how the other person thinks we *should* behave and, therefore, build a better model of them. However, as we noted right at the start of this chapter, it is very difficult to know in a social situation when we are receiving a 'signal' or just 'noise'. Jordan might ask to borrow the ruler (behave as they *should*) and Rosie does not pass it to them (not behave as she *should*). This does not necessarily imply that Jordan's sense of *should* is incorrect and they need to update their model (taking path 2). It may be 'noise' because, for example, Rosie may have just been so focused on her work that she simply did not hear Jordan!

Generally, the poorer the fit of our models of others and, therefore, our knowledge of how we *should* behave, the more likely we are to engage in behaviours that to them seem 'odd'. They will then reciprocate with behaviours that to us also seem 'odd' (not behaving as they *should*). We will be out of step, trying to dance together but listening to different tunes, each of us failing to accurately think through the mind of the other, akin to a double empathy problem (Heasman & Gillespie, 2018; Milton, 2012). We slip into the uncertainty tango. However, if each of us correctly models the other, we dance to the same music, we will be in sync, and connect. We can then better share our experiences and knowledge, and both build increasingly better fitting models.

Let's look now at how we build our social models, where it can go wrong and, therefore, where we might support our students who are struggling with social uncertainty.

Modelling me, modelling you

In order to build good models of others, all we need to do is know what they are thinking (!), know how they expect us to behave (how we *should* behave) and match this. Some key processes can help us to develop better models of others. The first is theory of mind (ToM). ToM is often described as the ability to infer the thoughts, desires and beliefs of another (Frith & Frith, 1999). There are many different ideas regarding ToM and how it comes about. Here we are going to look at it from the perspective of the PP story (see Chapter 1) and more broadly look to talk in terms of thinking through others' minds (TTOM; Veissière *et al.*, 2019). TTOM essentially enables us to more likely behave as we *should*.

According to PP, we use a prior model to help make a guess about other people. Our starting point for our model of *other people* is our model of *us*. Our body, and the interoceptive information it provides, gives us a set of embodied prior models (Allen & Tsakiris, 2019) for our model of *us* that we can then use as our prior model for *people*. This is why, in Chapter 4, we stressed the importance of interoception, as not only does it form the basis for our emotional world, but it also forms the foundation of our ability to understand others' emotional worlds and therefore the basis for social understanding. Essentially 'knowing the contents of another's mind can be demystified and simply recast as an optimal explanation for perceived (motor and visceral) behaviour in others – that would have been produced by ourselves, have we had been in the same intentional and emotional state' (Ondobaka, Kilner & Friston, 2017, p.66).

THEORY OF ~~MIND~~ BODY

Why is our model of our own body so important for understanding others? It is argued that theory of mind is more accurately described as being theory of body (Tsakiris, 2017). Trying to understand what is going on inside someone else's head, what they are feeling and therefore thinking ultimately comes down to understanding what is going on in their body, the interoceptive experience they are having. The trouble is, when we try to reduce uncertainty about what other people might be feeling (i.e. their internal bodily experience), there are fewer interoceptive cues that can be observed (through exteroception). The information we need is hidden. So, we must rely on our own prior models of bodily sensations, as the precision of the sensory input that other people give us is low. If we have a good understanding of the wide variety of our own emotional states (how they make us feel, what they look like and when we experience them and what situations might lead to them), it will make us better able to understand the multiple possible causes of the ambiguous sensory information other people give us about what is going on inside their body. For example, it can help us recognise that laughter does not necessarily mean someone is happy and enjoying themselves, it might also mean they are nervous.

If the model of ourselves, driven by our interoceptive awareness, is not as good as it can be, it will impact on all of the other social models we build from it (*the only cause of laughter is joy*). The relationship between our model of us and our model of others has also been identified as potentially providing a feedback loop between our interoceptive awareness and social uncertainty.

Once we have a good model of our internal state (good interoceptive awareness) we can find social life easier to manage. This may also then mean that when social life 'feels right', our understanding of ourselves will 'feel right' and this allows us to then make even better models of other people, leading to even better interoceptive awareness – a positive feedback loop. We then have a solid prior model about our internal information and so we tend to better manage any changes in this – essentially our emotions. This loop is known as the enhanced emotional discernment hypothesis (Arnold, Winkielman & Dobkins, 2019). It states that better understanding of bodily experience leads to better emotional understanding, which leads to a better understanding of others' emotions and therefore a richer social experience. This in turn provides more information to help build even better fitting models of the social world. This is where we want our students to be.

Good fitting models mean we can better manage the inevitable prediction errors that come from social interactions. We do not pay so much attention to the small details or a single occurrence (we keep our unexpected uncertainty glasses firmly in our back pocket), surfing confidently across the inevitably choppy waters of our social world. So, if our friend did not sit with us at lunch today, we are unlikely to run down path 1 and change our model of *our friend likes us*. We can recognise that this error likely occurred because of something outside us, independent of us, for example our friend may not have seen us because the lunch hall was busy, and they were distracted.

Interoception – why we look at Sensory in Social

Just as this interoception/social understanding feedback loop can be positive, it can also be negative. Once we start to experience uncertainty about our own body and the signals it is giving us, we can start to feel less certain about the signals being given to us from other bodies. This can explain why there is often a close link between social uncertainties and uncertainties around our own bodies, for example in eating disorders (Ainley & Tsakiris, 2013; Levinson & Rodebaugh, 2012; Meneguzzo *et al.*, 2020; Willem *et al.*, 2020).

Increased uncertainty and errors can then cause us to switch our attention away from our internal signals and overly focus on the external social signals (our cups shrink, see Chapter 4) to try to build a better fitting model based on this external information. We turn up the precision dial on this current external sensory input, upping our learning rate, turning down the precision on our prior models – we whip out our unexpected uncertainty glasses from that back pocket and hurriedly put them on. A growing body of research has explored this idea of social interaction difficulties being driven by us not setting our precision dial for our prior models, which would include that of our own body, to the place we should (Lawson, Rees & Friston, 2014; Palmer *et al.*, 2015; Pellicano & Burr, 2012; Quattrocki & Friston, 2014; Van de Cruys *et al.*, 2014).

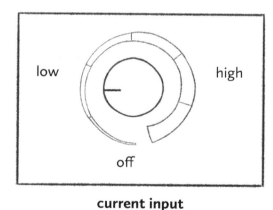

current input

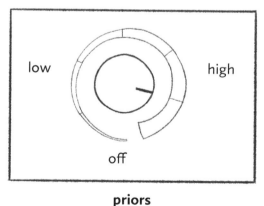

priors

As we discussed in Chapters 1 and 3, when we turn down the dial on our prior models we can end up overly focusing on sensory information that, alongside our small cups, can lead to a hypervigilance for social threat (Cacioppo & Hawkley, 2009). This may result in an overly negative bias when interpreting social situations. We see our friend not sitting next to us this lunchtime as being because **they do not like us**. We may over identify the prediction error (uncertainty), *they didn't sit* *with us*, as resulting from **us**; we must have been the cause. We struggle to think through our friend's mind (TTOM) and so look for certainty based on ourselves. We make ourselves the fixed, stable, certain cause of the problem. Although it may seem counterintuitive as it does not have a long-term positive impact on our wellbeing, making ourselves the centre of the problem brings, at the very least, some short-term certainty. It's all our fault.

What this means in practice is that, if we want to support our students who are experiencing social uncertainty, helping them to develop good interoceptive awareness will be key (see Chapter 4) to developing a good fitting prior model for others' bodies (and therefore minds) and can help us to more easily think through others' minds.

Learning the rules around *should*

If we want to make another person predictable, we need to behave in the way we predict they predict we will behave (behave as we *should*); we have to think through their mind. Developing a good internal model and therefore a good theory of body (mind) can help with this. However, we cannot predict every single person we ever encounter in the world, even if we have these great fitting models as a starting point. As our walking in the park example showed, the range of possible explanations for why people behave the way they do can mean our prediction space and the calculations required to accurately predict people's behaviour quickly reach levels beyond our capacity.

To make life easier we build broader, more general prior models that group people together. We then make quick judgements based on the person's physical features (such as their clothes, skin colour, hairstyle) which in turn might give us a clue as to their likely occupation and group membership, what broader model they might fit into. We use the prior models we have associated with those group membership judgements to then take a shortcut to what they might be like: kind, generous, rude. These board prior models are our stereotypes. They form strong predictions based on the external features of the person and where we encounter them (school, the shop, a religious setting). These help to make our compromise calculations easier when trying to resolve the uncertainty associated with another person and how we *should* behave. A stereotype 'prunes our prediction space, making others more predictable and making us less uncertain about how to act in their presence' (FeldmanHall & Shenhav, 2019, p.4).

We will also fall back on these stereotypes when uncertainty is particularly high, drawing more strongly on these prejudices.[1] It will make it much easier to

---

1   This explains how greater uncertainty, such as being faced with a threat, can systematically bias individuals, groups and whole societies towards strong yet inaccurate assumptions that resolve these uncertainties. This also explains why we love social rituals so much. They bring certainty – going to church, the football match, book club. The prediction space has been closed right down.

behave as we *should*. Learning the broader unwritten social rules of different places with different people can therefore help compensate for difficulties we might have in developing individual models due to difficulties discerning our own model.

Therefore, to support students who are struggling with social uncertainty, the second area (after interoceptive awareness) we can focus on is helping to understand the broader unwritten rules of social norms – trying to learn the rules. We can build some certainty in this area.

Finding our tribe

As we mentioned in the Introduction to the book, our teenage years are a time of increasing uncertainty, across all of our 3S's (the way the world works is being revealed as ever more complex – structure; our internal and external bodily state is changing – sensory; relationships are becoming more complex – social). This can help us understand why teenagers might be more prone to search for certainty within a stereotype, not only in making broad distinctions about others (*nerds*) but also desperately trying to find 'their tribe'. If a *skater* sees another *skater,* the prediction space they must manage in interacting with them is much, much smaller, so there is less room for uncertainty. Being in sync with another person makes predicting much easier; we are all hearing the same music and are all in step – no uncertainty tango.

Identifying other tribes, categorising people into them, helps us to understand how others *should* behave and, therefore, how we *should* behave with them. Equally, communicating clearly to others that we belong to a tribe with strong external identifiers (such as badges on our school bag showing what music we like) tells them how we *should* behave and therefore how they *should* behave with us. In clearly signalling to others how we are likely to behave (like the black and yellow stripes on a bumble bee), it potentially puts more of an imperative on them to behave as they *should* as it is in all of our interests to dance along in certainty. We have given a clear signal, we are a *skater*, so there should be a greater likelihood they should behave as we would expect them to, as we are showing clearly what they can expect from us.

What this draws attention to is the fact that, if we are unable to understand another person (because our interoceptive awareness is not as good as it could be), we will rely more on social norms and stereotypes. We will try to behave as others expect us to behave as this in turn will make others more predictable. If we have poorer models for both of these areas, so a poor model of me (and therefore models of others) and poor models of broader social norms, we may then look to actively make others more predictable. Rather than the passive, reactive way of making others predictable by behaving as we *should*, we can actively communicate to others that 'we are this type of person' or even more clearly 'this is the behaviour we are about to carry out'.

Communicating how we are going to behave serves the same function as behaving how we think others expect us to behave – it seeks to make our behaviour more predictable so as to make other people's behaviour more predictable.

Communicating, a need for control

Communicating our behaviour, removing the ambiguity around what we are thinking, in order to make ourselves more predictable to others, takes the opposite approach to the more passive 'behaving as others expect us to behave' to create social certainty. Communication, in all forms, is a more active way of guiding people's behaviour towards certainty. It can also be an easier way to reduce social uncertainty. Instead of having to understand how different people might predict us to behave in different situations (in order to know how best to match their prediction), communication involves guiding others to more accurately predict our behaviour, specifically by issuing unambiguous sensory signals.

We can do this in ways discussed above, displaying signifiers of our tribe: wearing certain clothes or listening to certain types of music. While this displays a clearer signal, it is nevertheless still a subtle form of communication; others might not know how people who listen to this music *should* behave. So if we want to make other people predictable by having them know what we are going to do, we need to have confidence that they will understand these subtle signifiers, using their theory of mind; however, this might be the area we are having a difficulty in.

We can guide people even more unambiguously to predict our behaviour (and therefore act more predictably themselves) by communicating our expectations much more clearly. We can use commands, order people to do things, 'boss' them around, make our expectations explicitly clear so as to make others more predict-able. This can help some students manage social uncertainty, especially in their younger years. However, the older we get the less likely our peers will respond to being bossed around. This might lead some students to have to resort to more and more explicit signalling of their behaviour (to increase the likelihood that others will then behave as they *should*). This might show in situations where students appear rude, aggressive, sexually 'inappropriate'. **What these behaviours are telling us is that they are communicating a need for control**. They are displaying increasingly extreme signals of how it is they are going to behave. In doing so, they also have closed down their prediction space. People's response to extreme examples of people not behaving as they *should* will create a huge amount of uncertainty for them. They are, therefore, going to display behaviours themselves that give them a strong sense of certainty. It may even make them withdraw from us (giving them certainty). For example, the response we get from someone when we punch them is going to be much more predictable than if we tell them a joke. These 'negative' extreme behaviours are driven by the same motivating factor as all of the other '*should-provoking*' behaviours – a need to create certainty. **They may seem like**

behaviours aimed to make people angry or sad, but it is not the sadness or the anger that the student wants to create in the other person, it is the certainty. These behaviours will cause such a high degree of uncertainty in others that it will likely result in a powerful certainty-seeking behaviour from them (withdrawing or rejecting us). It is just unfortunate that the behaviours that bring us the most social certainty are the negative ones, and the more extreme the negative behaviour, the greater the certainty they are likely to evoke.

So, as with all the 3S's, it is important when we see highly antisocial behaviours, we see them as just that, someone who is 'anti' social as it causes them too much uncertainty. Their behaviour will cause us uncertainty as the student is not behaving as they *should*, so we must take a step back and ask, '**Where's the uncertainty?**' Failing to do so means we are likely to seek inaccurate certainty by either normalising the behaviours – 'They are just a bad kid' – or immediately pathologising it – 'They have a disorder'. Either way, it then drives a wedge between us and the young person we work (or live) with, creating empathetic distance that makes it harder for us to provide support and even harder still to make a connection.

Building social certainty from the inside out and the outside in

As the introduction to this chapter has shown, the two underlying factors that will cause social uncertainty, and where we can provide support, are:

1 **Helping students to build good models of themselves (inside out).**

2 **Better understanding of the broader social rules of life (outside in),** understanding how we should behave, to make other people more predictable and reduce uncertainty.

Developing interoceptive awareness can take time and there are a lot of activities for this included in Chapter 4. Learning the social rules of the world and their worlds is something that, while not easy, we can teach more explicitly and may perhaps be more familiar to us. The positive feedback loop introduced above highlights the beneficial impact that this explicit teaching of social rules and expectations of how others might behave can, through helping to make their social world 'feel right', help to develop interoceptive awareness and a young person's model of themselves.

The remainder of this chapter works through ways we can build certainty in these two areas, particularly in helping to give more clarity to the structure of the social world and the hidden rules that underpin it. It begins by looking at behaviours that might indicate a search for social certainty and some ideas for providing it in the classroom or, for students who really struggle with the unpredictability of social communication, in smaller group work and more targeted support.

NEVAEH AND THE BENCH

Nevaeh came late to this school, at the start of Year 9. She'd had a difficult time at her last school and didn't really make any good friends (**social uncertainty**). Her parents hoped that this school would be easier as it was a bit smaller, though it was further from home.

She had been really excited about the change and was looking forward to the fresh start, but things hadn't gone too well. For a start, most of the girls in her year seemed much older than her, some wore makeup and did their hair in really complicated ways that took ages, but her mum said that her birthday was in the summer so maybe it was because of that.

Nevaeh's mum had always tried to help her with friendships, inviting other children to their home and giving her tips on how to act in a friendly and welcoming way when they came (**social certainty**). She knew that smiling was important, and that people liked it if you asked questions about them/their evening/their weekend (**social certainty**), but she couldn't work out how to move things on and conversations never really got going (**social uncertainty**).

Lessons were okay, she could do the work. Break times were hard, really hard. She didn't know where to go, what to do or what to say and so she just kept walking; round the playground, through the canteen, where she'd buy some chocolate (**sensory certainty**), past the sports pitches and through the library until the bell went and it was time for the next lesson where she could relax (**3S certainty**).

And then she found the bench by the science office. It started when she was waiting for a teacher to give her a lost textbook that had been found and she sat down for a bit; she felt good. It was warm because it was near a radiator (**sensory certainty**), it was also by a door to the playground so she could study the social groups as well as be near the adults (**social certainty**), and no matter what day of the week or time of day it was it was always free (**structural certainty**).

One Wednesday, a girl from another year came by. She was also waiting for a teacher, so she sat down on the bench too. The girls talked about the teacher as they waited. Nevaeh didn't need to worry about what her face or eyes were doing as they sat side by side and she liked having the chat with someone from a different year; she felt less 'judged' (**social certainty**). This became their place – sometimes a teacher or another student would stop and talk to them, sometimes one of them would bring something for them both to eat. They found they had some things in common and conversation seemed to flow (**social certainty**).

They are friends now and see each other at the weekends. Sometimes at break they meet in the library and use the computers or sit on the bean bags by the gerbils and sometimes they go out to the playground. But they usually meet at the bench first (**sensory**, **social** and **structural certainty**).

PRACTICE

I'm very impulsive and once I start I'm not finishing, I'll say stuff I don't mean. (Molly, Year 12)

THE SEARCH FOR SOCIAL CERTAINTY

What does it look like, what could it mean?

The chart in this section considers the 'Social' part of the 3S framework and works like this. Each line contains:

▶ a commonly observed behaviour which may indicate a search for social certainty

▶ the possible social cause of this behaviour, as the student seeks certainty

▶ a couple of ideas that might help a student with their social predicting – either by creating more social certainty around them or increasing their self-awareness and sense of agency.

You can use the 3S chart at the end to create your own record of behaviours that you observe, in terms of sensory, social and structure. These are included in each of the 3S chapters.

Not everyone who presents as 'socially different' needs an intervention. Some of the behaviours in the list below include things like 'dressing or acting in a very mature or immature way', which we include as we recognise that for some students, in some schools, their lack of awareness of 'typical' teenage behaviour can create barriers to a social life. However, in many school communities these types of differences are accepted as part of the natural variability of all humans and do not need to be changed or 'fixed'. We include the activities in this Social chapter to make sure that we are offering young people the choice (and the skills they need) to appear more predictable. This, plus some greater tolerance of social uncertainty, can be all you need to make a new friend or find a new tribe.

Sometimes we need to refer on. In some cases, students experience such extreme uncertainty that they are at risk of significant mental health difficulties. They may always be wearing their unexpected uncertainty learning glasses in social situations (see Chapter 1). It can take a long time to learn to take these off and use an expected uncertainty pair – building social models requires us to gather quite a lot of sensory input to start to notice social conventions, statistical regularities, to separate out the 'signal' from the 'noise'. A young person may be caught in the uncertainty loop and really benefit from structured, intensive and therapeutic one-to-one support in order to be able to move away from the certainty that withdrawal or other behaviour gives them. In this way, they can release some of their exaggerated need for control and experience different (more positive) social interactions and build better fitting models.

Many of the following behaviours also occur in similar sections of the book – 'The search for sensory certainty' and 'The search for structural certainty' – with a different analysis. Here we look at **social** certainty and uncertainty only, though in practice we always consider all three.

WHAT IT MIGHT LOOK LIKE	WHERE'S THE SOCIAL UNCERTAINTY?	IDEAS FOR CERTAINTY
Rarely contributing in class.	Uncertainty predicting social responses from peers/teacher, creating anxiety and withdrawal. *'I'm not certain I can interpret other people's responses correctly; I can't tolerate the uncertainty. If I don't contribute, I avoid this uncertainty.'*	**Offer written options for class feedback – on sticky notes/small group 'posters', use electronic feedback or token voting systems.** **Explain consequences of non-participation (what might a teacher think?) and negotiate small steps to participating, for example answering one prepared question a week/reading a prepared paragraph.**
'Constant' calling out in class, despite reminders.	Uncertainty predicting social responses from teacher, creating anxiety and desire for 'constant' feedback. *'Am I seen? Am I liked?'*	**Make social contact with student a priority, greet individually, remember facts/likes/dislikes/successes outside school and refer to them often.**

Demanding key roles in lessons/ projects/ performances/ family events.	Uncertainty predicting social responses in family or school community, creating greater desire for status, anxiety and need for wider feedback and acknowledgement. *'If I have an important role, I will have more status and feel more certain.'*	**Be very clear with positive feedback, give written version as back-up where appropriate. Assign roles supporting younger students/staff in favourite subject departments.**
Monopolising the conversation, talking over peers/teachers.	Uncertain of ability to follow rules for turn-taking, creating anxiety and need to control conversation. Uncertain of predicting social responses creating anxiety and need to control the conversation. *'Now I've got a turn to speak I need to keep this person here. Will they try and leave if I stop talking?'*	**In the moment: give feedback – for example, 'I'm interested, but when I get too much information, I feel overwhelmed and it's hard to have a conversation! Let's try again.'** **In a group: video 'free' conversation and use video feedback forms.**
Insistence on talking about favourite topics.	Uncertainty predicting suitable topics for conversation, searching for certainty in favourite topics. *'I don't know what to talk about. But I do know lots about...' 'It feels really good when I talk about...'*	**Give feedback – for example, 'I know you really like talking about..., but it's hard for me to take in that much information in one go. Maybe one or two facts at a time is enough. Then you could ask my (or someone else's) opinion?'** **Video 'free' conversation in a group and use video feedback forms. Encourage students in group to identify any 'information overload' from behaviour of others.**

cont.

WHAT IT MIGHT LOOK LIKE	WHERE'S THE SOCIAL UNCERTAINTY?	IDEAS FOR CERTAINTY
Talking to peers/acting as 'class clown' in lessons, despite reminders not to.	Uncertainty predicting social responses from staff and peers, creating anxiety and a desire for 'constant' feedback. *'Am I seen? Am I liked?'* *'If I'm seen and liked, I feel socially certain and I can focus.'*	**Be aware of the thoughts and feelings this provokes in you – avoid negative language as this may increase the anxiety and certainty seeking.** **Make social contact with student a priority, greet individually, remember facts/likes/dislikes/successes outside school and refer to them often. Ensure seating plan enables student to sit near socially certain peers.**
Rude/abrupt in discussions with teachers/family and other students.	Uncertainty predicting social responses from peers, creating anxiety and search for certainty. *'If they don't like me, it's because I've made them not like me. I have some certainty in this situation.'*	**Be aware of the thoughts and feelings this provokes in you. Avoid calling attention to rudeness in wider group.** **Use the thinking machine to analyse and look at positive and negative outcomes of this behaviour.**
Need to 'have the last word' and win arguments.	Uncertainty predicting social responses, creating anxiety, difficulties self-regulating, low self-esteem and desire for certainty. *'Being "right" is what's important in this conversation. Then I will feel certain of something.'*	**In the moment: be aware of the thoughts and feelings this provokes in you. Avoid calling attention to rudeness in wider group.** **Individually: use the thinking machine to analyse and look at both perspectives, as well as positive and negative consequences of this behaviour.**

Criticising peers in class or siblings in family.	Uncertainty predicting social responses from teachers, parents and peers, creating anxiety and search for predictability/ certainty. *'I can't tell what they think of me. If they don't like me, I'd prefer it to be because I've made them not like me. I have some certainty in this situation.'*	**Ensure student is seated next to familiar and accepting peers on a regular basis. Offer support to peers to manage negative behaviours.** **Individually: use the thinking machine to analyse positive and negative outcomes of this behaviour.**
Perfectionism and reluctance to admit mistakes/ defeat/not knowing something.	Uncertainty predicting social responses from teachers and peers creating anxiety and search for certainty in perfectionism and catastrophising. *'If I get everything right, I will feel certain of myself and my abilities.'* *'If I get one thing wrong, then everything in my existence will be wrong.'* *'I struggle with grey areas. I need to be right – or I'm wrong.'*	**Model tolerance of mistake making/winning/losing for all. Acknowledge difficult feelings. Be explicit on learning opportunity that comes from each.** **Look for opportunities to practise winning and losing – use the thinking machine to analyse thoughts and feelings.** **Individually: use 'What to do with worry' (Chapter 4) to raise awareness of thoughts and feelings.**

cont.

WHAT IT MIGHT LOOK LIKE	WHERE'S THE SOCIAL UNCERTAINTY?	IDEAS FOR CERTAINTY
Finds unstructured times/break time/weekends difficult, may seem more uncertain than during weekdays/ lessons. May regularly get into arguments at these times.	Uncertainty predicting social responses from peers, creating anxiety and search for certainty in different ways. May seem highly anxious or get into disagreements. *'I can't tolerate the uncertainty of unstructured times. I don't know what to do. I need certainty.'*	**Identify other students with similar difficulties and any jobs that need doing in the library/office/pastoral department/reception/art/ PE department (depending on students) and create informal teams.** **At home, create a loose structure to days, build in some certainty around free choice.** **Use the 'Thinking machine' to analyse any disagreements.** **Fade adult scaffolding once friendships appear established and encourage students to return to social spaces.**
Difficulties with inference.	Uncertainty predicting responses from social cues described in text, film or in real-life surroundings.	**Pause/freeze text, video or real life and ask 'What might happen next?' Analyse the clues we use to answer. Freeze mid-text/video and ask for feedback on emotions and intentions (based on face and body clues).**

Difficulties following plot of conversation/ film. May choose to avoid watching movies with groups/family, watch films for younger children or watch TV shows/films with unusually high repetition.	Uncertainty predicting responses from social cues (body language, facial expressions, tone of voice, etc.) and situational cues (props, settings, etc.). *'I can't follow like everyone else can and it makes me feel uncertain. If I don't watch/if I watch something else that I know well, I won't feel this uncertainty.'*	Discuss links between face, body and intentions day to day: 'The way you are sitting makes me think you're about to X' or 'When you have your head down like that I think Y.' Take random photos of group and analyse emotions and intentions based on body language and faces. Freeze video and ask group for feedback on emotions and intentions (based on face and body clues).
Use of unusually mature language, interests or dress sense if adversely affecting social relationships in school.	Uncertainty predicting social responses from peers, creating anxiety and the need for 'social formatting', copying those (in this case adults) around them for how to look and behave.	Individually: use the thinking machine to explain link between behaviour and social difficulties. Increase opportunities for social 'formatting' from slightly older young people. In school, offer peer mentoring or arrange skill-sharing to extend time spent together.
Use of unusually immature language/ interests/ dress sense if adversely affecting social relationships in school.	Uncertainty predicting teenage social behaviour, preference for the certainty of more structured (and familiar) social behaviour of early childhood.	Individually: use the thinking machine to explain link between behaviour and social difficulties. In a group: Finding my tribe activities.
Unusually messy hair/ clothes.	Unaware of social consequences.	Explain possible social consequences. Use the thinking machine to look at how other people might respond.

cont.

WHAT IT MIGHT LOOK LIKE	WHERE'S THE SOCIAL UNCERTAINTY?	IDEAS FOR CERTAINTY
Friendships that get described as 'obsessive'.	Uncertainty predicting social responses, creating anxiety and the intense 'study' of one person. Creates a socially predictable friend but does not develop other relationships.	**Use the social environment questionnaire to look for options to develop other friends in structured situations.** **Use the thinking machine to explain how intense friendship can feel from another's point of view.**
Gets on better with people significantly older/younger than them.	Uncertainty predicting social responses in peer group; feels less 'different' in the presence of adults and young children. Feels 'judged' in company of peer group.	**Look for new opportunities to develop social predictability in school, within and across year groups. Arrange clubs/skill development sessions in activities student enjoys (film-making, basketball, skateboarding, coding, cooking, singing, drumming, running, animation, etc.) to structure peer interactions.** **Assign roles supporting younger students in activities student enjoys.**
Openly criticises teenage rule-breaking. Does not attend social gatherings where rule-breaking may take place.	Uncertainty predicting social responses in peer group, prefers to stick to 'rules' established by adults for greater certainty. Experiences considerable uncertainty if others around them break these rules and may use this as justification for avoidance of parties/informal gatherings.	**In a group: Finding my tribe activity – extend to determine what kind of gathering each student might go to. Research reasons for adolescent rebellions.** **Use the thinking machine for exploring consequences of openly criticising peer behaviour.**

Difficulties with team sports (though may be 'sporty'), often has disagreements, especially during competitive games.	Uncertainty predicting required behaviour based on social cues and difficulties with other perspectives. May be misinterpreting the behaviour of peers. *'I can't tell what she/he is about to do and when the ball comes, it's a shock. Why are they angry with me?'* *'I didn't mean to foul them, why have I been given a foul?'*	**Individually: use the thinking machine to help understand other perspectives, especially for winning and losing.** **Suggest team sports with less emphasis on understanding social cues, for example running/ athletics/rowing/track cycling, or those that 'drill' whole-group participation: street dance, yoga, cheerleading, etc.**
Excessive use of social media 1.	Uncertainty predicting social responses from peers, creating anxiety and search for certainty by **studying online social behaviours of others.** *'By watching other people's reactions, I can learn about social behaviour and adapt my own.'*	**Be explicit about social responses in the environment. For example, 'I'm looking at his face now I've asked that question and it looks as if he is working hard to find the answer', or 'I knew as she came in that something good had happened – can you tell me why?'** **Watch carefully selected dramas appropriate for the group and analyse social behaviour.** **In a small group: video informal conversations, word games and role play and analyse social behaviour (see video feedback later in the chapter).**

cont.

WHAT IT MIGHT LOOK LIKE	WHERE'S THE SOCIAL UNCERTAINTY?	IDEAS FOR CERTAINTY
Excessive use of social media 2.	Uncertainty predicting social responses from peers, creating anxiety and search for certainty in a desire for **constant social feedback and approval**. *'If I get lots of "likes" I will feel certain and good. If no one likes my post or makes any comments, I will feel certain and bad, but at least I will feel certain that I am not liked.'*	**Look for new opportunities to develop social certainty, within and across year groups.** **Design lunch/after-school clubs around activities that student enjoys and encourage participation.** **Assign roles supporting younger students in activities the young person enjoys and is skilled in.** **Examples: film-making, trampolining, electronic music making, skateboarding, coding, cooking, singing, game development, drumming, running, comics, animation.** **Consider a peer mentor in school.**
Excessive use of social media 3.	Uncertainty predicting social responses from peers, creating anxiety and search for certainty through knowledge of any social exclusion. *'I can't tolerate the uncertainty – I need to know if I'm being left out of my social group. I'll feel bad but it's better than not knowing.'*	**Look for new opportunities to develop social certainty, within and across year groups.** **Design lunch/after-school clubs around activities that student enjoys and encourage participation.** **Assign roles supporting younger students in activities student enjoys.** **Consider a peer mentor in school.**

Excessive use of social gaming (where players communicate with each other).	Uncertainty predicting social responses from peers, yet strong desire for connection – creating a preference for social connections via gaming over real-life interactions. *'I want to make friends and connect with other people. I find it easier to do this online and it makes me feel good, so I want to do this all the time.'*	**Look for new opportunities to develop social certainty, within and across year groups.** **Design lunch/after-school clubs around activities that student enjoys, and encourage participation.** **Assign roles supporting younger students in activities student enjoys.** **Consider a peer mentor in school.**
Avoids social media completely.	Uncertainty predicting social responses from peers, creating anxiety and search for certainty through non-engagement. *'I can't tolerate the uncertainty I feel when I'm using social media, so instead of trying I'll just not get involved.'*	**Provide social media support in small groups. Encourage sharing of fears and ideas. (See 'What to do with worry' in Chapter 4 for a suggested format.)**
Inappropriate posts or comments online.	Uncertainty predicting social responses from others, creating desire for feedback and accompanying certainty, yet unaware of hidden social media rules or other perspectives. *'I want to feel "seen". I want to connect with other people. I feel invisible at school.'* *What's so bad about looking like this in front of strangers? I'll never meet most of them.'*	**Look for new opportunities to develop social certainty, within and across year groups.** **Design lunch/after-school clubs around any activities that student enjoys and encourage supported participation.** **Assign roles supporting younger students in activities student enjoys.** **In a group: use social media support activity.** **Consider a peer mentor in school.**

cont.

WHAT IT MIGHT LOOK LIKE	WHERE'S THE SOCIAL UNCERTAINTY?	IDEAS FOR CERTAINTY
Excessive non-social gaming (where players do not communicate with each other).	Uncertainty predicting social responses from peers, creating anxiety and search for certainty through non-engagement and withdrawal. Uses gaming as comfort behaviour. *'I feel anxious and isolated. When I'm gaming all this goes away. I want to do this all the time.'*	**Look for new opportunities to develop social certainty, within and across year groups.** **Design lunch/after-school clubs around activities that your student enjoys and encourage participation, for example gaming club, game design.** **Assign roles supporting younger students in activities your student enjoys.** **Consider a peer mentor in school.**
Avoidance of all non-essential social contact.	Extreme fatigue, interoceptive uncertainty, empty cups and out of their homeostasis state.	**Build in rest breaks throughout the day, at school and at home. Identify sensory activities that 'feed' and those that 'drain'. Help students understand which are which and support to self-monitor.**

Using the 3S framework to understand behaviour

The next page contains our 3S analysis sheet completed to look at the **social** aspects only of Jordan's behaviour at lunchtime only. This sheet repeats at the same point in the Structure and Sensory chapters, with a different analysis.

On the following page, there is a blank version for you to use to help you interpret your student's behaviour using a sensory, social and structural approach.

3S ANALYSIS

Name of student: Jordan   Year group: 10   Date: 10 Jan
Adult(s) completing checklist: Ms B, Mr H

WHAT'S THE BEHAVIOUR?	WHERE'S THE SENSORY, SOCIAL AND STRUCTURAL UNCERTAINTY?	IDEAS FOR CERTAINTY?
Avoids lunch — spends time in bathroom or sits at back of classroom. Talks about feeling ill.	Sensory: Social: Uncertain of who to sit with in the canteen. Fear of judgement. Structure:	Social: 1) Identify days when Jordan is able to navigate lunchtime. 2) Find out what works on these days and develop skills to build on this. 3) Identify a new lunch club with peer support — increase social connections. 4) Link with other students — consider a rolling peer support programme for lunchtime seating, if difficulty persists.
	Sensory: Social: Structure:	

cont.

WHAT'S THE BEHAVIOUR?	WHERE'S THE SENSORY, SOCIAL AND STRUCTURAL UNCERTAINTY?	IDEAS FOR CERTAINTY?
	Sensory: Social: Structure:	
	Sensory: Social: Structure:	

3S ANALYSIS

Name of student: Year group: Date:
Adult(s) completing checklist:

WHAT DOES IT LOOK LIKE?	WHERE'S THE SENSORY, SOCIAL AND STRUCTURAL UNCERTAINTY?	IDEAS FOR CERTAINTY?
	Sensory: Social: Structure:	
	Sensory: Social: Structure:	

cont.

WHAT'S THE BEHAVIOUR?	WHERE'S THE SENSORY, SOCIAL AND STRUCTURAL UNCERTAINTY?	IDEAS FOR CERTAINTY?
	Sensory: Social: Structure:	
	Sensory: Social: Structure:	
	Sensory: Social: Structure:	

THE SOCIAL ENVIRONMENT

This is a framework for understanding and recording how a young person's social environment might be affecting their ability to take part in school life, helping us to create opportunities for developing social predictability and certainty. When understanding social uncertainty, we need to always be mindful of the prior models we bring to the situation, our own bias and stereotypes. We need to try to think through our students' minds.

Why

Because we experience social certainty when we engage in behaviours that are socially predicted **within our environment**.

Why does this matter so much to educators? Because it's hard to feel good and learn if you are using up all your energy on social anxiety, so we look for ways of providing social certainty and reducing this. The framework is useful because it takes a broader view of where a student finds it hard to predict social behaviour, so recognising and understanding their uncertainty can help us to design better support.

How

→ **Think of a student** you feel is struggling with predictable social behaviour.

→ **Unpredictable behaviours** – record what these are. When and where do you observe them?

→ **Identify possible causes of uncertainty** in the tricky situations, either sensory, social or structural.

→ **Predictable behaviours** – notice times when socialising seems to go well.

→ **Involve others** – get as many other teachers, parents and other adults to fill in a form.

→ **Identify or create opportunities together** and help build social certainty.

THE SOCIAL ENVIRONMENT

Name of student: Alex   Year group: 9   Date: 3 Feb
Person completing form: Ms A, Mr G

UNEXPECTED BEHAVIOURS Record what these are. When and where do you observe them?

Spends break times alone, avoids classroom and wanders corridors (possibly hides in toilets). Prefers to talk to teachers, usually about pets or politics. Seems to almost push other students away in break times — makes 'unfriendly' face if spoken to and gives short answers. Other staff say he eats near students from same year group at lunch but does not speak to them, keeps head down and eats quickly.

CONSEQUENCES?

Seems unhappy at break times and more distracted at lessons straight after. Concerned about social relationships in school.

WHERE'S THE UNCERTAINTY? Sensory, Social and Structure

Might be finding it hard to process conversations at noisy unstructured times? Sometimes puts hands over ears if a video comes on at an accidentally high level in class. Uncertain of response from classmates? Uninterested in topics of conversation in peer group and unsure how to join in.

EXPECTED BEHAVIOURS Notice times when socialising seems to go well

Works okay in a small group. Seems happier in most lessons.

Music teacher says he seems very happy in rehearsals for school play (in orchestra) and talks to students from lower years, laughs and seems to enjoy socialising.

IDENTIFY OR CREATE OPPORTUNITIES FOR SOCIAL CERTAINTY

Possible ideas:

- Talk to music department about jobs that might need doing in lunch break and any other music students who might also like something structured at this time.

- Talk to music department about 'helper' role in any lunchtime or after-school clubs with younger students.

- Encourage Alex to join brass club.

- Investigate mentoring group for social confidence/peer mentor.

THE SOCIAL ENVIRONMENT

Name of student: Year group: Date:
Person completing form:

UNEXPECTED BEHAVIOURS Record what these are. When and where do you observe them?

CONSEQUENCES?

WHERE'S THE UNCERTAINTY? Sensory, Social and Structure

EXPECTED BEHAVIOURS Notice times when socialising seems to go well

IDENTIFY OR CREATE OPPORTUNITIES FOR SOCIAL CERTAINTY

THE ASSESSMENT CHECKLISTS

We begin with tick lists, which not only give us an idea of how we and our students feel about their social abilities but introduces them to the type of behaviours we might be thinking and talking about in future sessions.

We need some form of baseline. Social behaviours are hard to measure; we can isolate discrete skills such as eye pointing to signal someone else's turn to speak, use of gesture for emphasis, asking questions in class, but overall social competence (and confidence) is harder to quantify.

This checklist, based on *Talkabout for Teenagers* (Kelly & Sains, 2017), forms the basis of a qualitative baseline assessment. Qualitative because it reflects a level of awareness, rather than success or failure at a certain skill. For example, a student may tick 'always good' for sentence 5 – 'I use facial expression and body language to show I'm interested' – but after a term of video work this may get revised to 'sometimes good'. We look for change in either direction as a measure of success as it can signal a shift in attitude or behaviour.

Some terms may need explaining the first time: the concepts of **small talk** and the **social fake** may be new to students, but once they hear some examples they usually understand.

Small talk

Will: Did you see the new season of (insert current show here) is out?

Luke: Yeah, I know.

Will: Can't believe that beginning, did you see the bit when...

(...conversation about something they've both seen then takes place)

Q: Why did Will start that conversation?
A: To signal to Luke that he wants to spend time with him (this makes Luke have good thoughts about Will).

Q: Why did they talk about the show when they've both seen it? What was the point?
A: To signal to each other that they share a common interest (this makes Will and Luke have good thoughts about each other).

The social fake

Imagine you open a present from your auntie/uncle/friend and it's bad. It's something you would never use/wear but they are looking at you with a big smile and wide-open eyes, ready for you to say how much you like it. Do you:

1   Say nothing – you don't trust yourself – you just put it away and move on.

2   Say, 'Thanks but I don't really like it. Could you get me something else?'

3   Say, 'Thanks so much – that's really original!'

4   Say something else.

Hopefully you guessed that 3 is the social fake answer – done to keep people having good thoughts about us. Encourage your students to come up with others, too.

Students complete the first form, parents, carers and teachers the second.

Name: Class/group: Date:

COMMUNICATION CONFIDENCE	MOSTLY NO ☹	SOMETIMES 😐	MOSTLY YES ☺
1 I feel confident about the way I look			
2 I find it easy to choose the right clothes for the situation			
3 I can use 'small talk' at the start of a conversation			
4 I am good at looking at people when I'm talking to them			
5 I use facial expression and body language to show I'm interested when someone else is talking			
6 I feel confident joining in with other people's conversations			
7 I am good at doing the 'social fake'			
8 I am good at looking relaxed			
9 I am confident meeting new people my age			
10 I find it easy to make friends			

11	I am good at dealing with feelings and can stay calm if I need to			
12	I can ask for help and say if I haven't understood			
13	I have a few close friends I can talk to if I'm upset about something (in real life and/or online)			
14	I am good at handling disagreements with my friends			
15	I am good at handling disagreements with my family			
16	I find it easy to talk about how I feel			
17	I am confident speaking in class			
18	I am good at paying attention and not daydreaming			
19	I feel confident using social media (write down what you use most)			
20	I think there are lots of good things about being me			

Anything else you would like to say?

Name of student: Class/group: Date:
Parent/carer completing checklist:

COMMUNICATION CONFIDENCE	MOSTLY NO ☹	SOMETIMES 😐	MOSTLY YES ☺
1 They seem confident about the way they look			
2 They find it easy to choose the right clothes for the situation			
3 They can use 'small talk' at the start of a conversation			
4 They are good at looking at people when talking to them			
5 They use facial expression and body language to show they are interested when someone else is talking			
6 They are confident joining other people's conversations			
7 They are good at doing the 'social fake'			
8 They are good at looking relaxed			
9 They are confident meeting new people their age			
10 They find it easy to make friends			

11	They are good at dealing with feelings and can stay calm if needed			
12	They can ask for help and say if they haven't understood			
13	They have a few close friends they can talk to if upset about something (in real life and/or online)			
14	They are good at handling disagreements with friends			
15	They are good at handling disagreements with my family			
16	They find it easy to talk about how they feel			
17	They are confident speaking in class			
18	They are good at paying attention and not daydreaming			
19	They are confident using social media What do they seem to use most?			
20	They seem happy being them			

Notes:

BUILDING SOCIAL CERTAINTY

The following activities are designed to engage students in developing awareness of their own social behaviour, understanding the impact of social uncertainty and using this awareness to better understand what types of behaviour they can use to help others feel less uncertain. This, in turn, will make others more likely to behave in line with their predictions, ultimately leading to more certainty, connection and understanding for everyone.

This is not just about teaching 'social skills', nor is it about homogenising quirky individuals to better resemble their peers, but we believe more than anything that young people need to have a **choice** when it comes to fitting in. As Temple Grandin says on her website,[2] 'The focus should be teaching people...to adapt to the social world around them, while still retaining the essence of who they are.'

Recognising the neurodiversity within us all (and that we all create our own models) helps us understand that it is the disconnect between an individual and their environment that is the primary cause of any difficulties, rather than an 'impairment' in that individual. Social differences may be accounted for in the same way, and often our students become excellent social communicators when they find their tribe (see Gabby and the club below as an example of this).

We try to increase the social certainty in our students' lives by providing knowledge and opportunities for them to understand the complex social world around them. The aim of our work is also to increase **tolerance** of social uncertainty by developing greater self-awareness and sense of agency.

The following pages contain examples of the many activities we have developed over the years and we hope you will find some of them useful. Many will need adapting to make sure that you use examples and language relevant to your teens and your community. This is not an exhaustive list – we create new ways of working all the time – but we hope it gives you some ideas and a starting point for your own resources.

The support activities are divided into four sections:

Step 1: Understanding me

Step 2: Understanding other people

Step 3: Being predictable: reducing other people's uncertainty

Step 4: Social practice.

---

2   www.templegrandin.com

GABBY AND THE CLUB

Gabby wasn't making many social connections in school. She walked around with her head down, avoided eye contact and rarely initiated conversations (**social uncertainty**). If anyone asked her a question, she would answer it, factually and politely, and move on.

She was a good student, she loved art and would usually choose to draw during break times, rather than talking to anyone else (**social uncertainty**). She said she found the noisy classroom challenging (**social uncertainty**) but did not take up the offer of going to the library during these times, saying she liked being around the others (**social seeking**).

By using the 3S framework, and talking to her teachers and parents, we decided that at break times Gabby was probably experiencing uncertainty in all three areas:

- **sensory** – unpredictable noise and movement

- **social** – 'chit chat' that was hard to follow and participate in

- **structure** – unstructured break times.

Gabby was bringing in and working on her Japanese art, which was giving her great pleasure (and **3S certainty**). She connected with other artists online, but it was not helping her connect with any other students in school. Her desire to stay in the classroom at break, surrounded by the chatter, made us think that she had an unmet desire for social connection. So, we set up a lunchtime Manga Club. **We used the certainty of Manga as a bridge to the uncertainty of social interaction**. It was very popular.

From the very beginning, Gabby seemed to have more certainty. She came in with open and confident body language and eye contact, smiled, asked spontaneous questions, volunteered information about herself and now runs the club with another student from a different year group. They plan to visit exhibitions and one day want to go to Comic Con together.

Understanding me

This section contains activities to develop (social) self-awareness and certainty in our students.

Chapter 4 focused on **interoception** – the ability to interpret the feelings in our bodies as thoughts and emotions. It's only by doing this that we know what makes us feel good (or bad) and are able to make the choices in life that are right for us.

We also use this internal information when we think about people in the past or the future:

'Do I get a good feeling in my body when I'm with this person?'

'If I think about going out with them instead of revising, does it make me feel good or not?'

'Do I get a good feeling when I think about that afternoon?'

'Would I like to go out with them again?'

For 'live' communication in the present, a crucial skill our students need to develop is the ability to rapidly **switch their attention** between this 'inside' feeling (interoceptive information – how is this making me feel?) and the 'outside' feeling (exteroceptive information – what information is this person giving me?) in order to make judgements and form better predictions about others.

Without this ability, our students find it hard to predict so much of the social environment, how it makes them feel and their place within it. This chapter builds on the interoceptive work in Chapter 4 and hopefully helps build a little more social certainty.

Personality activities

In order to develop a stronger self-concept and the capacity to manage different social situations, it's important that all our students have a good sense of where their talents (and difficulties) lie. Lower interoceptive awareness means that they may not only find it difficult to work out what they (and others) are thinking or feeling, but also find it hard to understand what kind of person they are.

Our academic systems reward those with good word and number skills before they recognise the students who exhibit extreme bravery and persistence every morning by just getting up and facing the uncertainty (possibly across all 3S's) of coming into school. For someone who is also struggling academically, it may be particularly difficult for them, and us as educators or parents, to appreciate the importance (and usefulness) of the other skills they possess – skills which are often overlooked in an academic environment.

The following pages contain cards for you to download or copy, print out and cut up. Each of these cards contains an attribute, a personality label, which someone may or may not feel they possess. There is a matching set of cards which contains definitions. These activities are based on those found in Victoria Honeybourne's excellent book *A Practical Guide to Happiness in Children and Teens on the Autism Spectrum* – which has lots more good ideas for self-awareness and wellbeing.

In addition to these activities, we sometimes find it useful with older teens to carry out online personality-type questionnaires. There are many different options available, and you will need to look and see which you think your students will find most accessible. Encourage the students to select the first answer that comes into their head as we find they often get 'bogged down' with giving a general answer that captures them most of the time. This in itself can be a teaching opportunity.

Students often really enjoy completing these questionnaires – if you can do it as a group it can spark some interesting conversations about individual difference, even before the scores arrive. The website https://psychology-tools.com has several free, online personality tests, which students often find interesting.

PERSONALITY PAIRS

This activity uses the cards on the following pages and is a good introduction to the topic of personality types. It also develops character vocabulary and could be run in a literature class as much as in a mentoring session, a speech and language therapy group, or as part of a PSHE curriculum.

Why

Many of our students find 'character' as a concept difficult to relate to. Difficulties with interoception and theory of mind make it hard to get a certain sense of what 'type' of person someone might be. We need this information when we are trying to work out who in our social space might be a good fit as a friend; we need it for social certainty.

How

→ **Download and print or photocopy the cards** that follow and cut them up.

→ **Either select a few descriptors or put them all down on the table** (face up).

→ **Students take a description from the pile of definition cards** and try to match it to the corresponding personality descriptor.

→ **If a student struggles to make a match, offer a choice of three personality descriptors**, either closely or distantly related, according to your knowledge of the student.

Extensions

→ Once a match is made, each person draws an emoji/cartoon/stick person that describes this personality type to them.

→ If using in a literature lesson, you can ask the students to choose which they could apply to certain characters or hold up an attribute and ask them to decide which characters it might describe.

→ You can further extend this activity by asking students to describe a time when someone around them displayed this personality attribute.

   • 'I think my friend is **reliable** because once he waited for me after school, even though I was late out.'

   • 'Mr G is really **fair**. He gives us all the same amount of attention and doesn't just listen to the really smart kids.'

   • 'My dog is always **enthusiastic**.'

→ Doing this in drama? Give out the attribute labels and ask students to act theirs out. Keep a list on the board to remind everyone of the options as they guess.

→ Doing this as a small-group warm-up? Give descriptors to one group and corresponding definitions to another and see how quickly they can find their match.

Personality descriptors

Brave	Creative	Curious	Emotionally intelligent
Enthusiastic	Fair	Flexible	Forgiving
Funny/humorous	Generous	Grateful	Honest
Independent	Individual	Kind	A leader
Modest	Objective	Organised	Patient
Reliable	Resilient	Responsible	Self-controlled
Sociable	Spiritual	A team player	

Definitions

Being able to do things you find difficult or scary	Being original and good at finding new ways of doing things	Interested in new ideas and asking questions	Being aware of and dealing with your emotions
Doing things with energy and passion	Giving everybody an equal chance, regardless of what you think	Being open to trying things another way	Understanding when other people make mistakes and giving them a second chance
Finding life amusing and making others laugh	Sharing your time or your things with other people	Appreciating what's good in your life	Telling the truth
Being happy to do things by yourself	Being happy to stand out in a crowd	Doing good things for other people and looking out for them	Being happy in a leadership role
Not showing off when good things happen	Being able to see things from other people's points of view	Being ready for what comes next	Being able to wait for things to happen
Doing what you say you will do, when you say you'll do it	Learning from mistakes and keeping on trying even when it's hard	Being trustworthy – knowing what is right and wrong	Being able to control your thoughts and feelings when you need to
Enjoying being with other people in social situations	Believing in a higher power, maybe a religion	Being able to work well in a group	

Building a predictable relationship

Sometimes, when we are working with a student who struggles with uncertainty in school, we discuss with them which lessons are easier and which are harder to manage and how different classrooms and teachers affect their learning. When we ask which are the 'best' teachers for that student we often find that it's not the creative, risk-taking and innovative teachers that get mentioned (although they do too) but the teachers that have been in the school for a while and are more (you guessed it) predictable.

Our students don't just struggle with uncertainty across the 3S's in school. It's easy to forget that some have very uncertain housing situations and are often on the move, some have just arrived from uncertain countries, some live in very unpredictable families and some don't even know if there will be an adult at home that night.

One of the problems is that our students don't always seem uncertain and the search for certainty can look like all kinds of more deliberate and difficult behaviour. However, we need to overlook the feelings these behaviours provoke in us and **act certain** if we are to engage and support these young people. We need to be a port of certainty in a storm of uncertainty. This means being predictable and consistent with our teaching structures (see Chapter 3 on Structure) but also with our own social behaviour.

Many of our students describe coping better in classes where they '**feel seen**', where they get a sense of connection (social certainty) from a teacher. Often this is established with a simple bit of specific praise early on in their teacher–student relationship or they have something in common: they might support the same football team, have family in the same country or both play the drums (these allow the student to draw on broader social 'norms' for a group that can be used to reduce uncertainty about a specific member of that group). This doesn't take extra staff or special groups – once we know who our more uncertain students are, we can use some specific strategies:

▶ Regularly greet them with a smile and by name as they enter the classroom.

▶ Be very clear: avoid using idioms and casual sarcasm and leave less room for ambiguity in our vocabulary, body language and tone of voice unless we are absolutely sure the student understands what we mean.

▶ Use clear, simple, written comments and sticky notes to increase certainty about what was meant when giving feedback; anxiety often means that positive verbal comments are seen as ambiguous or are even interpreted negatively.

▶ Remember something good that they did in class a while ago, and mention it.

▶ Remember that they are really good at something outside school, and ask about it.

▶ Remember that they were doing something special and ask how it went.

▶ Use the information we have about their interests (see Chapter 2), and bring it into teaching examples.

I AM...

Building social certainty through better self-understanding.

Why

With support we can help students develop a more certain awareness of self, which in turn helps develop a growth mindset and fosters greater self-compassion. Making friends requires us to hold ourselves in good esteem, and positive affirmations are well proven to have a positive effect on mental wellbeing. This activity creates a nice, permanent, visual reminder of 'what's good about me' for the student to refer to outside the session.

How

→ **Give each student a piece of A4 paper and ask them to write 'I am...' at the top,** or download the worksheet on the next page.

→ **Ask them to draw an outline of themselves in the middle.**

→ **Get creative.** Show examples of bubble writing/modern calligraphy to encourage creative lettering and look up different types of stick person/body outline to fire the imagination.

→ **Provide the list of personality labels** on a screen or on paper. Ask the students to copy down the attributes they **currently** possess around their outline.

→ Then ask them to turn their paper over and write down the words they don't think describe them **at the moment.**

→ **Emphasise to students how some elements of our personality change over time.** Maybe share a story about how you became more (or less!) organised, flexible or objective as you moved from adolescence to adulthood.

→ **Encourage students to date the sheet and keep it** – perhaps inside a locker or on their bedroom wall as a reminder of all their positive attributes.

I am ...

ME AND NOT ME (YET)

Students learn to use their areas of strength to help with the challenges they face.

Why

In order to develop good self-awareness and self-compassion, we need to know what our strengths are, and low interoceptive awareness can make it difficult to do this. Once we know, we can also use the information to develop our own strategies for when we experience uncertainty. By carrying out these activities in groups, students can develop their ability to think through other minds – learning that a) other people think differently from them and b) **everyone** has challenges.

How

→ **Put all the attributes cards up on a screen or on a table and explain that you are each going to pick out three to describe your strengths.**

→ **Model how to do this** and share your top three strengths.

→ **Ask each student to do the same.** Record all strengths.

→ **Repeat, this time asking the students to identify three things which they feel they struggle with,** modelling as before.

→ **Now get each student to write down one of the attributes they currently struggle with in the middle of a piece of paper and then write their positive attributes around it.** See if they can find a way to use what they are good at to help what they find difficult. Use sticky notes for extra interest and colour, or encourage drawing of weird and wonderful shapes to hold the words.

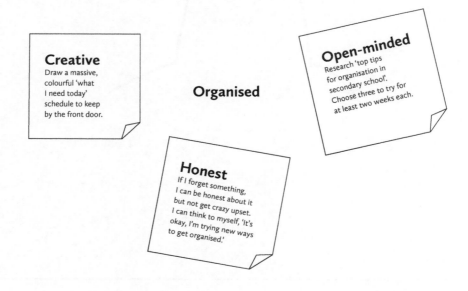

Creative
Draw a massive, colourful 'what I need today' schedule to keep by the front door.

Organised

Open-minded
Research 'top tips for organisation in secondary school'. Choose three to try for at least two weeks each.

Honest
If I forget something, I can be honest about it but not get crazy upset. I can think to myself, 'It's okay, I'm trying new ways to get organised.'

WOULD YOU RATHER...?

A game which opens up conversations about attitudes to sensory needs, socialising, popularity, image, friendship, the future, love, wealth, happiness and work, as well as exploring some of the implicit social rules we live by.

Why

Social uncertainty can cause our students to be uncertain of their own likes, dislikes and beliefs, and lots of social communication involves sharing our opinions:

'oh, I hate it when that happens...'

'I've never liked...'

'Wouldn't it be good if...'

This type of structured activity can help young people learn to access their own thoughts and beliefs as well as practise expressing them, building a better model of themselves. In addition, understanding that other people have different thoughts and beliefs to us can help develop greater certainty through the ability to build models that generate better predictions about what these could be. It's also a nice structure to use when practising specific skills (e.g. for video sessions).

How

→ **Photocopy or download the 'Would you rather...?' cards**. Go through them and remove any that you feel are not relevant to your group or community. Add some of your own.

→ **Place a number of cards face down on the table** or, if using with a whole class, put them in a hat/box/bowl/envelope. Students take it in turns to select a card at random and answer. Encourage students to explain their answers, maybe asking for two or three points.

→ **Encourage other members of the group to speak up if they feel differently**. Negotiate how you get a chance to speak – will this be formal (hand up?), informal (call out and try and get a turn?) or very structured (having to signal non-verbally that you want a 'talking stick' and have it passed to you before you can speak?)?

→ **If you are using this in a debate session, select students to argue two different sides** regardless of whether they agree. There are many websites devoted to these kinds of topics[3] but we have also had great success with asking students to write their own questions, once they are used to the format.

---

3   https://improb.com is a good place to look

Would you rather watch TV or listen to music?	Would you rather own a rat or a snake?	Would you rather live in Narnia or go to school at Hogwarts?
Would you rather go without TV or without junk food for the rest of your life?	Would you rather only be able to whisper or only be able to shout for a day?	Would you rather go without your phone for a week or not be able to speak for a week?
Would you rather be hairy all over or completely bald?	Would you rather be the most popular person or the smartest person you know?	Would you rather live in an amusement park or a zoo?
Would you rather have an unlimited number of crisps or sweets?	Would you rather always be cold or always be hot?	Would you rather only eat sweet or savoury food for the rest of your life?
Would you rather see the future or change the past?	Would you rather be three inches taller or three inches shorter?	Would you rather not be allowed to wash your hands for a month or wash your hair for a month?
Would you rather have unlimited respect or unlimited power?	Would you rather have a rewind or pause button you could use at any time?	Would you rather not be able to see colours or taste?
Would you rather find your dream job or your true love?	Would you rather lose all of your teeth or all of your hair?	Would you rather have a permanent splinter under your big toenail, or have a permanent bad haircut?
Would you rather be able to breathe underwater or fly?	Would you rather know every language or know how to talk to animals?	Would you rather be able to see your own future or be able to see everyone's future but your own?
Would you rather partner with someone whom you don't love or with someone who doesn't love you?	Would you rather always have really slow internet or a really old phone?	Would you rather always stink and not know it or always smell something that stinks that no one else smells?

Would you rather lick your best friend's foot or let a stranger lick your foot?	Would you rather receive £5000 every week for the rest of your life, or you and your best friend receive £1000 every week for the rest of your life?	Would you rather get a paper cut between your fingers every time you turn a page or bite your tongue every time you eat food?
Would you rather wear what makes you feel comfortable or wear the best outfit in the room?	Would you rather wake up in the morning as a dog or as a cat?	Would you rather travel in time and meet your great-great-great grandparents or your great-great-great grandchildren?
Would you rather never be able to feel any emotion or never be able to show any emotion?	Would you rather be able to take back anything you say or hear any conversation that is about you?	Would you rather always be able to tell when someone is lying or be able to lie without anyone knowing?
Would you rather be part of a big family or a small family?	Would you rather lick and seal 1000 envelopes or fold 1000 pieces of laundry?	Would you rather always be one hour early or always be ten minutes' late?
Would you rather be able to taste colours or see smells?	Would you rather buy all your underwear used or buy all your toothbrushes used?	Would you rather go on a cruise with everyone from your class or go to the beach alone?
Would you rather your skin could change colour like a mood ring or change colour like a chameleon?	Would you rather know now who you will partner with, or know how many kids you will have?	Would you rather be invisible to people of the opposite gender or be invisible to people of the same gender?
Would you rather always cook or always wash up?	Would you rather look young and feel old or look old and feel young?	Would you rather stay in a room that's really brightly lit for a whole week or stay in a room that's kept almost completely dark?

Understanding other people

Thinking through other people's minds

Difficulties with building a model of ourselves and then of others can have a real impact on our ability to 'read' other people and social situations. Having established a foundation of greater self-awareness through the activities in Chapter 3 and the 'Understanding me' section above, we now suggest some ideas to help our students understand more about the behaviour of people around them.

This is primarily for social reasons, but these skills go further than helping someone join a new group. Robyn Steward (2013, p.22), in her important book *The Independent Woman's Handbook for Super Safe Living on the Autistic Spectrum*, is clear about the need for this kind of work:

> Not being able to read and understand body language or missing information conveyed via body language can cause difficulties from a safety perspective because some of the danger signs about a person might be conveyed in body language.

Greater social certainty increases our chances of making informed decisions about the intentions of those around us and we need to make sure that all our school-leavers (whatever their gender) have as much opportunity to develop their ability to 'think through others' minds' as possible.

The next few pages contain a mixture of creative activities, games and debates to help explore some of these issues with your students.

MANNEQUIN CHALLENGE

A creative activity to explore the connection between how people look and the thoughts we might have about them as a result.

Why

Understanding the image we project is important, if we are to become socially certain. Everything we wear, how we wear it, our hairstyle, the presence or absence of make-up, the bag we carry, the bike we ride communicates something about us, and it's important to practise de-coding the images of people around us too.

This activity considers how other people look and the assumptions we make, rather than focusing on the individuals in the group. In this way, we can study the links behind what people wear and the image they project as a concept, without encouraging direct comment. If your students are comfortable with giving and receiving supportive feedback, you may like to try making it personal to members of the group, but it's not necessary to do this.

How

→ **Download or photocopy a mannequin figure** for each student and the group leader.

→ **Students use colour pens or pencils** to 'dress' a figure in any way they like.

→ While they are doing this, **encourage them to think about the person they are dressing.** What kind of personality might they have? What do they like doing outside school? Would you want to be their friend? (Make sure these questions are written down and visible throughout the activity.)

→ **Ask students to make brief notes on their character**, on a separate piece of paper.

→ **You can create word banks** for spare time activities and personality types or use the personality descriptor cards earlier in this chapter.

→ Student A presents their image, talking through the person's appearance only, and all the other students write notes on what kind of person they think they are, using answers to the questions above.

→ **Everyone shares their answers.** Discuss how we made these assumptions (what specifically made you think that?) and share the similarities and differences.

→ **Repeat** with Student B presenting their image, and so on.

MANNEQUIN CHALLENGE

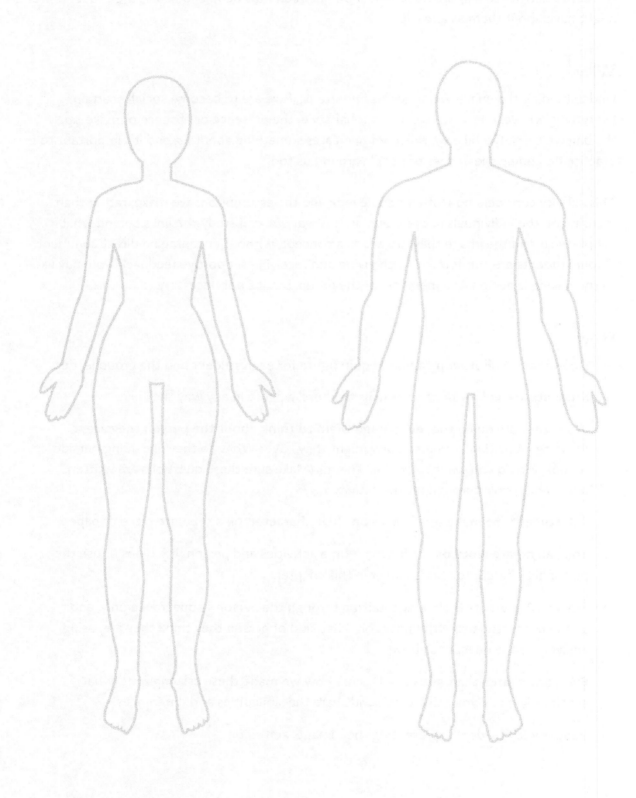

FINDING MY TRIBE

Another simple activity, looking at how we make predictions about people, based on the way they look. What are some of the broader social stereotypes that people use to close down the predictive space around understanding others?

Why

It can be useful to consider the mismatch between the communication style of an individual and their social environment as the cause of any uncertainty, rather than a lack of skill. If we can help students understand this and help them 'find their tribe', we are hopefully increasing their sense of agency, as well as teaching a useful life skill when trying to find new people to talk to or make friends with.

> I don't really get on with the other girls in my year. At home, I'm still friends with some of the boys from my primary school. We game together online and sometimes meet up. (Natalie, Year 7)

How

→ **Choose photographs of different young people** from the internet who represent as many different 'types' or 'tropes' as you can think of. Look for obvious differences in teens and pre-teens who look: sporty, fashion conscious, not bothered about fashion, heavily made up, natural, goths, dancers, city and country dwellers, clubbers, skaters, have loads of piercings, heavily tattooed, and so on.

→ **Save the photos** as a PowerPoint or insert them into one of the 'Finding my tribe' sheets and print off for each student.

→ **Choose one picture** and, using the 'Finding my tribe' sheets, ask the students to fill in the answers to the questions, independently or in pairs. Provide personality word banks.

→ **Share the social predictions** you've made, one by one – notice the similarities as well as the differences in the predictions we make based on what someone wears, as well as their body language and facial expression in the photo.

→ **Draw attention to the different ways** that we interpret each other's choices and how people will make assumptions about us, even if we think we aren't doing anything remarkable. This is social predicting and it's what we all do.

→ **Talk about options for finding new friends.** Where are we likely to find people with whom we have things in common?

Extension

→ Spread all the photos out on the floor/screen and ask students to put them into imaginary friendship groups or pairs, based on the social predictions they've made, and explain why.

FINDING MY TRIBE

LOOK AT THE PHOTOGRAPH AND ANSWER THE FOLLOWING QUESTIONS	
What kind of personality do you think this person has?	
What makes you think that?	
Do you think you would be friends?	
If so, why and what might you like to do together?	
If not, why not?	

SOCIAL INFERENCE

An activity that practises interpreting non-verbal communication.

Why

Lots of people find it hard to interpret facial expression and body language, which are often ambiguous clues as to what a person is really thinking. This can create social uncertainty. By increasing awareness of some of the common non-verbal behaviours people use to communicate, we can increase social certainty.

How

→ **Find a video clip** that your students will find engaging but not necessarily know in detail. Movies and online streaming series about people their age can be a good place to start but **you need to have watched the clip carefully to make sure it's appropriate**.

→ **Watch it twice with no sound.** First time around, encourage students to write down what they think is the theme of that scene – where are they? What is going on? (This is good practice for students who struggle with central coherence.) Second time around, you can ask them to answer specific questions – 'Is Joey feeling happy or sad?' 'Why?'

→ **Ask students to share their answers**.

→ **Watch it once with the sound on** and give lots of positive feedback to students who guessed correctly, pointing out how different facial expressions or body language were the key to understanding the plot.

UK series such as *Waterloo Road* and *Ackley Bridge* have been good sources of British teen behaviour and older US TV shows like *Friends* or *The Fresh Prince of Bel Air* have been really useful with younger students due to the slightly less subtle communication style. *The A Word* and the US show *Atypical* have also been popular with our groups and can be a good way to talk about neurodiversity.

SOCIAL FILTERS

A sorting activity, to help introduce the concept of 'thinking through others' minds' and filtering what we say. It is useful when a group of students are having friendship difficulties.

Why

Some of the disagreements that arise between students can occur due to uncertainties with what other people are thinking and therefore how they are going to behave – thinking through others' minds. Our more impulsive students may have this understanding but find it difficult to put it into practice. This activity raises awareness of social consequences, and it can also provide the vocabulary to help us prompt ourselves and others to behave in a way that takes the thoughts and feelings of other people into account to bring greater certainty for everyone.

There are no fixed answers for this type of activity as the group will decide, for their community, what is acceptable and what is not. What's important is that students understand that what they say has implications for other people (and therefore, them too) and that what may be factually true is not always appropriate to say.

How

→ **Begin by talking about the general concept of a filter:** what examples can they think of and what is a filter for? Avoid any discussions about how they filter out the 'bad' stuff, as we are focusing on how they separate different types of substances.

→ **Give each student a sentence.** You can use the examples below or write your own, though this works much better if you use phrases you have heard your students actually use around school.

→ **If you like, you can set up two boxes at the front of the room.** One has THINK ONLY written on it and one has THINK AND SAY. If you don't have time, just mark two piles. You can draw pictures to make this very clear.

→ **Ask each student to come up and read out their sentence.** They then say if they think it's something they would 'think only' or 'think and say'.

→ **Encourage students to give their opinion** and as a group decide which box (or pile) it goes in. If you like, you can choose to focus on what we say when we are talking to 'people I don't know well' or 'people I know well' as this will change the outcome.

→ **How might someone feel if we didn't use our filter** on each 'think only' phrase? Choose from: good, okay, annoyed, upset, angry.

Extension

→ Ask students to write their own sentences on sticky notes. Once the group has decided, stick it on the board under one of the two headings.

→ Once this game has been played, the vocabulary 'Remember to use your filter' can be a useful one, for students and staff alike.

Social filter phrases

You always finish your work so quickly!	Didn't you wear that all last week?
Is that a new coat?	Your bag's a weird colour.
That drawing is really good.	She's late.
You've cut your hair.	That's a really low mark.
That looks good.	I got the best mark in the class!
How do you do that?	Why do you have to ask all the time?
You're always so organised.	The teacher has already answered that.
It always looks so easy for you.	I can't believe you're still into that.
That's a really stupid question.	Where did you get that jumper?
I guess I'm better than you at maths.	Those trainers are interesting.
Gold doesn't suit you.	Brown eyes are the worst colour.
Your handwriting's really messy. I don't know how anyone reads it.	You still have a home button on your phone?

THE THINKING MACHINE

This activity was named by one of our students. We use it often to help review 'what went wrong' in tricky situations and to help young people become **more reliable social predictors**.

Why

Many of the students we work with find it difficult to see things from another person's point of view, particularly when they are feeling at their most stressed or uncertain. An accidental shove, an ambiguous comment or a confusing tone of voice can be interpreted as something more deliberate and can have dramatic consequences.

Students are often referred to pastoral or behavioural teams when they are regularly involved in misunderstandings and arguments, or where someone feels they might not be understanding what's going on socially. We can use these calmer moments (we need to make sure everyone **is** calm before we start) as opportunities to unpick what might have happened from more than one perspective. We have to make sure this is in no way framed as a punishment. We can instead put it within the context of self-compassion. **If something went wrong, it went wrong because we are human, and all humans make mistakes**.

How

→ **Write the names or initials of the people** involved in the spaces at the top of the sheet.

→ **Support your student to describe what happened** in objective, factual terms. Break it down into steps, and using the format on the sheet. Put anything that was said or done in the middle box using the student's own words.

→ **Write the short- and long-term consequences** in the final box. It will be easiest if you draw the machine yourself digitally, on a whiteboard or on a large piece of paper so you have the right number of spaces.

→ **Go back to the first step** and help your student work out what **they** were thinking. Fill in the box in their own words.

→ **Ask the student to imagine what the other person might have been thinking** and write this in the think bubble. Continue down the sheet.

→ If your student is finding this difficult, you have two choices: **offer a number of suggestions** or **involve the other person** in the activity. Both can be powerful and have their place. Either way, the point is to get the student to understand that there might be lots of options for what the other person was thinking – and not necessarily what they had assumed. You can write a variety of thoughts in the other person's bubble, if needed.

→ **Review the narrative**, reading both sets of thoughts as you go. Make sure the student is happy with the wording. This may be enough to help them understand that other people have different thoughts and interpretations of the same event. If not, draw their attention to it.

→ **Decide with the student what to do with the thinking machine drawing**. You can keep it for future reference, throw it away or shred it.

→ **Create a second thinking machine**, this time to help your student work out a different (happier) sequence of events and what the new consequences might have been (see example).

Extensions

→ Let the student draw their own machine – they can do this digitally or get creative with shapes on a large piece of paper.

→ Draw comic strip figures in the central boxes to support the writing.

THE THINKING MACHINE

Dani   Eva

In English

Dani's thoughts:
- This is fun. I like Eva. She makes me laugh.
- I'm laughing but that's not funny anymore.
- I'm so angry. She has to pay for that.
- I feel better that I've told her.

In English (centre):
- We were messing about in the back row, being rude about each other's families — for a joke.
- At the end of the session, Eva said something about my brother, like 'Yeah, but he's PROPERLY stupid', or something like that.
- I went into the classroom and emptied her bag onto the floor. Everyone looked at me.
- I ran at her shouting and tried to hit her. Sienna got in the way and stopped me.

Eva's thoughts:
- This is fun. Dani thinks I'm funny. It's all good.
- We're still joking. It's funny.
- Why is she doing that? What have I done?
- I'm scared and I don't know what's happened to Dani.

Consequences...

We both got in trouble. Eva's not speaking to me. I feel confused about what happened. I still want to be her friend but I think I've ruined it.

THE THINKING MACHINE

Dani _____   Eva _____

_____ In English _____

We were messing about in the back row, being rude about each other's families — for a joke.

This is fun. I like Eva. She makes me laugh.

This is fun. Dani thinks I'm funny. It's all good.

At the end of the session, Eva said something about my brother, like 'Yeah, but he's PROPERLY stupid', or something like that.

I'm laughing but I have a weird feeling inside me.

We're still joking. It's funny.

I could have said, 'oh leave him alone, he's alright.'

I'm upset. I need to tell her how I feel.

I feel bad I made that joke.

We would have gone to lunch as usual.

I feel better that I've told her.

I'm glad she told me. It could have been awkward.

Consequences...

We stay friends. It's easy.

THE THINKING MACHINE

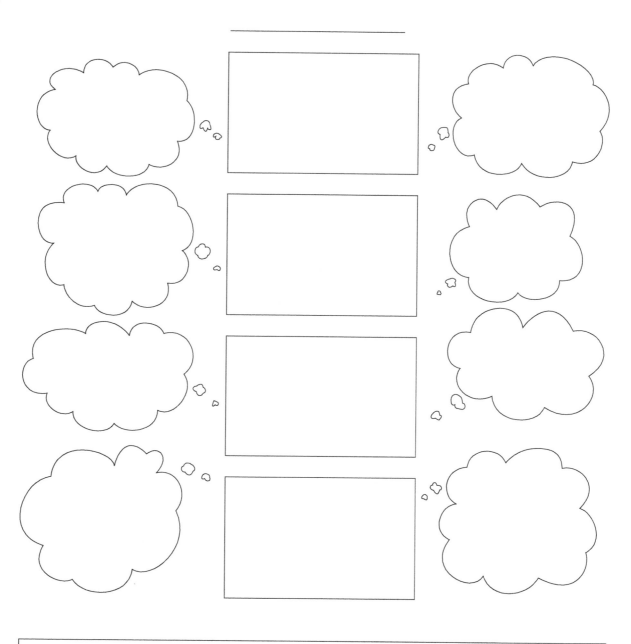

Consequences...

Being socially predictable

We are trying to build social certainty to help our students behave in socially predictable ways with people they may not know well. It's a life skill and one that for some people needs to be taught.

However, this doesn't always make sense to our students, so we borrow these words from Michelle Garcia Winner's (2007) *Social Thinking* programme to help explain some of our activities:

We want to make other people have good thoughts about us.

If other people have these good thoughts, they will behave in a socially predictable way, as everyone follows the broader social norms of how to treat 'people who are good to us'.

The activities in this section are particularly useful for students with low interoceptive and social awareness, who may not appreciate that they can come across as demanding, rude or unfriendly. These students can experience low self-esteem and find it hard to self-reflect and they can also be more vulnerable to bullying or abuse than their more socially switched-on peers. These activities begin by using stories about other people, and don't obviously require any self-reflection or disclosure.

Everything we do gives people an impression. This impression is made up of the social predictions people make about us, based on our appearance and behaviour. Even sitting still and not moving communicates information about us (imagine doing this at a party). This does not mean that we have to go around worrying about everything we do, but it does mean that we have to spend some time thinking about the impression we create.

As you will have read in Chapter 1, we humans are 'predictavores'; we feel calm, relaxed and certain when we are around people whose social behaviour we can predict and they feel comfortable around us when we are predictable too.

Conversely, we tend to feel uncertain when we are around people whose social behaviour isn't predictable and may feel uncomfortable, annoyed or angry.

predicted behaviours = social certainty

unpredicted behaviours = social uncertainty

For example, in some cultures, when we meet someone for the first time, we might do some of the following things: *smile, make eye contact, say something like 'hi', use an open body posture and touch; maybe a social touch on their arm or sometimes a handshake*. After this we usually engage in some form of small talk, often related to the situation we find ourselves in.

In other words, we engage in **highly predictable behaviour**, in order to create immediate social certainty – a predictable (and therefore positive) impression.

Some elements of social predictability are easy to explain and practise and we are more likely to run explicit 'teaching' sessions on topics like these:

▶ Meeting someone for the first time (with careful attention to the context)

▶ Attending an interview

▶ Making a presentation

▶ Asking a teacher for help.

Predicting the behaviours that are expected in informal social situations is harder; it's a very uncertain area. Many of our students like rules (because they give them certainty) but find them hard to apply flexibly, so it can be dangerous to simply 'teach social skills'.

Instead, we try and run activities that help young people explore social uncertainty in a safe environment, where they know they will not be judged. The groups aim to give participants more certain evidence that:

▶ other people think differently to them

▶ there is no straightforward answer when it comes to 'social'

▶ we aim to make others think good thoughts about us

▶ other people also struggle to get all this right

▶ we all make social mistakes.

We begin with the building blocks of **conversation**.

CONVERSATION JENGA

A role-play activity to look at the building blocks of conversations and how we use different types in our conversations.

Why

Learning how to interact in a socially predictable way in unfamiliar situations can be really hard for some of our students, so it's useful to try and break it down in order to give them some strategies.

Over-analysing the highly complex mechanics of how we make conversation can be counterproductive, yet we have found that explaining the basics can help our students feel more certain of how to get involved and present a more certain image to those they don't know well. The aim of this activity is not to teach our students how to prepare and pre-build conversations (which can be counterproductive) but more to raise awareness of the options available to them if they are 'stuck'.

Most of the things we say in social 'chit chat' fall into one of these groups, so we think of them as the building blocks of conversation. We use a range of these to make conversation flow. If we just use one repeatedly it can make our conversation sound boring or weird.

This next activity is best with a Jenga game (or similar) but wooden blocks will also do.

How (part 1)

→ **Lay out some Jenga pieces** in a rough pile on the table. Demonstrate the difference between building the tower with one piece directly on top of each other and the traditional way where three blocks go one way and the next three lie across these in a different direction. See how high your students can go using each method.

→ **Explain** how conversations are made up of blocks – we need to use a mixture of the different types of blocks above to make a conversation flow.

→ **Go through the types of blocks.** Ask students to come up with their own examples after you have introduced these examples. You can mix them up and ask students to identify which is which, if you have time.

Positive comments

'I like your haircut', 'I had fun on Saturday', 'I'm feeling good about that test.'

Neutral comments

'There's an extra rehearsal', 'Football's cancelled', 'School's closed tomorrow.'

Negative comments

'That exam was terrible', 'Her make-up's rubbish', 'There's no way you'll be able to do that.'

Factual questions

'When's the next season out?', 'What time do we have to be there?', 'What's the homework?'

Social questions

'What did you think?', 'Why did you do that?', 'What was that like?'

→ **Model a conversation** where you are Person A and you only lay one direction of block. Choose a student to be Person B – they can respond with the script or spontaneously.

Person A	Person B
'I like your bag.'	**'Thanks.'**
'Those pockets are my favourite colour.'	**'Are they? Oh.'**
'Your last bag was nice too.'	**'Yes, it was.'**
'It's my favourite lunch today.'	**'Really?'**
'That lesson wasn't too bad, was it?'	**'That lesson was okay.'**

→ **Ask Person B how they felt during that conversation and ask other students to rate the conversation as 'good', 'okay' or 'weird'.** Talk about the thoughts they might have had about Person A. How likely is the conversation to continue?

→ **Explain how if we vary the blocks we use the conversation might be more stable and last longer.** Use the example below or use your own.

Person A	Person B
'That's a nice bag.' (positive comment)	**'Thanks.'**
'Where did you get it? (factual question)	**'From the vintage market.'**
'Oh, I love those kind of markets.' (positive comment)	**'Yeah, me too.'**
'Which one would you go to for jewellery?' (social question)	**'That weekend one near you.'**
'Is it on both days? (factual question)	**'Think so.'**
'Might go this Sunday, want to come?' (social question)	**'Yeah, I might do.'**

→ **Ask Person B to explain the difference in this conversation** and get feedback from other students.

→ **Play Jenga as a group.**

How (part 2)

→ **Download or photocopy** the cards on the following page and cut them up.

→ **Cut each label to size and stick to a Jenga block.**

→ **Distribute the blocks to all members of the group** so that each person has at least two different blocks. Ask students to invent a situation, perhaps going to a new lunch club, talking to someone at a family gathering or being friendly to a neighbour in the street.

→ **Go around the group one by one and build a scripted conversation**, step by step. Students can only make a contribution if they have that kind of block in their pile. So, if a student has a FACTUAL QUESTION and a NEUTRAL COMMENT card, they can only add those type of contributions. Participants add their block to the pile as they make their comment.

→ **Record the conversation (in writing).** Talk about which types of block are most useful and likely to develop a conversation.

→ **Play Jenga.**

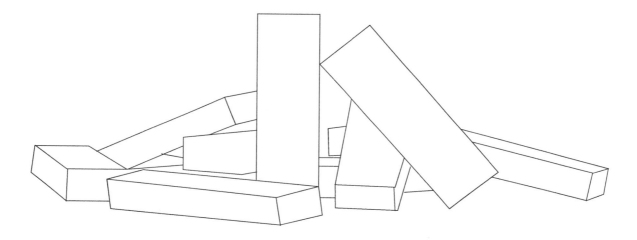

Positive comment	Neutral comment	Negative comment
Factual question	Social question	Factual question
Positive comment	Neutral comment	Negative comment
Factual question	Social question	Factual question

THE BAD NEWS SANDWICH

This is useful for when we need to say something, but we are uncertain of what the listener's response might be. It is a good visual reminder of how we need to sandwich any 'tricky message' between two slices of positive feedback. This also acts as a good warm-up exercise for assertiveness.

Why

Some of our students experience such great social uncertainty that it can cause them to avoid 'tricky' situations such as telling a teacher they don't understand, telling a parent that something hasn't gone well or explaining to a friend the effect that a certain behaviour is having on their friendship. When we are helping students develop a more assertive communication style they can really benefit from some structural certainty, such as this sandwich.

How

→ Ask students to draw a sandwich. Here is an example:

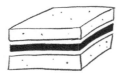

→ **Explain** how if we are worried about how our message will be received, we can say something positive either side of it to make the listener feel okay. This may make it easier for them to hear our message. We sometimes even come up with a possible solution as the last part of the conversation. Give your own examples or use the ones below.

- **Example 1:** 'I like sitting next to you on the coach (positive bread), but I really can't handle the smell of your egg rolls (tricky filling). Will you bring something else next time? I'll bring some crisps (positive and possible solution bread).

- **Example 2:** 'I know you love it when I stay in and watch *Strictly* with you, but I feel I need to go out and be with my friends a bit more at the weekends. I'll be in tomorrow night and we can do something then.'

→ **The tricky filling has 'how we feel' as the main message.** So instead of 'Your sandwiches are disgusting' we say, 'I can't handle the smell.' Instead of 'I don't want to stay in with you' we say, 'I feel I need to socialise with my friends.'

→ Consider the scenarios on the following page, and make up some of your own.

→ **Ask students to design a sandwich** by coming up with ideas for the positive bread as well as the tricky filling, for each scenario.

→ Using this approach offers structural and social certainty to students who struggle to speak up or who create their own certainty in a way that's perceived as rude.

Bad news sandwich scenarios

You just can't eat something your mum has cooked for dinner.	Your friend wants to watch something you think looks really frightening.	You've forgotten your PE kit.
Your teacher thinks you didn't hand in your homework (you did).	Your auntie is visiting for the weekend but you don't want to cancel a plan with your friends.	Your teacher has explained twice but you still don't understand.
Someone is humming next to you and you are finding it distracting.	Your neighbour has accidentally spilt something all over your artwork.	You don't want to go to a party, but your friend wants you to go.
Your grandma gave you a present but says she's happy to change it if it's not right.	You're in a pizza restaurant and your food was late and cold.	You think your teacher has given you the wrong homework.

PASSIVE, AGGRESSIVE OR ASSERTIVE?

This topic appeals to many of our students because of its certainty – we can define these three terms, look them up in dictionaries, give examples and sort them into piles.

Why

Because of their social processing differences, many of our students are uncertain of times when they may be acting passively or aggressively. By giving clear guidelines for how to explain when something's 'not right' we can help them fix it in a more assertive way, and by sharing our feelings about situations we create more social certainty – 'It's not just me that struggles like this.'

How

→ Explain how being assertive means '**standing up for ourselves, but in a way that still makes other people have good thoughts about us**'. Give an example from your life, or make one up involving the students in the room.

→ **Encourage the group to explore the definitions of assertive and passive** and note these down for future reference.

→ **Explain the bad news sandwich** (previous activity) as a structure for assertive communication.

→ **Look at the scenarios on the next page**. Remove any that aren't relevant to your school community and add some of your own. Print out and cut up the cards.

→ Each student takes a turn to read out the scenario.

→ **Round 1:** everyone makes up an aggressive response – discuss.

→ **Round 2:** everyone makes up a passive response – discuss.

→ **Round 3:** everyone makes up an assertive response – discuss.

→ **Share your answers and discuss the consequences** for everyone 'in the story', then move on to the next scenario.

Extension

→ Students write their own scenarios plus a solution and read them out one by one (check them first to make sure they are appropriate; some of our students are uncertain about what information is suitable for sharing in a group).

→ Everyone in the group decides if it was passive, aggressive or assertive and discusses other options for a solution. Keep the scenarios for other activities/role play.

→ Use the emotions cards (Chapter 4) to decide how the passive or aggressive answers might make other people feel.

Passive, aggressive or assertive scenarios

Your drama teacher has told you again what you need to do for homework, but you still don't understand. You're starting to feel anxious.	Your sister keeps coming to swimming with you and your dad. It's something you really like doing just with him.
Your mum keeps asking you to look after your baby brother in the evenings. You are worried you won't have time to study.	Your friend keeps borrowing money from you and not paying you back. It's starting to bother you.
Your friend keeps posting pictures of you without asking. You're starting to feel annoyed.	Your friend is having a big 16th birthday party. You don't like loud noise but you like your friend. You don't want to go.
One of your friends wants you to keep playing FIFA online, even though you know you're supposed to be doing revision. You're feeling stressed.	You're feeling left out of a friendship group, but then one of them asks you to go and buy food for them. You feel annoyed.
Your teacher tells you off for a rude drawing on a textbook. It was your neighbour who did the drawing.	Your friend keeps messaging you to go out but you don't want to go.
Your dad keeps turning up late to fetch you after running. It stresses you out.	You're out with your friends and it's time for your curfew. You want to go home but you're worried about what they will say.

SOCIAL DILEMMAS

Social differences are harder to talk about than learning differences. Students will happily talk about their struggles with science, maths or languages but it's rare to hear anyone discuss their difficulties understanding the hidden social rules within their school community. These activities are a chance to unpack 'doing the predictable thing' as a group.

Why

Some of our students find it hard to make social predictions and can struggle to balance out what they need or want against what will make other people think good thoughts about them. It can be hard for them to work out what's expected of them in different situations and cause uncertain and uncomfortable feelings. This activity hopes to develop the following ideas:

There are no right answers. The group decides what is usually predicted of us in each situation. This is a useful way to develop someone's tolerance of social uncertainty – we aren't providing a 'set of rules', instead we practise this kind of social problem solving.

People think differently. This can increase a sense of agency (as a result of realising that other people find this tricky too).

Practising 'how' to say something can help us with social predictability. By working out what the options are for each scenario we develop the social part of our brains. We then find it easier to predict the social world and feel more certain.

How

→ **Print out and cut up the cards,** remove any that you feel are not appropriate for your community or setting and make up some of your own.

→ **Explain** that this is an activity to work on social problem solving.

→ **Level 1** uses multiple-choice questions and is easier to access.

→ **Students take turns** to read out a social dilemma and the available options.

→ **Make the options visible** to all for the rest of the activity, either on a board or on paper.

→ **Write down your answers.** Everyone in the group (facilitators included) writes down what they would do in that situation. They can choose from one of the suggested answers, or come up with their own.

→ **For each answer ask,** 'What kind of thoughts would the other person/people in this dilemma have about you if you did this?' **Good, okay, weird, annoyed, upset** or **angry**?

→ **For each answer then ask** 'What might happen as a result?' and discuss possible short- and longer-term consequences for every option.

Extension

→ Move on to level 2. Once a group is used to the concept via the multiple-choice format, you can progress to open questions that require more individual thought.

SOCIAL DILEMMAS, LEVEL 1

Someone in your class keeps asking you to message them photos of your maths homework answers.

Do you:

A tell the teacher – it's wrong to copy

B tell your friend you don't want to do it – how would you do this?

C let them copy – it's their problem, not yours

D something else

One of your friends has body odour. You don't think they notice the smell, but other people do.

Do you:

A put some deodorant in their bag when they aren't looking

B tell them – how would you do this?

C do nothing – it's not your problem

D something else

You are watching a live show on the family TV that you can't get on any other device. Your older brother walks in and changes the channel.

Do you:

A get an adult to change the channel back

B get angry – you were there first

C offer to find a different device for them

D watch their show but complain the whole time

E something else

Your friend is really late to meet you in town and didn't answer any of your messages while you were waiting. They do this often.

Do you:

A get angry when they arrive – you were stressed out by their thoughtlessness

B leave – they will just have to go to the shops alone

C smile and say nothing about it

D something else

You are asked to do the dishes more than your brother/sister because they always leave the table first.

Do you:

A just do the dishes, it's not worth it

B refuse – it's not fair

C do the dishes but complain to the adult the whole way through the job

D something else

Your art teacher compliments you in front of the whole class on a piece of work.

Do you:

A get embarrassed and look down as you hate to be singled out

B smile and say 'thank you'

C worry about what the other students will think

D something else

You don't know what the homework is, because you copied it down too quickly and can't read your writing. You're worried about what the teacher will say.

Do you:

A not do the homework – you'll just have to get in trouble but it's better than asking again

B ask a friend to message it to you

C explain to the teacher that you find it hard to copy from the board – how?

D something else

You have broken your laptop screen. It was expensive and you worry about your mum's reaction.

Do you:

A say nothing – you can use the family computer and she might not notice

B cry and hope she feels sorry for you

C explain what's happened – how?

D something else

Your mum insists on choosing your clothes.

Do you:

A tell her you've had enough – you refuse to wear anything she chooses

B ask her if you can look online together

C carry on – it's not worth the fuss

D something else

Your parents want you to do more subjects than you think you can cope with. You worry that they will be disappointed if you say this.

Do you:

A ask your teacher to email them

B get angry or upset and hope it makes a difference

C carry on – it might work out

D something else

Your parent is critical of the friends you choose.

Do you:

A start spending more time with the friends they think are good for you

B tell them it's none of their business

C tell your parent why you like them and carry on as you are

D something else

Someone in your class has asked you to their party. They don't have loads of friends so you feel sorry for them, but you don't really want to go.

Do you:

A go to the party but leave early

B say you'll go but don't turn up

C try and get some of your friends to go with you

D something else

The person you sit next to in science has a habit of tapping their pen on the desk. You've already asked them to stop twice.

Do you:

A get angry – it's annoying you

B tell the teacher

C ask them if they can find something quiet to twiddle instead

D something else

Your friend always says they'll do something with you, but lets you down at the last minute.

Do you:

A tell them you feel disappointed when they do this

B get angry – you're sick of being let down

C say nothing – it's just how they are

D something else

Your teacher says your work is scruffy, but you find it hard to write neatly.

Do you:

A keep trying harder – you might get there eventually

B feel angry – don't they know you have trouble writing neatly?

C get upset – you're sick of people telling you this

D tell the teacher – how?

You forget to wait for a friend at the end of the day. They had to go home alone.

Do you:

A apologise and buy them a really expensive present

B do nothing – it's not that big a deal

C explain the reasons why you think you forgot – how?

D something else

You've been invited to a party. Your mum insists on talking to the parents about where the party is. Your friends' parents are happy to let them go if they let them know the address.

Do you:

A not go, it's only a party

B let your mum call the other parents. It's embarrassing but at least you get to go

C go to the party but tell your mum you're staying with another friend and hope you don't get found out

D something else

You don't enjoy going on sleepovers to a particular friend's house.

Do you:

A tell her you don't like staying at her house

B get your mum to make up an excuse each time

C suggest another friend comes too – it might help

D something else

Someone has brought a firework into school and asked you to keep it in your locker.

Do you:

A tell the teacher – it's dangerous

B help them and hope you don't get caught

C tell them you don't want to get involved – how?

D something else

You drop your food on the floor in the canteen and the whole place laughs.

Do you:

A laugh too – you didn't do it on purpose

B shout at everyone to stop laughing

C pretend it didn't happen and walk off

D something else

SOCIAL DILEMMAS, LEVEL 2

Someone in your class asks what you think of their haircut. You think they looked better before. *Be honest, but kind.*	Someone in another class is always making fun of your height. *Refuse to be put down.*
One of your friends has decided not to go to school tomorrow and wants you to sneak into town with them for the day. *Say no without hurting their feelings.*	Someone has borrowed your calculator and hasn't returned it. You need it for your science homework. *Ask for it back.*
You and your friend have been given the job of clearing up the hall after the school play. You are doing most of the work, and they are just looking at their phone. *Complain to them.*	You did well in a test. Your friends are really pleased for you but you're embarrassed. *Accept their compliments.*
You're really pleased because you've got into the college you wanted. Your friend didn't. *Give them the news while showing you understand their feelings.*	A friend spills their inky water over your sketchbook, ruining some work you spent a long time on. *Explain how you feel.*

A friend criticises your best friend for being a 'show-off'. *Stand up for your friend.*	Your younger brother borrowed your bike and left it at his friend's house. *Let him know you are annoyed.*
Your parents have asked you to be back from a birthday party at 10pm, but your friend doesn't have to be home until 11. *Negotiate a later home time.*	Your dad has a new girlfriend who is usually there when you visit. You'd like some time for just you and him. *Explain how you feel and why.*
You are regularly asked to babysit your younger brother and sister. You'd like more time to spend with your friends. *Explain how you feel to your mum.*	Your mum is considering a new job. It would be a promotion for her but it would mean moving house and starting a new school. *Let her know you are happy for her, but explain how you feel.*
Your best friend gets upset if you suggest that you spend time with other people too. *Explain how you feel, and find a way to resolve the situation.*	Your best friend has started spending time with a group you don't feel comfortable with. You'd rather not go to their parties but your friend wants you to go. *Explain how you feel and why.*
Someone in your class has posted something on social media and the rest of the class are making fun of her behind her back. *Explain what you would do and say.*	Your friend is upset because you've started 'seeing' someone and you are spending less time together. *Find a way to help her feel better.*

Your friend keeps asking you to play a game online but you want to try and revise. *Explain how you feel.*	The wi-fi at home keeps dropping and, though your mum keeps promising to do something about it, she hasn't. *Negotiate for better wi-fi.*
You are finding a science module really challenging. Although your teachers have explained it again to you, you still don't get it. *Ask for more help.*	All your friends seem to be coping with the level of work but you are really struggling. *Talk to them and find out more.*
You've got a babysitting job and the parents keep coming back later than they say. You get paid but you'd rather know when they were coming back. *Explain this to the parents.*	One of your friends is always trying to convince you all to do crazy stuff so he can film it and post it on social media. It's getting dangerous and you're worried something bad will happen. *Explain how you feel.*
Someone in your class keeps making comments on your friend's online photos that make her feel uncomfortable. *Help your friend work out what to do.*	You've seen on social media that there was a party in your year, but you weren't invited. One of your friends was there, but hadn't told you she was going. *Explain how you feel to your friend.*

A framework for talking about online social communication.

Why

Online interactions can be very appealing to our more socially uncertain students. They get to prepare and edit what they want to say, there's no confusing non-verbal communication to integrate with spoken language and they can take their time to respond. However, there are still 'hidden' rules and any misunderstandings arise in a much bigger arena than the school environment.

Our students tend to divide into two camps: those who use social media constantly (either to observe the social behaviour of others or to gauge their own social status) and those who use it in a very limited way (either avoiding it completely or restricting their interactions to a single channel). Either way, we need to be clear about the advantages and disadvantages of using this kind of technology, reinforcing basic safety guidelines as we go.

How

Tech changes, fashion changes and it's hard to predict what channels our students will be drawn to. We offer this as an opportunity to promote information sharing and debate.

→ **Use the framework on the worksheet.** Choose one or two topics for each session/ lesson.

→ **Encourage every student to contribute** either verbally or in writing.

→ **Advantages might include:** you can stay connected with friends all the time, you can make friends with people who live in different countries, you can find out about things you're interested in, you can talk to people who are interested in the same things as you, you can talk about how you feel with people you will never meet.

→ **Disadvantages might include:** everything is public, you can't always control who's looking at what you say or do, people's lives online can look more perfect than they really are, we can feel bad about ourselves in comparison, we might feel left out of social events that get posted by our friends, you can't always take back what you post, it causes 'drama'.

→ **Guide the students to build a list of their own social media 'rules'.** Include, but go beyond, the standard internet safety guidelines: What do you do if you text someone a couple of times and they don't answer? What do you do if someone posts a picture you aren't happy with? How do you manage someone's feelings if you post a picture of an event they weren't invited to? What do you do if you see someone being made fun of online? How do we deal with unkind messages on our own accounts? What upsets you? What are the rules in your community?

→ **Research different internet safety rules and discuss them.**[4]

→ **Provide each student with a typed and printed copy of the group rules to take away** at the end of the module.

---

4   See, for example, University College London: www.ucl.ac.uk/grand-challenges/sites/grand-challenges/files/rough_guide_to_social_media_use.pdf

WHAT'S SO GREAT ABOUT SOCIAL MEDIA?

List every social media platform you and your friends use. What's the difference between them?

Is there anything you don't use? If so, why?

What's good about social media?

What's not good about social media?

What would you share?

What would you not share?

What are the internet safety rules?

What are your own personal rules? What's not okay?

Social practice

The students we see typically divide into two groups – those who find the unwritten rules of a social community hard to understand:

'I'm not sure what to do in social situations.'

and those who know what to do, but find it hard in practice:

'I know what to do, but I just can't do it.'

The activities in this section are useful for both sets of students, but the second group may need less information before they practise. Discussing and running role plays based on real-life (and completely invented) situations can lay a foundation for a change in behaviour outside the sessions. In an ideal world, some practice sessions would happen outside the school environment – for example, in a coffee shop or park – to facilitate the transfer of skills. This is sometimes possible, if we and our students are prepared to be flexible and school safeguarding policies are closely followed.

Many of the students we know find it difficult to flexibly apply prior models or effectively generalise skills from one situation to another. They may also experience social uncertainty due to not very precise models of themselves ('How do I know how I'm feeling and behaving?') and subsequent difficulties thinking through others' minds ('How are they seeing this situation?' and so, 'What are they thinking or feeling?').

Teaching our students too many 'top-down' social skills and expecting them to remember them, before applying them flexibly in many different situations, has its pitfalls. It may simply be giving them more models to inaccurately apply and may increase their social uncertainty. This doesn't mean we don't ever teach skills, but we try to do this by raising awareness using games, role play, plenty of discussion and video whenever possible. This section provides you with some ideas for what and how to practise, in order to help students develop more social behaviours that others should find more predictable, and therefore they are likely to behave more predictably, so bringing more certainty to a situation in times of need.

The key message here is not that we want to fundamentally change our students, nor their communication style, more that we want to help them learn how to behave in an expected way and manage other people's uncertainty for them. We do it for them so that they in turn will end up behaving more predictably for us. It's a life skill thing.

USING VIDEO

Reasons (and some ideas) for using video

▶ **Nothing compares to the instant impact of watching yourself on screen**. It is **possible** to convince students that the feedback they get from you or their peers is valid, but as anyone who has ever been filmed knows, video is a powerful and non-judgemental force – and one that's more difficult to argue with.

▶ **Using video and a feedback form** (see the first worksheet) with any of the activities in this section boosts their effectiveness. We ask students to rate themselves and each other, to increase general social awareness and certainty. The 'notes' section encourages students to record their own ideas for future improvements.

▶ **You can video a group of students doing almost anything and make it a social learning experience** as you watch it back. This means you can bring activities they truly love into the sessions. This could mean putting on make-up or even sharing holding a guinea pig is part of learning – really useful with reluctant groups.

▶ **Students usually experience social uncertainty at the prospect of being filmed** and you can use this as an exercise in tolerating the uncertainty, teaching positive self-talk, while doing everything you can to make it a fun experience (by providing lots of social and structural certainty within your activity).

▶ **Students sometimes prefer to watch video with the sound off first**, and then again with sound. We often have a conversation about how much we all 'hate the sound of our own voice' and research why we sound different on recordings (frequencies, bandwidths and bone conduction).

▶ **We can break down and analyse the 'conversation chain'** as we are able to freeze/pause and rewind film to its component parts in a way we can't do with real life.

▶ **You can watch your students' favourite shows with the sound off**, to practise interpreting facial expression and body language and coming up with predictions (best, though, if they don't know every episode by heart for this).

▶ **You can watch recordings of school events** or national events without sound, watching the background characters and guessing what they might be thinking or feeling.

▶ **It can be really fun.**

Things to be aware of when using video

▸ Each educational establishment will have its own privacy policies and protocols; make sure you are clear about consent before making a video recording.

▸ You will need to make sure that any recordings are securely stored and agree with parents/carers what happens at the end of any project/group.

VIDEO FEEDBACK

What I did well

What I could do differently

What the others did well

Notes:

THINGS I COULD HAVE DONE WELL...

Looking at other people when I talk

Showing interest in other people with my face

Showing interest in other people with my body

Asking factual questions

Asking social questions:
- 'What did you think of that?'
- 'Why did you do that?'
- 'How did you feel when that happened?'

Answering questions

Making supporting comments/sounds/gestures

Saying when I didn't understand

Showing that I wanted to speak with my face/body

Giving someone else a turn to speak

Noticing when someone was bored

Choosing topics other people are interested in

SOPHIA AND THE INTERVIEW DRILL

Sophia avoided socialising, she said it was 'too much hassle' and she would rather spend time alone or with her family when not in school (**social uncertainty**). School staff noticed that she had a narrow range of facial expressions, rarely made eye contact and she spoke very quietly unless with one of her friends (**social uncertainty**). Despite this, she was an able, academic student and was preparing for university applications.

Sophia had two close friends in school (**social certainty**) and enjoyed spending time with them, but was clear that once she was away from school, she had no interest in seeing them and didn't feel the need for more social activities when the school day or week was over. She would message her friends occasionally, but usually about homework or school events (**social certainty**).

When she reached sixth form, she began to worry about what she would do after school and how she would cope with meeting new people (**social uncertainty**), so she reluctantly (**social uncertainty**) joined a sixth-form mentoring group run by pastoral staff.

Her 'How confident is my communication?' questionnaire revealed that she felt confident in almost all areas but knew, because other people had told her, that her eye contact and body language could do with work. Her teachers and a parent also completed a questionnaire and the results suggested that Sophia was unaware of some aspects of her more unpredictable communication style.

The group leader asked the group to identify what skills they would like to master by the end of the group and they agreed to work on 'interview practice'.

Each group member was recorded taking part in an interview role play. Filming began as they opened the door and ended as they closed it at the end of the interview. The video feedback form was completed, so the students could identify (for themselves and each other) 'what went well' in their interview.

Every student was invited to choose one thing they would like to practise. Sophia chose 'coming into the room' and rated it at 4/10, so the component parts were discussed and identified (head up, make brief eye contact and smile – say hello and sit where indicated).

This phase of the interview was then drilled – each week she was asked to prepare her 'open' face and body at the other end of the corridor before receiving group feedback.

At the end of the group, all students were recorded again and rated their new skills. Sophia scored herself 8/10 for coming into the room, and said that she had started using this entrance style as she arrived in most of her lessons. A few teachers commented on a more confident approach in her interactions with them, too.

Low **interoceptive awareness** and uncertain **theory of mind** mean that many of our students are unaware that their social style may be unpredictable to others. While older students (from the age of 15 or 16 onwards) are often able to discuss difficulties and identify specific strategies they'd like to develop (see 'Sophia and the interview drill'), younger students may need a more indirect approach.

The next few pages of this chapter contain games that we play to explore different aspects of social behaviour. As with all our work, they are designed to build social certainty and predictability as well as further develop tolerance of social uncertainty.

Either explicitly or implicitly, we work on understanding and practising the following aspects of social communication:

▸ facial expression

▸ body language

▸ volume and rate of speech

▸ tone of voice.

This can help our students become more socially certain and predict more reliably when:

▸ making small talk

▸ doing the social fake

▸ managing conversations with unfamiliar people

▸ asking questions

▸ asking for help

▸ managing disagreements

▸ talking about feelings.

Games for social certainty

The following pages contain examples of some of the activities we have used over the years. We also play these commercially available games, especially with younger teenagers, who may initially find it difficult to engage in more discussion-based sessions (some use a time limit which can be useful for discussing more uncomfortable feelings, such as stress and 'failure'):

▸ Think Words

▸ Last Word

▸ Rhyme Time

▸ Should I or Shouldn't I? (social thinking)

▸ Linkee/Dinkee

▸ Pass the Biscuits.

THE HAT GAME

A fun, student-led game to consider use of language and body language. Good for an early group session.

Why

Some of our students find it hard to use their bodies to express their thoughts and feelings and sometimes being in a new group is tricky. Playing competitive games can be more motivating (for some students) and also give us the opportunity to talk about things like 'how we deal with anxiety' or 'dealing with not winning'.

How

→ **Everyone in the group writes down the name of a well-known person or character** on a small square of paper and passes it to the adult who checks it for suitability and folds it in half twice (so you can't see what's written on it).

→ **Encourage students to think about the people in the room**, and only to write down names that they think everyone will recognise (this may be difficult for students who do not have secure theory of mind). Repeat until everyone has written at least ten.

→ **Take all the squares in and mix them in a hat (or bag or box).** Form two teams.

→ **Round one:** A student from Team 1 takes their turn by picking names from the hat and describing them to their team – as many as they can in 60 seconds. They may not use any words written on the square (e.g. if describing Iron Man, you must not say the words 'man' or 'iron'). Score one point for each name guessed correctly.

→ They can 'pass' if they don't recognise a name and put the square back in the hat.

→ After one 60-second turn, the hat passes to someone in Team 2 who describes as many as they can, and so on, until all the squares have been used up.

→ Once all the squares have been used, count how many each team guessed correctly and score.

→ **Round two:** Put all the squares back in the hat and play again, but this time students can only use **three words** to describe the characters (e.g. for Iron Man: 'Marvel. Strong. Guy').

→ Score as before and add to round one scores.

→ **Round three:** Put all the squares back in the hat and play again, but this time students can only use mime and gesture to describe the characters. Add all scores and find your winning team.

PLUSHIE EMOTIONS

An old game, but a simple game – good for quick warm-ups, using and 'reading' facial expressions.

Why

It builds social certainty. Some of our students don't understand, or express themselves by using, the full range of facial expressions. This activity raises awareness of 'communicating with our faces' and offers social practice in a simple game format. Playing this (or other simple warm-up games) at the start of **every** session can also help provide structural certainty to students who experience social uncertainty in group situations.

How

→ **Get hold of a plushie/bean bag/large squishy football/cushion** or other item that won't cause damage to anything if it's thrown off course (students can bring favourite items from home).

→ **Everyone stands in a circle**, arms width apart.

→ **Explain that you are going to play a game to look at how different people show different emotions.** It's important because we need to be able to 'read' other people to know how they are feeling, as well as express how we feel in a way that's understood.

→ **Place a prompt card with emotions written in large letters on it in the centre of the circle**, so that everyone can read them. Use emotions level 1, 2 or 3 from the sensory section (page xx) or your own, enlarged to fill at least A3 size.

→ **Find the youngest/oldest/tallest/smallest player** – they start.

→ **The first person calls out an emotion** and throws the plushie to someone else in the group who must then make a face that demonstrates the emotion called.

→ **The receiver then calls out a new emotion and passes it on**.

Extensions

→ The receiver can win points by thinking of a situation when they might feel that emotion.

→ All group members copy the 'receiver' and compare faces as they look around.

→ Adult records a video of the game. Review it the following week, randomly freezing on faces and getting students to try and guess or remember what emotion was called in each case.

PASS THE FACE

Another quick activity for awareness and practice of predictable behaviour.

Why

Many of our students find it hard to mirror other people's non-verbal communication. It's important because this is part of how we signal to someone that we are listening and thinking about things from their point of view. If we don't do this, we may seem unpredictable and the listener may experience social uncertainty. (Are they listening to me? Are they interested?) They may not end up having good thoughts about us. It's also a good 'group awareness' activity for warm-ups.

How

→ **Everyone sits or stands in a circle.**

→ **Start with a group wave** (or clap) to warm up and establish a physical presence in the group.

→ **Explain that you are going to play a game about making different facial expressions.** This is important as it's one way we show other people what we are thinking and feeling when we are in conversation. It makes us more predictable.

→ **Place a large card with emotion words on it in the centre of the circle,** so that everyone can read them. Use emotions level 1, 2 or 3 from the sensory section (Chapter 4) or your own.

→ **Find the youngest/oldest/tallest/smallest player** – they start.

→ **First person chooses an emotion** (keeps it secret) and makes a face to go with it. They then 'pass' this face to the next person and it travels round the circle.

→ **At the end of the 'round', everyone writes down what emotion** they thought went round the circle. Score points for correct answers.

→ **Encourage discussion** if people disagree on the faces other people are matching to the emotion word. Model assertive and socially predictable ways of disagreeing.

EMOTIONAL SENTENCES

A game that looks at tone of voice and how it changes the meaning of the words we say.

Why

Some people find it hard to de-code people's 'tone', which leads to uncertainty understanding things like sarcasm and other more subtle meanings. This activity raises awareness and also provides an opportunity to develop social predictability.

How

→ **Print off or photocopy and cut up the sentences on the next page.**

→ **Make a set of the emotions cards** from Chapter 4 into a bag/hat/small box/envelope. Add some of your own.

→ **Hand a sentence out to each member of the group.**

→ **On each turn, the student picks an emotion and reads out the sentence in that manner.** So, if the emotion is 'disappointed', the student reads their sentence in a disappointed tone of voice.

→ **The other students try to guess the emotion** and can try saying the sentence/emotion combination themselves. Talk about what 'story' could be built around the sentence, and what it could mean when someone says it like that.

→ **The student keeps the same sentence but selects different emotions on each subsequent round.** Use the emotions cards from Chapter 4 and add your own, if you like.

Emotional sentences

That test was really hard.	My friend's not coming for that sleepover.
The bus is coming.	We are going on holiday next week.
I have to give a talk in front of the class.	Have you seen the homework?
He's been at the gym for more than an hour.	My dad is cooking meatballs for dinner.
I'm going to the dentist this afternoon.	I got an email from that kid in Canada.
It's parents' evening tonight.	My brother always wins this game.
I fell off my bike last weekend.	There's a spider in the shower.
They haven't arrived yet.	My cat is on my bed.
Their class has no homework.	She's waiting to hear about the tickets.
He's online.	We are going to a Japanese restaurant for my brother's birthday.
My neighbours are moving to Australia.	We've got to do a presentation tomorrow.
I said it wasn't me, but actually it was.	Yeah, I think she's great.
I can't believe it; she got tickets to the premiere.	My sister got a new phone.

BODY LANGUAGE HAT GAME

A game to look at social predictions based on how we use our bodies. Comedy bell buzzer optional.

Why

Some of our students find body language difficult to de-code and use in a predictable way. This adds to their social uncertainty. Becoming more aware of the impact our body language can have on other people, and vice versa, can help build social certainty.

How

→ **Download, print out/photocopy and cut up the instructions on the next page**. Put them in a hat, bag or box.

→ **Practise using the bell/buzzer** and check that all students are happy with the sound. You may like to play without it, to begin with.

→ **Students take turns acting out the instruction**.

→ **Other students race to ring the bell/buzzer** or shout out a chosen word to interpret the 'message' and win a point.

→ **Students can then all try out the action** and discuss alternative interpretations.

→ There is no 'right' answer to this activity – the objective is for the group to determine, for their community, what is 'assumed' when we engage in various body postures.

Body language hat game instructions

Fake smile	Hands clasped behind head	Lips pressed tightly together	Look down
Tap foot	Slumped over	Pull on ear	Fold arms across chest
Raise eyebrows, head on one side	Hand over mouth	Hand on heart	Head down, eyes shut
Roll eyes	Yawn	Head on one side	Hands over ears
Shrug shoulders	Push bottom lip out	Chin up	Bite lip
Fingers out, palm facing out	Fidget with hair	Drum fingers on table	Stare into space
Keep looking at door	Hands on hips	Tap fingers together quickly	Bite fingernails

AWKWARD MOMENTS

A game for social predictability practice, as well as an opportunity for students to share any 'awkward moments'.

Why

Sometimes we all have to deal with uncertain social situations. Working out some options for how to respond can be really helpful. We may need to 'fake it' or learn to deal with the uncomfortable uncertainty (or both), and for some of our students knowing when and how to do this causes them social uncertainty.

How

→ **Download, print out/photocopy and cut up the cards on the next page.**

→ **Explain that there are times when we all have to pretend**, in order to make other people have good thoughts about us. This is not the same thing as being upset and hiding it. If we are really upset we need to tell people (see passive, aggressive or assertive activity for more on this).

→ **Talk through a scenario**, taking turns to share how you would react.

→ **For each, identify:** how you might be feeling, why you might need to 'fake it' and how you might make the other person have good thoughts about you in these situations.

→ **Ask students to add their own awkward cards.** Shuffle them up and encourage students to take turns picking from the pile.

Someone gives you a present you already own.	Your friend is five minutes late to meet you after school.
Your auntie has dyed her hair but you don't like it.	Your friend didn't text you back last night.
You say 'hi' to someone and they don't respond.	Your friend lets you down, cancelling her visit to your house (you were really looking forward to it).
Someone asks you if you're going to 'the party' but you haven't been invited.	You think someone is waving at you and you wave back, then realise they were waving at someone else.
You accidentally send a photo of yourself doing something stupid to someone you really like/don't know that well.	You say something in class that makes everyone laugh but you don't think it's funny.

SMALL TALK

What it is, why we do it and opportunities for practice.

Why

Most people experience some degree of social uncertainty when trying to connect with people they don't know well. Many of our students find it hard to understand the concept of small talk. Indeed, it seems ridiculous that they would bother to tell someone what they did that weekend or the route they took to get somewhere, when they have no actual interest in the subject. Many of our more logical students express themselves very clearly on this subject. But it's a life skill, part of the communication 'dance' that we participate in to create social certainty and predictability, so we try to teach it as part of this social curriculum.

How

→ **Explain the concept. Ask students to take turns reading the following sentences and discuss as a group**. Do they agree? Would they add anything?

- When we first meet someone, we want to make a connection with them, so they have good thoughts about us.

- We may not know much about them, we might not know what they like to talk about, or we might just need to warm up to a conversation.

- We need something to talk about so we can show them our open and friendly body language and facial expressions. Then they will have good thoughts about us.

- We choose a topic that's neutral but relevant to the situation. This is the small talk.

- Sometimes when we use small talk we find we have something in common with the other person. Then we can talk about something we both like or agree on and we can make a connection.

- People use small talk all the time, even with people they know well. They might use it to work out if it's a good time to talk and get some clues to how someone is feeling, before they ask a question.

- Small talk can be useful to make people have good thoughts about us.

→ **Work out your scenarios:** Ask students for examples of times when they didn't know what to say. Develop a 'scene' with imaginary names and back stories for two or more characters.

→ **For each scenario, come up with conversation starters** using this structure, using a mixture of open and closed questions.

→ **Challenge** the students to develop the conversation based on what they discover with their openers.

→ **Role-play** some to see how far the conversation goes and, if you can, use video for review.

→ **Example:** First day of rehearsals for school musical:

Past	Present	Future
Were you in the last show? Have you been in many musicals? What other parts did you try for?	Do you play any instruments? What do you think of the teacher/story/dances?	What time will we finish tonight? How many rehearsals will we be needed for?

JOINING IN

A listening, thinking and doing activity which helps students build awareness of non-verbal as well as verbal skills.

Why

When we do our self-assessment questionnaires, this is something that the majority of students say they feel uncertain about. Joining in with other people's conversations requires many different skills, which is why so many people find it tricky. It's hard to 'teach' due to its complexity, but fun to practise. As always, video helps.

How

→ **Ask two students to start a conversation** about something, before you leave the room. Ask your students to choose the topic or use the 'Would you rather...?' topics from earlier in the chapter.

→ **Adult enters the room and models joining in (version 1).** Make sure you go through some or all of the following steps:

- Walk in and immediately approach the pair – stand very close.

- Without looking at the speaker, start talking about your views on the topic.

- Keep going for as long as you can.

→ **Ask your students to rate your joining-in skills** – video is really useful here as you can rewind and pause your behaviour as well as the group reactions. Students can explain some of the thoughts they had about your behaviour.

→ **Adult enters the room and models joining in (version 2).** Make sure you go through some or all of the following steps:

- Turn your head to show interest once you are in the room.

- Approach the group slowly, turn your body to face the speaker.

- Use head nodding and facial expression to show interest.

- Try and make eye contact with one of the speakers.

- Wait for one of the speakers to look at you and then make a comment or ask a question.

→ If your first attempt is ignored, try again until you get a turn.

→ **Ask the students to describe some of the steps** you went through to get a turn. Again, video is useful.

→ **The students then take turns to become the 'joiner'.** Use video if you can, and give lots of positive feedback on all and any skills observed as well as asking the students to give feedback to each other.

→ **Repeat** until the process starts to feel natural, part of a 'social muscle memory'.

SOCIAL DEBATE CARDS

Cards to stimulate conversation about social resilience, 'rules', being different, fitting in and everything else.

Why

Many of our more uncertain students respond well to the structure of debate-style conversations; they like the semi-formality of a conversation where it is clear who gets a turn to speak, rather than having to negotiate this. The activity promotes the sharing of opinions on various aspects of social behaviour and promotes greater understanding of ourselves and those around us.

How

→ **Download, print and cut out the cards on the next page**. Look through them and select those that you feel would be useful for your group. Add some of your own.

→ **Spread the cards face down on the table**, make a pile or hide them around the room (to allow for movement).

→ **Students take it in turns to select a card** and agree or disagree with the statement before asking someone else in the group for their opinion.

→ Depending on the size of the group, you can set how many more students you'd like to contribute to each topic and ask the students to 'pass the debate on' until the limit is reached.

→ For a more 'freestyle' approach, ask students to join in and contribute as they wish.

→ Identify and model as a group how we might get a turn or pass the debate on – asking questions, turning towards someone, eye pointing, using facial expression, etc.

Extensions

→ This activity works well with students who find it hard not to interrupt. Make it clear that we can only contribute if we have the question passed to us and talk about how we feel when we are interrupted before we have finished speaking.

→ Videoing these types of activities can be a really good way to give feedback.

Social debate cards

It's important that I am liked by everyone I know.	We all judge other people.
Being yourself is more important than fitting in.	It's more important to listen to other people than to say what we think.
It's bad to talk about people when they are not there.	It's not important to have friends.
Popular people are superficial and usually not clever.	Acting friendly will always make people like us.
If I know I'm right I don't have to compromise.	It's better to pretend that things don't bother us than to complain.
How we look is how we feel.	Being honest is always the right thing to do.
There are some topics we should never talk about.	If someone tells us a secret, we can never tell anyone.
It's better to exclude someone than explain why you don't like them.	If someone is late to meet you, it means they don't care about you.
We should never talk about our successes in public.	Some people never get anxious.
First impressions last.	It's never too late to apologise.

IF YOU ONLY HAVE FIVE MINUTES

Tips for dealing with social uncertainty in the classroom, where we can help by doing the following:

1 **Talk about the hidden rules** that some people seem to automatically understand. Point out when you do the 'social fake' or make small talk. Explaining things like how you knew another teacher wasn't angry when they came to fetch a student from the class by their body language, tone of voice or facial expressions can really help students who struggle with social uncertainty.

2 **Be explicit about classroom social behaviours** beyond the basic 'school rules'. This can be really useful in developing social predicting skills, as can modelling and role play of situations that didn't go well. Brainstorm solutions to disagreements – our students are much better at coming up with these than we are – and gradually draw up a protocol of how to give each other feedback with sentence starters like 'When you do this it makes me feel...'

3 **Avoid idioms** when giving directions or key information without checking for understanding. Can you find the double meanings in the following phrases? 'We need to wrap this up', 'I bumped into her yesterday', 'You need to be more on the ball', 'Go in with an open mind'.

4 **Be very clear with requests**. Use visual back up for maximum certainty.

5 **Teach 'social'**. Most schools run some form of personal and social curriculum and there is often space in the timetable here to carry out some of the activities in this chapter in order to build social certainty.

6 **Work with mentors or coaches**. Some of our students already get this type of extra support, but group mentoring can make it more cost effective and is often more beneficial to the students, who get to develop new friendships and share difficulties. Student mentors are also a great way to offer social support; in our experience, it works best where the age gap is one of at least two or three school years.

7 **Use time outside the classroom as a learning experience**. We suggest to schools that where they have a student who is regularly required to leave the classroom, they offer this type of work as part of their behaviour support programme (either in a small group or one-to-one sessions) so that their time outside the classroom contributes to greater social certainty in school.

8 **Use drama lessons**. These can be an excellent way to practise some of the 'social faking' we all need to do to get by in different situations (at a party, in the park, on a bus) as well as physical activities to increase interoception (see Chapter 4 for details).

9 **Offer safe spaces**. For students with high anxiety, identify a space that is available during both lessons and break times, where they can go if they need to deal with feeling

overwhelmed. Many of our students use the toilets, but with some imagination it is often possible to find an alternative, be it a library, a wellbeing space or a social 'hub' for vulnerable students.

10 **Provide friendly faces.** Encourage students who may need occasional, but urgent, human support to develop relationships with a suitable (and willing) non-teaching member of staff. They might work in the library, school office, wellbeing team, art/science technical team, medical team or premises management team. This can be done by setting up 'work experience'-type projects (during break times), and if a good relationship develops, arrangements can be made for how a student can get urgent access to their 'friendly face'.

FURTHER READING

Gray, C. (1994). *Comic Strip Conversations: Illustrated Interactions that Teach Conversation Skills to Students with Autism and Related Disorders.* Arlington, TX: Future Horizons. (More ideas for perspective taking and making 'social' visual.)
Kelly, A. (2017). *Talkabout for Teenagers: Developing Social and Emotional Communication Skills.* London: Routledge. (More ideas on specific skill development for social and emotional development in adolescence.)

REFERENCES

Ainley, V. & Tsakiris, M. (2013). Body conscious? Interoceptive awareness, measured by heartbeat perception, is negatively correlated with self-objectification. *PloS One, 8*(2), 1–9.
Allen, M. & Tsakiris, M. (2019). The Body as First Prior: Interoceptive Predictive Processing and the Primacy. In M. Tsakiris & H. De Preester (eds) *The Interoceptive Mind: From Homeostasis to Awareness* (first edition, pp.27–45). Oxford: Oxford University Press.
Arnold, A. J., Winkielman, P. & Dobkins, K. (2019). Interoception and social connection. *Frontiers in Psychology, 10*, 2589.
Cacioppo, J. T. & Hawkley, L. C. (2009). Perceived social isolation and cognition. *Trends in Cognitive Sciences, 13*(10), 447–454.

Conant, R. C. & Ross Ashby, W. (1970). Every good regulator of a system must be a model of that system. *International Journal of Systems Science, 1*(2), 89–97.

FeldmanHall, O. & Shenhav, A. (2019). Resolving uncertainty in a social world. *Nature Human Behaviour, 3*(5), 426–435.

Frith, C. D. & Frith, U. (1999). Interacting minds – a biological basis. *Science, 286*(5445), 1692–1695.

Heasman, B. & Gillespie, A. (2018). Perspective-taking is two-sided: Misunderstandings between people with Asperger's syndrome and their family members. *Autism, 22*(6), 740–750.

Lawson, R. P., Rees, G. & Friston, K. J. (2014). An aberrant precision account of autism. *Frontiers in Human Neuroscience, 8*, 302.

Levinson, C. A. & Rodebaugh, T. L. (2012). Social anxiety and eating disorder comorbidity: The role of negative social evaluation fears. *Eating Behaviors, 13*(1), 27–35.

Meneguzzo, P., Collantoni, E., Bonello, E., Busetto, P., Tenconi, E. & Favaro, A. (2020). The predictive value of the early maladaptive schemas in social situations in anorexia nervosa. *European Eating Disorders Review, 28*(3), 318–331.

Milton, D. E. (2012). On the ontological status of autism: The 'double empathy problem'. *Disability & Society, 27*(6), 883–887.

Ondobaka, S., Kilner, J. & Friston, K. (2017). The role of interoceptive inference in theory of mind. *Brain and Cognition, 112*, 64–68.

Palmer, C. J., Paton, B., Kirkovski, M., Enticott, P. G. & Hohwy, J. (2015). Context sensitivity in action decreases along the autism spectrum: A predictive processing perspective. *Proceedings of the Royal Society B: Biological Sciences, 282*(1802), 20141557.

Pellicano, E. & Burr, D. (2012). When the world becomes 'too real': A Bayesian explanation of autistic perception. *Trends in Cognitive Sciences, 16*(10), 504–510.

Quattrocki, E. & Friston, K. (2014). Autism, oxytocin and interoception. *Neuroscience & Biobehavioral Reviews, 47*, 410–430.

Steward, R. (2013). *The Independent Woman's Handbook for Super Safe Living on the Autistic Spectrum.* London: Jessica Kingsley Publishers.

Theriault, J. E., Young, L. & Barrett, L. F. (2020). The sense of should: A biologically-based framework for modeling social pressure. *Physics of Life Review*, doi: 10.1016/j.plrev.2020.01.004.

Tsakiris, M. (2017). The multisensory basis of the self: From body to identity to others. *The Quarterly Journal of Experimental Psychology, 70*(4), 597–609.

Van de Cruys, S., Evers, K., Van der Hallen, R., Van Eylen, L. *et al.* (2014). Precise minds in uncertain worlds: Predictive coding in autism. *Psychological Review, 121*, 649–675.

Veissière, S. P., Constant, A., Ramstead, M. J., Friston, K. J. & Kirmayer, L. J. (2019). Thinking through other minds: A variational approach to cognition and culture. *Behavioral and Brain Sciences*, 1–97.

Willem, C., Nandrino, J. L., Doba, K., Roussel, M. *et al.* (2020). Interoceptive reliance as a major determinant of emotional eating in adult obesity. *Journal of Health Psychology*, 1359105320903093.

Willey, L. H. (2014). *Pretending to be Normal: Living with Asperger's Syndrome (Autism Spectrum Disorder)*, expanded edition. London: Jessica Kingsley Publishers.

Winner, M. G. (2007). *Thinking About You, Thinking About Me.* San Jose, CA: Think Social.

6

CONCLUSIONS...
AND HOPES FOR THE FUTURE

As we go to press, uncertainty is high on the international agenda and likely to remain there for a while. We hope that having read the book you have an even greater understanding of what might cause structural, sensory and social uncertainty in the young people you live and work with. We also hope that you now have some new ideas for how to help them cope with the deeply uncomfortable feelings uncertainty can bring.

We put this book together in the hope that the emergent shift in focus from need for diagnosis to diagnosing of need continues, and that the types of transdiagnostic strategies described here become universal and commonplace – both in schools and in the home. Yes, diagnosis can be a part of self-discovery (and helps us access specific interventions) but, since the exact diagnostic label we receive is not always a particularly good shorthand for much about us as individuals, our specific situations, life experiences and ways of thinking, it may not be the most reliable indicator for wider future support and interventions.

Using the question '**Where's the uncertainty?**' releases us from the complexities of who can reach the threshold for which diagnosis and helps us focus on the here and now. This simple approach helps us to address the fundamental aim of everything we are trying to do, helps us find out what we can do today that will help this young person reach their potential.

We also hope that this book can help reduce uncertainty in you, the adults who support teenagers and young people, by offering our new understanding of some of the reasons behind the behaviours (that we all find difficult to manage) in a new way – not deliberately 'difficult' and **always** stemming from uncertainty.

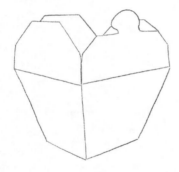

KEY POINTS TO TAKE AWAY

Why uncertainty?

▸ The world is uncertain – this we cannot change, but we can change how often we experience uncertainty and our capacity to manage it.

▸ We see the world by guessing the world. These guesses are based on a compromise calculation between our existing models (beliefs) and current sensory information.

▸ Uncertainty, prediction errors, come around when our models do not fit the sensory information we are experiencing.

▸ Differences in how good a fit our models are and how we experience sensory information can make us more prone to prediction errors – uncertainty.

How to help

▸ Try to find the uncertainty. Is it **structural**, **sensory**, **social** or all three?

▸ Reduce how much uncertainty students experience by building certainty: look at environmental change, develop skills, support needs and build on strengths.

▸ Develop capacity to manage uncertainty: build self-awareness (knowledge) and self-efficacy (agency).

▸ Recognise and then celebrate the fact we are all different, we all have our different strengths and needs.

...the idea of human unity should not efface the fact of its diversity and the idea of its diversity should not efface the idea of its unity [...] Understanding what is human means understanding our unity in diversity, our diversity in unity [...] Education should illustrate this unity-diversity principle in all spheres. (Morin, 1999, p.54 as cited in Sandri, 2014)

REFERENCES

Morin, E. (1999). *Les sept savoirs nécessaires à l'éducation du futur*. Paris: Seuil.
Sandri, P. (2014). Integration and inclusion in Italy: Towards a special pedagogy for inclusion. *Alter, 8*(2), 92–104.

GLOSSARY

Action uncertainty Uncertainty about which action to take in one's current state (e.g. turn left or right). For social stimuli, these actions include possible verbal or non-verbal communications, aggressive or affiliative actions and transactions (e.g. lending money) (FeldmanHall & Shenhav, 2019).

Active inference The way we can actively (i.e. through action) minimise errors in our predictions. We can perform actions to bring about sensory states in line with our predictions. For example, if you hear a bump in the night and wake up expecting (predicting) not to see a monster, but instead see a monster-like outline, you can take action and turn the light on. This will then (it is hoped) confirm your prediction that there is not a monster there. In this way, you can act to make the world more similar to your model of the world, as opposed to the other option, which is to update the model to make it more similar to the world. Active inference can be seen as the generalisation of predictive processing to explain cognition and action.

Agency Control over actions and their consequences. We exercise agency when we intentionally influence our own functioning, environments and life circumstances. The sense of agency refers to the sense of oneself as the agent, that is, the initiator, executor and controller of one's own actions or movements and the associated effects in the outside world (Gallagher, 2000).

Agentic uncertainty Uncertainty about the extent to which we have control over actions and their consequences.

Allostasis The dynamic regulation of bodily states through change – achieving stability through change. This can be seen as the way we get to the state we want to be in (homeostasis) and describes the process of adjusting bodily states made in response to actual and/or anticipated demands. For example, allostasis could be used to describe the changes to our heart rate and blood pressure if in the middle of the night we jump out of bed and run away from a monster.

Autonomic nervous system (ANS) The autonomic nervous system regulates our ability to adapt to environmental changes via its parasympathetic and sympathetic branches. These branches function together to promote adaptation and self-regulation in response to environmental demands (both internal and external). These two branches are often simplified as the rest-and-digest and fight-and-flight systems respectively. ANS activation occurs in response to a variety of changes in both the internal and external environment that require adaptation in order to survive, when we need to move out of our home state (temporarily), such as the need to increase our breathing rate once we find ourselves running so we do not pass out. The sympathetic system is the call to arms and gets us ready for action, while the parasympathetic system then calms us down and guides us back home. It could also be seen as holding back the sympathetic system following exposure to a stressor (the thing that kicked us out of our home state), as it reduces our metabolic (energy) output and heart rate, drawing us gradually back to homeostasis (Porges, 1992, 1995a, 1995b, 2007).

Bayesian inference Generating predictions about potential states of the world by weighing the probabilities (likelihood) of new evidence against one's a priori beliefs (priors) to form an updated set of predictions (posteriors) (FeldmanHall & Shenhav, 2019). It is based on Bayes's theorem. We widely accept that the process of having beliefs about the world, interacting with it and then updating these beliefs is a fundamental component of learning. Bayes's theorem is a mathematical formula that describes an optimal way of updating your beliefs given new evidence. It is essentially an equation to optimise our existing beliefs (priors) by ensuring we revise them (creating posteriors – essentially now new priors) in the light of sensory evidence. It describes our **compromise calculation**.

Compromise calculation see above.

Expected uncertainty Expected uncertainty arises when events occur probabilistically, rather than deterministically. So, there is not a clear one-to-one relationship between an event and the hidden cause of that event. Gathering more experience does not reduce expected uncertainty, which has resulted in it sometimes being called 'irreducible uncertainty' (Pulcu & Browning, 2019). The uncertainty is an inherent part of the thing we are learning about.

Explore-exploit dilemma The tension between choosing an option that has a known (certain) reward distribution (e.g. one's default menu item; exploiting) or choosing an option with an uncertain reward distribution (e.g. new item on the menu; exploring) to collect new information and reduce one's uncertainty. In social environments, these can manifest in terms of choices to interact with close friends or unknown acquaintances (FeldmanHall & Shenhav, 2019).

Generative model Generates predictions about incoming sensory input. To better predict future sensory input, the generative model is potentially updated by the mismatch between the generated prediction and the received sensory input, prediction errors.

Hidden process Any process that we cannot directly observe but that influences observations is a hidden process. Examples include how enjoyable a party will be or what the weather will be like (Pulcu & Browning, 2019).

Homeostasis The stability of bodily states (physiological systems) that are essential to maintain life, such as body temperature, oxygen tension and glucose levels. It can essentially be seen as the state we want to be in where all these elements are kept within a stable, balanced, safe range, and if we ever move from it we look to get back to it. We can think of it as our physiological '**home**'-ostasis.

Hyper-prior This is a strong prior constraint or pre-existing belief that influences or constrains all subsequent beliefs.

Interoception The sense of the internal physiological condition of the body. Our 'inner-selfie'. It is the process by which the nervous system senses, interprets and integrates signals originating from within the body, providing a moment-by-moment mapping of the body's internal landscape across conscious and unconscious levels.

Interoceptive accuracy How reliably and accurately you can detect internal signals, such as heartbeats. This is measured objectively through performance on behavioural tests, most commonly heartbeat detection tests such as judging when you experience a heartbeat and a tone ('a beep') at the same time.

Interoceptive awareness Metacognitive (thinking about thinking) insight into your own interoceptive skills – knowing that you are good when you are good, or knowing when you are bad when you are bad.

Interoceptive sensibility How good at interoceptive processing you **think** you are. This is a subjective measure that can be looked at through questionnaires. Questions that ask the extent to which you agree with statements such as: 'I can feel myself swallowing a lot' or 'I can feel how fast I am breathing.'

Learned helplessness A sense or belief that you are incapable of changing what you perceive as uncontrollable conditions (where you have little to no agency). This sense is often developed when people are exposed to uncontrollable and aversive/negative experience and then generalise that experience – effectively learning to be helpless in similar situations even when they might be controllable. This can then form a negative feedback loop. The less capable they feel they are, the more they assume the situation to be uncontrollable, and therefore the less capable they are of controlling that situation.

Likelihoods In Bayesian terms, this refers to a conditional probability, that is, the degree to which event A is consistent with event B, and if we believe A to be true what are the chances of B happening? So given that you don't believe monsters exist (A), what are the chances that a monster-like outline you are seeing is a monster (B)?

Motor (planning) uncertainty Uncertainty around planning motor actions, movement.

Neurological threshold The volume of stimuli needed for a neuron or neuron/system to respond. A lower threshold requires less sensory input for a response (hyper-sensitivity). A higher threshold needs more sensory stimulus for a response (hypo-sensitivity).

Outcome uncertainty Uncertainty about what kinds of rewards or punishments one could receive (e.g. amounts of monetary gain or loss). For social stimuli, these outcomes can be concrete (such as money gifted or stolen) or abstract (e.g. appreciation or approbation), and they can affect future rather than immediate states (e.g. having your reputation enhanced) (Pulcu & Browning, 2019; FeldmanHall & Shenhav, 2019).

Over (hyper)-sensitive When discussing sensory needs, this refers to being overly responsive to sensory information. You may respond to sensory input faster, more intensely, and for a longer period. It may take less sensory input to register it. This in turn can lead to sensory avoidant behaviours, looking to avoid sensory input so as to avoid being overwhelmed.

Parasympathetic nervous system This could be essentially considered as the 'flip-side' of the sympathetic nervous system. The parasympathetic system is responsible for stimulation of 'rest and digest' or 'feed and breed' activities that occur when the body is at rest.

Perceptual uncertainty Uncertainty about features of stimuli in one's environment (such as shapes or colours). For social stimuli, these may include labels (e.g. names or group affiliations), facial expressions (e.g. smiling or frowning) and social norms associated with environmental settings (e.g. church or bar) (FeldmanHall & Shenhav, 2019).

Posterior In Bayesian terms, this is one's updated prior in light of having experienced (sampled) some data.

Precision Essentially this reflects the reliability of something. We can think of precision in terms of the strength of the conviction we have in something. The precision of a prediction error describes the reliability of the prediction error; that is, the weight given to a prediction error (how high up the dial is turned) when revising or updating beliefs. The higher we turn up the precision dial, the more certain we are of the information. While it may look similar, precision is different from accuracy: a prediction can be precise but inaccurate, imprecise but accurate, or any other combination.

Prediction error This represents a sense of surprise or expectancy violation, it results in uncertainty. It is the discrepancy between expectation and reality. It can potentially then drive learning to remove the uncertainty and to improve future predictions.

Predictive coding Broadly speaking, this is a framework around how we think that describes how the brain draws on past experience (prior models) to make predictions. New experiences affirm or violate those predictions (prediction errors), and the brain refines its models to make better predictions in the future.

Predictive processing (PP) Very generally PP considers the brain as a probabilistic machine constantly making predictions about its environment. According to PP, perception comes about through the brain combining prior knowledge or expectations, including knowledge about the present context (current prediction) with incoming sensory evidence to give a perception that reflects its best available guess concerning the most probable state of the world. This view proposes that the brain does not passively receive sensory input and then work out what it is experiencing, but it holds a generative model of causes and consequences of the world that it proactively updates and uses to predict or prepare for upcoming experiences.

Prior (model) Information we already hold. It represents your level of (un)certainty about some belief (or bit of information) before you have experienced (sampled) any data round it. A prior belief (i.e. that monsters do not exist). It is important to note that you hold this information along a distribution of probabilities that define strength of your beliefs before you experience any new information.

Sensory diet A type of sensory intervention that is aimed at supporting regulation through sensory activities that are specifically chosen to target particular sensory needs, for example bouncing on a gym ball.

Sensory modulation The process of perceiving sensory information and generating responses that are appropriately graded to, or in line with, the situation. Sensory modulation reflects adjustments made in response to continual physiological processes to ensure adaptation to new or changing sensory information. It is the regulatory component of sensory processing and is explained in terms of neurological thresholds for hyper-sensitivity, hypo-sensitivity and a behavioural response continuum of sensory avoiding and seeking (Champagne & Koomar, 2012).

Sensory processing The means by which we acquire information about the environment through our senses. How we organise information from all eight senses (multiple inputs) to give us usable information to manage ourselves within an environment.

Surprise A measure of the absolute difference between what occurred and what was expected. It is an expression of uncertainty and akin to a prediction error.

Sympathetic nervous system This is essentially our bodily system of mobilisation. It prepares the body for action in an emergency by increasing cardiac output, stimulating sweat glands and inhibiting the metabolically costly gastrointestinal/ digestive tract. This system has always been associated with emotion. The label 'sympathetic' reflects the identity of this system as one 'with feelings' and contrasts it with the parasympathetic nervous system, a label that reflects a system that 'guards against feelings' (Porges, 1997).

Temporary uncertainty Essentially the uncertainty we have as a result of an initial lack of knowledge or experience. This type of uncertainty can be reduced through experience and gathering more information.

Theory of mind The ability to infer another person's mental states (thoughts, perceptions, motivations).

Under (hypo)-sensitive When discussing sensory needs this refers to being under-responsive to sensory information. You may respond to sensory input more slowly and/or less intensely. It may take more sensory input to register it. This in turn can lead to sensory-seeking behaviours looking for more sensory input.

Unexpected uncertainty Unexpected uncertainty arises when the thing we are learning about changes.

Volatility The changeability of a process. It is a source of unexpected uncertainty.

REFERENCES

Champagne, T. & Koomar, J. (2012). Evaluating sensory processing in mental health occupational therapy practice. *Occupational Therapy Practice, 17*(5), 1–9.

FeldmanHall, O. & Shenhav, A. (2019). Resolving uncertainty in a social world. *Nature Human Behaviour, 3*(5), 426–435.

Gallagher, I. I. (2000). Philosophical conceptions of the self: Implications for cognitive science. *Trends in Cognitive Sciences, 4*, 14–21.

Porges, S. W. (1992). Vagal tone: A physiologic marker of stress vulnerability. *Pediatrics, 90*, 498–504.

Porges, S. W. (1995a). Cardiac vagal tone: A physiological index of stress. *Neuroscience and Biobehavioral Reviews, 19*, 225–233.

Porges, S. W. (1995b). Orienting in a defensive world: Mammalian modifications of our evolutionary heritage. A polyvagal theory. *Psychophysiology, 32*, 301–318.

Porges, S. W. (1997). Emotion: An evolutionary by-product of the neural regulation of the autonomic nervous system. *The Integrative Neurobiology of Affiliation, 807*, 62–67.

Porges, S. W. (2007). The polyvagal perspective. *Biological Psychology, 74*, 116–143.

Pulcu, E. & Browning, M. (2019). The misestimation of uncertainty in affective disorders. *Trends in Cognitive Sciences, 23*(10), 865–875.

SUBJECT INDEX

AUTHOR INDEX

ACTIVITY INDEX

of related interest

The Incredible Teenage Brain
Everything You Need to Know to Unlock Your Teen's Potential

Bettina Hohnen, Jane Gilmour and Tara Murphy
Illustrated by Douglas Broadley
Foreword by Sarah Jayne Blakemore

£15.99/$21.95 | PB | 360PP | ISBN: 978 1 78592 557 3 |
eISBN: 978 1 78450 952 1

This book is a must read for anyone parenting, teaching or supporting teens, who wants to empower them to reach their potential. Written by a team of clinical psychologists, it leads you through tried and tested strategies to build strong relationships and improve communication with young people as they develop, learn and grow.

In the book we learn that the 'teenage brain' is unique which gives us an incredible opportunity for change and development, but it is also a time when young people are particularly sensitive and potentially vulnerable. It guides you through ways to communicate effectively with teens without negatively affecting their self-esteem. There are plenty of tips about what to say, what not say and the best mindset to use with teens, day to day.

The authors draw from the latest research in neuroscience and psychology, years of clinical expertise and first-hand parenting experience. It's relatable like your best friend's advice, and informed by scientific evidence – easy to read, hard to put down.

The Mentally Healthy Schools Workbook
Practical Tips, Ideas, Action Plans and Worksheets for Making Meaningful Change
Pooky Knightsmith
Foreword by Norman Lamb

£19.99 / $27.95 | PB | 200PP | ISBN: 978 1 78775 148 4 | eISBN: 978 1 78775 149 1

This book is the perfect starting point for anyone looking to promote and encourage mental health in their school, or evaluate their existing provision, in line with current government priorities. It covers not only the day-to-day practical steps you can take to meet the mental health needs of learners, but also a provides a whole bank of ideas for ensuring you adopt a whole-school approach to positive mental health.

Pooky Knightsmith lays out tried and tested tools you can use to evaluate the overall mental health of a school, showing how to improve and support the mental health of staff, and how to ensure that the voice of every learner is heard and valued, including the most vulnerable - and that everyone involved with the school feels safe, healthy and happy. Pooky's simple 'litmus test' framework lays out six practical areas you can explore to implement change within your own school, with explanations, sheets to fill in, tips from loads of school staff, and case examples that break these ideas down into easily digestible chunks. This much-needed book is a jumping off point for meaningful change in all aspects of your school community that will promote, support and strengthen mental health at whole-school level.

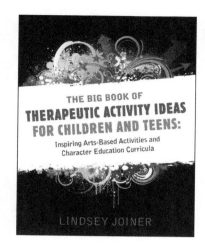

The Big Book of Therapeutic Activity Ideas for Children and Teens
Inspiring Arts-Based Activities and Character Education Curricula
Lindsey Joiner

£19.99 / $35.00 | PB | 256PP | ISBN: 978 1 84905 865 0 | eISBN: 978 0 85700 447 5

For difficult or challenging children and teenagers in therapeutic or school settings, creative activities can be an excellent way of increasing enjoyment and boosting motivation, making the sessions more rewarding and successful for everyone involved.

This resource provides over one hundred tried-and-tested fun and imaginative therapeutic activities and ideas to unleash the creativity of children and teenagers aged 5+. Employing a variety of expressive arts including art, music, stories, poetry and film, the activities are designed to teach social skills development, anger control strategies, conflict resolution and thinking skills. Also included are character education activities and ideas for conducting therapeutic day camps, including sample schedules and handouts. The activities can be used in many different settings with all ages, are flexible, and can be adapted for use with individuals or groups.

Brimming with imaginative ideas, this resource will be invaluable to anyone working with children and teenagers, including school counselors, social workers, therapists, psychologists and teachers.

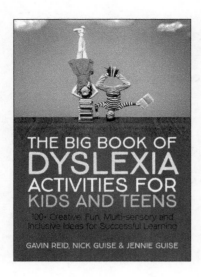

The Big Book of Dyslexia Activities for Kids and Teens
100+ Creative, Fun, Multi-sensory and Inclusive Ideas for Successful Learning
Gavin Reid, Nick Guise and Jennie Guise

£22.99 / $32.95 | PB | 320PP | ISBN: 978 1 78592 377 7 | eISBN: 978 1 78450 725 1

Packed with fun, creative and multi-sensory activities, this resource will help children and teenagers with dyslexia become successful learners across the curriculum.

The authors provide over one hundred tried-and-tested fun and imaginative activities and ideas to unlock the learning of children and teenagers with dyslexia in creative ways. The book is split into parts addressing literacy, numeracy, learning and cross curricular subjects. With fun activities like 'Spelling Ping-Pong' and 'Class Got Talent', it focuses on key skills such as listening, memory, spelling, writing and key board skills.

Each activity includes a 'red herring' that will keep dyslexic children and teenagers entertained, extending them in interesting ways that will appeal to those who think outside of the box.

Brimming with imaginative ideas, *The Big Book of Dyslexia Activities* is an essential toolkit for any teacher or parent working with children and young people with dyslexia.